John Crawford, Geo Eyvel, John Steele Sweeney

Debate on the Points of difference in Faith and Practice

Between the two religious Bodies known as the Disciples of Christ and the regular

Baptists

John Crawford, Geo Eyvel, John Steele Sweeney
Debate on the Points of difference in Faith and Practice
Between the two religious Bodies known as the Disciples of Christ and the regular Baptists

ISBN/EAN: 9783337128630

Printed in Europe, USA, Canada, Australia, Japan

Cover: Foto ©ninafisch / pixelio.de

More available books at **www.hansebooks.com**

DEBATE

ON THE

Points of Difference in Faith and Practice

BETWEEN THE TWO RELIGIOUS BODIES KNOWN AS THE

DISCIPLES OF CHRIST

AND

THE REGULAR BAPTISTS;

EMBRACING

THE SUBJECT OF CALVINISM AND THE DESIGN OF BAPTISM.

Held in the Village of Springfield, in the County of Elgin, Ontario, from the 10th to the 12th September, 1874,

BETWEEN

Prof. CRAWFORD, Woodstock, Ont.,

AND

Elder JOHN S. SWEENY, Paris, Kentucky, U.S.

W. E. MURRAY, Esq.; Aylmer, President.

Reported by Mr. Geo. Eyvel, of the "Journal," St. Thomas.

TORONTO:
PUBLISHED BY EDMUND SHEPPARD.
1875.

PUBLISHER'S PREFACE.

It is right that the readers of this debate should know the reasons why it is not published jointly by the two religious bodies represented in the controversy.

It was mutually agreed upon before the discussion commenced that the services of a reporter should be obtained, and that one-half of the expenses incurred for the stenographic report should be paid by each party, and that in the event of either afterwards declining to proceed with the publication, the report should be handed over to the other party.

At the close of the debate, before the audience dispersed, the writer, on behalf of the Disciples, publicly stated that it was the desire of his brethren that the addresses should be printed. Mr. Holmes, of Aylmer, as the representative of the Baptists, also publicly announced that they desired the publication of the debate.

Two or three days after the discussion closed, the following note was addressed to Mr. Holmes, which was copied and attested by Bro. T. C. Scott, of Toronto :

KINGSMILL, 15th Sept., 1874.

Dear Sir,—Since you have stated that your brethren are willing to publish the debate recently held in Springfield, I write to ascertain whether you will find responsible persons to pledge themselves to meet one-half the expenses of reporting and preparing the said debate for the press.

The expense of reporting, already incurred, is twenty-four dollars ;[*] the reporter's charge for writing out and

---

[*] This amount was afterwards reduced to eighteen dollars.

fitting for publication will be about one hundred dollars more.

I further wish to find out whether you will agree to the appointment of a committee of five persons whose business shall be to make all necessary arrangements connected with its publication : the committee to consist of two Baptists, two Disciples, and a fifth party chosen by these four. If there are any other and better arrangements that you can suggest, please to do so.

You will oblige by answering by first mail.

Yours truly,

E. SHEPPARD."

This note was *never answered*, and as we indirectly learned that the Baptists had abandoned all thought of publication, our brethren appointed a committee of ten who directed the reporter to proceed with his work.

As the expenses incurred were quite heavy, an appeal for pecuniary aid, was made to some of our churches in the Provinces, which appeal was so nobly and generously responded to, that the writer felt safe in complying with the request of the committee, and taking the whole responsibility of the publication into his own hands. From Mr. Holmes' letter which is quoted in Mr. Sweeny's first speech, it will be seen that all the arrangements for the debate were *ex parte*. The Disciples were not allowed to have a voice in the matter. The positions for debate were all definitely and unchangeably arranged by Mr. Crawford,—this will account for frequent references to those positions in the course of the discussion.

The debate will speak for itself. Some of the issues are of vital importance and call for a careful consideration.

The writer concludes by calling the attention of every reader to the following noble thoughts of Archbishop Whately, on the subject of " The Love of Truth in Religious Enquiry."

"As any one may bring himself to believe almost anything that he is inclined to believe, it makes all the difference whether we *begin or end* with the enquiry, 'What is truth?'

There should be an endeavor to preserve the indifference of the *judgment*, even in cases where the *will* cannot, and should not, be indifferent.

The judgment is like a pair of scales, and evidences like the weights; but the will holds the balances in its hand, and even a slight jerk will be sufficient, in many cases, to make the lighter scale appear the heavier.

Men are too apt to ask as the first question, not how far each doctrine is agreeable to *Scripture*, but to *themselves;* not whether it is conformable to God's will, but to their own.

When comparing opinions or practices with the standard of God's Word, we must beware, lest we suffer these opinions or practices to *bend the rule* by which they are to be measured.

Some persons follow the dictates of their conscience, only in the same sense in which a coachman may be said to follow the horses he is driving.

It makes all the difference, whether we pursue a certain course *because we judge* it right; or judge it to be right *because we pursue* it"; and to the still nobler words of a higher authority: " Prove all things; hold fast that which is good."

EDMUND SHEPPARD.

January 21st, 1875.

PROF. CRAWFORD'S PREFACE.*

According to agreement I have the privilege of prefixing a brief preface to this controversy; but as neither party is at liberty to insert any debatable matter, I feel it to be unnecessary to write more than a few words.

In revising my addresses I observed some portions which I would have liked to enlarge and improve were this admissible; but, as both parties are to abide by the reporter's copy, unless with such slight revision as he may sanction, it must go to the press just as delivered, according to his impartial verdict.

I do not make this remark by way of apology; as I do not wish to see any alteration made in the arguments which I employed in debate, as I believe them to be held in strict harmony with the Word of God, whatever they may lack in finish, owing to their being necessarily delivered extempore.

I would observe that in my last address, being anxious to introduce another important topic before the termination of the debate, viz : the nature of saving faith, I was obliged to leave some of Mr. Sweeny's arguments, which he delivered in his preceding address, unanswered ; but no argument I think of any importance. As he was, according to arrangement,

---
*NOTE.—When Prof. Crawford learned that the debate was to be published he asked the privilege of writing a preface for insertion in the work, which privilege was granted, and though it will exceed the space asked for, it is given *entire*.   E. S.

entitled to close the debate, I had, of course, no opportunity of replying to his last address.

Throughout the controversy also, I was obliged to pass by some points of minor importance, simply for want of time.

I would say that when requested to enter upon this debate, I yielded, from an urgent sense of duty, and not because I have any delight in controversy for its own sake. I honestly believe that the doctrines maintained by my opponent are both dishonoring to God and ruinous to the souls of men. I opposed them, therefore, with all my ability; but it is far from my intention to entertain any hostile feelings either towards him or towards those who hold his views. If my language, in any part of the debate, may appear strong, I wish the reader to set it down to my hostility to the doctrines which I opposed, and not to those who hold them.

I would remark with respect to the numerous quotations which I have made from the works of the late Mr. Alexander Campbell, that they have all been quoted before by Dr. Jeter, in his "Campbellism Examined," and that during the life-time of Mr. Campbell, although he reviewed Dr. Jeter's work, in the "Millenial Harbinger," he never complained of misquotation. The quotations which I made from Mr. Franklin are all from his volume of sermons now in extensive circulation.

It will be observed that I have employed the term Campbellism in this debate; although I consented, for the time being, in order to avoid a needless waste of time in disputing the propriety of using this appellation, to employ instead of it the word "Disciples."

I would say, however, in the words of Dr. Jeter, that "the term Campbellism has been used, not as a term of reproach, but of distinction." " From the word Disciple, indefinite as an appellative, no term can be derived to signify the views of those who adopt the name."

The system which I have opposed has been, and I think with great propriety, termed Campbellism, from the late Mr. Alex. Campbell, the author and most eminent proclaimer of the peculiar system of doctrines represented by the term. I have not, however, used the word either for the purpose of irritating my opponents or doing them any injustice, but simply for want of a more appropriate distinctive appellation.

I have, I think, endeavored to realize throughout this controversy, a sense of my responsibility to my Heavenly Master. It is, indeed, a very small matter to be judged of man's judgment; but we must all stand before the judgment seat of Christ. I commend my part in this controversy to Him. May He be pleased to employ it for His own glory, for the advancement of His truth, and for the salvation of souls.

JOHN CRAWFORD.

Woodstock, Ont., Dec. 4th, 1874.

DEBATE.

ADDRESS.

Thursday, 10th Sept., 10 *o'clock, A.M.*
(PROF. CRAWFORD'S FIRST ADDRESS.)

Professor Crawford.—It is unnecessary for me to occupy any time in the beginning of this debate, in stating the reasons why we have entered upon it. I may say, briefly, that a challenge was given by Mr. Sheppard to Mr. Holmes, who, along with others of my ministerial brethren, requested me to take it up. My hands were full, for I don't think there is a man in Canada who works harder than I do; but after taking a few days to deliberate, I thought it my duty to accede to the request. In order that I might know exactly what I was to do, I examined carefully the doctrines held by the Campbellites, and laid down certain positions that will cover the whole ground they occupy. I shall not, at this time, encumber myself with minor points, upon which even all Baptists are not agreed, but shall pass on to the consideration of the more important questions of difference between the Campbellites and myself.

It will be my duty and endeavour to show in the first place, that certain doctrines constitute Campbellism; and secondly, to show that these doctrines are false. It will be the part of my opponent to show, either that these doctrines are not Campbellism, or, if they are held by that body, to show that they are true.

I feel the full weight of the responsibility which rests upon me in this matter. I trust I have not come here merely to show my debating powers, but as a servant of Christ, to vindicate what I firmly believe to be the truth, and to expose what in my inmost soul I am convinced is unsound. I come here earnestly desiring to imitate the spirit of my Master, determined to say or do nothing unworthy of a Christian or a gentleman; and I believe my opponent will be guided by the same determination. I sincerely hope I, and all present, feel our responsibility, and that we are here to examine with devout impartiality the truths of God's word. The subjects of the debate upon which we are entering are not of little importance; they are the very kernel of the Truth, and therefore we ought to proceed in prayerful dependence upon Almighty God, remembering that we must all stand before the great judgment seat to answer for what we say and for what we hear in this house. I would simply say, before proceeding to the discussion which has brought us together, that I shall utter nothing that I do not utter with the full persuasion that it is perfectly true. I shall not employ a single sophistical argument, that I know to be sophistical. I say let Christianity be banished from the earth rather than that its advocates should employ arguments which they know to be false, in order to defend it, or to gain a victory over an opponent.

First, then, as to the doctrine of the Spirit's influence. *We* hold that God by His powerful influence, acting directly upon the soul, and using the Truth as His instrument, converts the sinner. *Their* view is that God works in man's conversion, simply through the Truth : that is, that the Truth is the power; that there is no influence of the Spirit to make the sinner's soul willing to receive the Truth. I will first establish that this is Campbellite doctrine, and then endeavour to show from God's Holy Word that it is unsound. I will read extracts from the writings of Alexander Campbell, the founder of the sect, to prove my first position. Mr. Campbell was President of their College for the training of their young preachers.

"Christianity Restored," page 348 :—

"Because arguments are addressed to the understanding, will and affections of men, they are called moral, inasmuch as their tendency is to form or change the habits, manners, or actions of men. Every spirit puts forth its moral power in words; that is, all the power it has over the views, habits, manners, or actions of men is in the meaning and arrangement of its ideas expressed in words, or in significant signs, addressed to the eye or ear."

Again, he says on page 349 of the same work: "The argument is the power of the spirit of man, and the only power which one spirit can exert over another is its arguments. How often do we see a whole congregation roused into certain actions, expressions of joy or sorrow, by the spirit of one man. Yet no person supposes that his spirit has literally deserted his body and entered into every man and woman in the house, though it is often said he has filled them with his spirit. But how does that spirit located in the head of yonder little man, fill all the thousands around him, with joy or sadness, with fear and trembling, with zeal or indignation, as the case may be ? How has it displayed such power over so many minds ? By words uttered by the tongue; by ideas communicated to the minds of the hearers. In this way only can moral power be displayed."

The writer's meaning is unmistakable; that is, that it is simply the power that is in the words of Truth; no power of the Spirit of God, to apply that truth to the soul. He goes on:—

"From such premises we may say that all the moral power which can be exerted on human beings, is, and of necessity must be, in the arguments addressed to them. No other power than moral power can operate on minds; and this power must always be clothed in words addressed to the eye or ear. Thus we reason when revelation is altogether out of view. And when we think of the power of the Spirit of God, exerted upon the mind of human spirits, it is impossible for us to imagine that the power can consist in anything else but words or arguments. Thus in the nature of things, we are prepared to expect verbal communications from the Spirit of God, if that Spirit operates at all on our spirits. As the moral power of man is in his arguments, so the moral power of the Spirit of God is in His arguments."

The meaning of these passages is very clear from the illustration which the writer uses. The man who moves an audience moves it only by his arguments; his own spirit does not leave his body to go into the audience, but simply the power which is in his words.

Again, in "Christianity Restored," page 351:—

"We plead that all the converting power of the Holy Spirit is exhibited in the divine record."

And on page 360 of the same work:—

"Hence it follows that to be filled with the Spirit, and to have the word of Christ dwelling richly in one, are of the same import in Paul's mind."

Again, on pages 362, 364, and 365 :—

"All the power of God or man is exhibited in the truth which they propose. Therefore we may say that if the light or the truth contain all the moral power of God, then truth alone is all that is necessary to the conversion of men, for we have before argued and proved that the converting power is moral power."

"Assistance to believe! This is a metaphysical dream. How can a person be assisted to believe? What sort of help and how much is wanting? Assistance to believe must be either to create a power in man which he had not before, or to repair a broken power. * * * *
The Holy Spirit was not given until the day of Pentecost. Hence, if the Holy Spirit aided men to believe in Jesus Christ, it must have been subsequent to that date."

As I wish to be clear that this doctrine is taught by Mr. Campbell, let us have another quotation:

"Christian Baptist," page 529 :—

"Can men, just as they are found when they hear the Gospel, believe? I answer boldly—yes, just as easily as I can believe the well attested facts concerning the person and achievements of General George Washington. I must hear the facts clearly stated, and well authenticated, before I am able to believe them. The man who can believe one fact well attested, can believe any other fact equally well attested."

The next quotation, and the last I shall give from Mr. Campbell's works, is on page 350 of "Christianity Restored."

"As the spirit of man puts forth all its moral power in the words which it feels with its ideas; so the Spirit of God puts forth all its converting and sanctifying power in the words which it feels

with its ideas. * * * * *
If the Spirit of God has spoken all its arguments; or, if the New and Old Testaments contain all the arguments which can be offered to reconcile man to God, and to purify them who are reconciled, then *all the power* of the Holy Spirit which can operate on the human mind *is spent*; and he that is not sanctified and saved by these, cannot be saved by angels or spirits, human or divine."

I shall give you one quotation from Mr. James Hemshill's "Scripture Reformation," page 23:—

"If they (the Samaritans) were converted before baptism, they were converted without the Holy Spirit, for they had been baptized, and yet the 'Spirit had fallen upon none of them.' * * This passage (Gal. 2, 2.) ought alone to decide this controversy about the work of the Spirit. The passages are abundant which teach the nature of the Spirit's work, and all are like the above, conclusive to the fact that the Holy Spirit dwells in the saints, and that he does not come to sinners to convert them."

That is, the Samaritans were baptized; they were believers, justified, washed in the blood of Christ; they had all this, but not the Spirit of Christ; therefore they were "none of his," (Rom. 8, 9.) I leave my Campbellite brethren to reconcile these two views. When the Apostle John says:—"The Holy Ghost was not yet given, because that Jesus was not yet glorified," (John 8, 39.) he does not refer to the ordinary gracious operation of the Holy Spirit; but to the fuller measure of Holy Spirit, consequent upon the completion of Christ's finished work and ascension, by which the fuller revelation objectively made on the cross of Christ was to be applied.

Believers had the gracious operation of the Divine Spirit in the past dispensation, as well as in this. Hence David prays, "take not thy Holy Spirit from me," (Psalm 51, 2.) The writers of the Old Testament, moreover, were inspired, for in that dispensation, according to the Apostle Peter, "holy men of God spake as they were moved by the Holy Ghost," (2 Peter 1, 21.)

I shall quote next from the sermons of Mr. Franklin, whose doctrines have never yet been disavowed by the Campbellites, for the quotations are made from the seventh edition of his works in full circulation. I understand, also, that Mr. Sheppard does not hesitate to acknowledge his belief in the soundness of Mr. Franklin's teachings; and I contend, that if I show that, in these modern days, these doctrines of the early Campbellites are accepted and preached by the Campbellites, I have shown what Campbellism is. In looking over this book I was anxious to ascertain whether the doctrines set forth by Mr. Campbell have ever been repudiated, especially the doctrine that a man is converted without the direct influence of the Holy Spirit. I have, with this object in view, made a careful search, and I find that his views are one with Mr. Campbell's on this doctrine and have never been repudiated by their followers. I will read you a quotation from Sermon III, page 57, 7th edition:

"There are two theories about this" (viz: How persons are made believers,) " so widely different that if either one of them is right the other is wrong. One of these theories asserts that God puts forth an *immediate* power or influence of His Spirit from Himself, or a direct influence to the soul of the unbeliever and makes him a believer. The other theory asserts that God puts forth His power or influence through Christ, the Apostles, through the Holy Spirit that was in the inspired Apostles, and makes believers. These two theories are wholly irreconcilable. If the one is correct the other is a delusion, a deception, a cheat."

The next quotation is from Sermon III, page 59 :—

"We all admit that God makes believers by His Holy Spirit. Nor is it whether he does it by His power. We all admit that God makes believers by His power. But does He put forth His power through Christ, through the Apostles, through the Spirit in the Apostles, through the Gospel preached by the Apostles? Or does He put forth his power or influence to make believers, immediately from Himself to the soul of the sinner, not through Christ, nor through the Apostles, nor the Word? This is the question to be seetled by Scripture.

I have made this quotation not so much to bring out the author's views on the subject as to show how very unfairly he states our side of the question. He speaks as if we believed that God did not convert the soul through Christ, through His teachings and that of the Apostles; in short, through the Truth ; whereas, we believe that a regenerate man is born of the "uncorruptible seed of the Word;" but the question is, does not the power of the Spirit accompany this Word? I find that this kind of one-sidedness prevails wherever he pretends or attempts to state our views, as though we entertained the belief that a man could be saved without the reception of the Truth. I say if he did not know our belief he should not have attempted to give it ; and if he did know it, he should have stated it fairly. I would not attempt to review Campbellism if I was not prepared to show exactly what it is. I know what Campbellism is, and after stating what it is, I shall review it in the light of God's Word.

In the same sermon, when commenting on Acts 11, 14, "When He is come He shall tell you words whereby thou and thy house shall be saved," he goes on to say, "Any theory proposing to make believers and save men without words, cannot be received, while the Lord's system, in which men are saved by words is regarded. The question is not whether the Lord can save men without words, but whether he does in the system revealed in the Bible. The angel says *by words*, and let him who says *without words* bring his proof. And in the same sermon, when discoursing on Rom. 10, 17: "Shall the great Apostle of the Gentiles be called to testify in the case as to how faith comes? He says in Rom. 10, 17: 'So then faith cometh by hearing, and hearing by the Word of God.' If he had said faith comes by feeling, by an immediate influence of the Spirit, or by anything else *besides hearing*, it would have been just as easy so to preach."

Here again, as you will observe, he misstates our views, whether purposely or not I cannot say. The question is not whether a man cannot be saved without the Word; we believe that the Word is needed in the salvation of sinners; but the question is, can a man be saved without the Spirit operating upon his heart and preparing it for the reception of the Truth? Is not such want of candor on the part of one claiming to be an expounder of the Truth, to say the least of it, very unbecoming? In page after page he goes on to attribute to us doctrines that have no existence save in his own brain. In the same volume, in discoursing upon Romans 10, 17: "So then faith cometh by hearing and hearing by the Word of God," he argues that because the Apostle uses the word "hearing," and does not say that faith cometh by feeling or by the immediate influence of the Spirit, therefore a man can be saved by hearing and nothing else,—no influence of the Spirit of God. Then in Sermon III., pages 66 and 67, he says:

"But was it not granted at the outset that he makes believers by the Holy Spirit? It was, and without any reservation. He unquestionably does it by the Holy Spirit. But can it not be that he makes believers through the Gospel and by the Holy Spirit? There can be no difficulty in this, for the Gospel itself was preached by the Holy Spirit sent down from Heaven, which things the angels desire to look into. See I Peter, 1, 12. Paul says of these things, 'But God has revealed them to us by His Spirit; for the Spirit searches all things, yea, the deep things of God.' See Cor. 2, 10. The very same gospel preached by the Apostles was preached also by the Holy Spirit, speaking in them. Indeed it was not the Apostles that spake, but the Spirit that spoke in them; and the *person who believed the words which the Holy Spirit spoke, certainly was made a believer by the Holy Spirit.* The Holy Spirit operates on men by words or through words."

Here I would observe that I hold as high views on the doctrine of inspiration as Mr. Franklin or the Campbellites possibly can. I believe and teach that every word of Scripture both of the Old and New Testaments as they came originally from the pens of the inspired writers were not their words only but also the words of the Holy Ghost, by whom they were inspired. But the question is not whether the Truth is of God, but whether that Truth alone can convert. The

Word is the divine instrument and is admirably adapted to its work; but can the instrument alone, however excellent, perform the work executed by its instrumentality? True, the Apostles preached the Word of God; or rather the Holy Ghost that was in them preached through them. But it is also necessary that the same Spirit, operating upon the souls of men and bringing the truth home to their hearts and consciences, converts them. The Word is the divinely appointed instrument; but the Word does not perform the work of conversion only instrumentally. We might as well say that the man who makes an axe cuts down the tree that another chops down with it as to say that a man is converted by the Holy Ghost when no power of the Spirit is exerted but only the power of Truth, the divine instrument.

And on page 69, of the same sermon:—

"The influence or power, then, of these words of the Holy Spirit, is the influence or power of the Holy Spirit, and a man *made a believer by these words of the Spirit, is made a believer by the Holy Spirit.*"

Again on page 71:—

"Is the power that God exercises in making believers, and turning men to God, the power of intelligence addressed to the human understanding? Or is it a subtle power of the Spirit, immediately from God, that takes effect on man, as heat, cold, or electricity, not in words addressed to the human understanding, that makes believers, and turns men to God?"

Again, page 75:—

"But some one objects saying, 'Do you think there is power in the mere Word to quicken a sinner, dead in trespasses and sins, and turn him to God?' Men of faith never say 'the mere Word,' nor the 'bare Word,' when speaking of the Word of God, which is quick and powerful, and sharper than a two-edged sword, but call it the Word of God. The power of God is in it, the power of Christ; and the power of the Holy Ghost is in it." Here I would remark that when we charge the Campbellites with teaching that a man is converted by the "mere Word" or "mere Truth," we mean the mere Word or Truth of God, or mere Word of the Holy Ghost. And in this do we misrepresent their views? If conversion is effected by the operation of God's Truth alone, without any direct or immediate operation of the Holy Spirit on the heart, what is this but the operation of the "mere Word" of God?

REPLY.

Thursday, 10th Sept., 10 o'clock, A. M.

(MR. SWEENY'S FIRST REPLY.)

Mr. Sweeny.—I accord fully and heartily with the gentleman whom I am to call my opponent in the discussion upon which we are entering, in his remarks as to the spirit and manner in which such discussions should be conducted. I would not have you construe anything I may say, in the hurry and heat of debate, as intended to offend any one, whether agreeing with me or not; whether Christian or not; for I shall certainly say nothing intentionally to offend any one who may listen to us. I think I can also join my opponent in earnest and heartfelt prayer to Almighty God, that His blessing may attend us both while contending for what we believe to be His Truth, as well as all who shall hear us.

We were informed that this discussion was originated by a challenge given by my Brother Sheppard to the Baptist Pastor at Aylmer. Well, as I understand the matter, Brother Sheppard did (after some antecedent correspondence or other communication between them, that need not be now recited,) formally challenge the Aylmer Pastor to discuss a proposition relating to Spiritual influence in conversion, and the challenge was accepted, and while as yet no preliminaries had been agreed upon, such as the time when the discussion should begin, how long it should be continued, who should be the representative men in the discussion, and all such matters as in which, of course, both parties have rights, Brother Sheppard received notice from the Aylmer Pastor that all these matters had been arranged, and that he had nothing to do but come to time, and in a very short time at that. That this may appear, and that all present may understand the exact attitude of my brethren in the discussion, I will read the letter of the Aylmer Pastor, together with that of Professor Crawford, asking you to bear in mind that it came to Bro. Sheppard just at the time when he was expecting something as to the preliminaries to the discussion of the propositions he supposed were to be debated. But here is the letter:

AYLMER, August 31, 1874.

REV. — SHEPPARD :

Dear Sir: I regret that my engagements are such as to prevent me coming personally to see you. I enclose the positions Prof. Crawford is prepared to take. They embody clearly the matter in dispute between the two bodies and *involved in this controversy.* In reference to them, I have to say that the Professor will consent to no modification or alteration; they are *definite* and clear, and the Professor calls upon you to meet and defend them.

We have fixed Thursday, September 10th, 1874, as the date of the controversy, and on that day the Professor will be in Springfield at ten o'clock in the morning, prepared to make good his positions, whatever your decision may be. I will read a copy of this and the propositions at Springfield to-night, and also give notice as above.

Respectfully yours,
GEO. HOLMES.

Here is the Professor's letter, containing his positions:

WOODSTOCK, 29th August, 1874.

I undertake to prove, and defend, in public debate, the following positions.

1. That the direct operation of the Holy Spirit, by his actual personal agency, on the human soul; opening the heart to the cordial reception of Divine Truth, and enlightening the mind, through the instrumentality of that Truth, is indispensably necessary, in the conversion of a sinner to God. And therefore,

That the Word of Truth alone, or mere moral suasion without direct spiritual agency, cannot effect the renewal or conversion of a soul, dead in trespasses and sins; and also

That the teaching of the late Mr. Alexander Campbell, President of Bethany College, Virginia, and his followers, is, upon this vital doctrine of the Christian religion, unsound, evasive, and contradictory.

2. That no person is a fit and proper subject of Christian Baptism who has not previously become the subject of converting and regenerating grace, by the operation of the Holy Spirit, through the instrumentality of Divine Truth; and that, therefore, baptism is not conversion, nor regeneration, although this ordinance represents this spiritual change in a figure; nor do we receive the remission of sins in and through baptism, only in a figure.

3. That the teaching of Mr. Campbell and his followers, on the import and use of Christian baptism, is unsound, evasive, and contradictory.

4. That the basis of Christian faith and hope, as set forth by Mr. Campbell and his associates, is, as such, in the highest degree defective and delusive.

5. That the tendency of the so-called "Reformation," originated by Mr. Campbell, and carried on by him and his associates, is to substitute a heartless, formal religion, for true spiritual piety; and to sow the seeds of many pernicious errors.

JOHN CRAWFORD.

The letter of Mr. Holmes shows that he and Prof. Crawford took the whole matter of preliminaries and propositions into their own hands, rather arbitrarily, not to say arrogantly, extending but the courtesy of ten days previous notice to my brethren. They are, therefore, responsible for the somewhat novel character of our debate; which, it seems, is to be a discussion without a distinct logical proposition.

The letter of Mr. Crawford is, I suppose, to be the ground of our discussion. That letter contains some things in which I suppose, he and I agree, and some concerning which we differ. He proposes to make an attack all along the line of what he chooses to call Campbellism; while I will, of course, defend at only such points as I shall feel that the interests of the cause I advocate require me to defend. I shall resist him only where I shall believe him to be wrong. He, of course, has his points of attack well in mind, his method of attack all planned, and his material and munitions arranged; while I am to watch my whole line, and be ready, without a moment's notice, to defend it at any point. But I don't complain. I feel no fears. I shall aim to advocate only truth, and that is easily defended. Who wars against that cannot have enough advantages to put firm upon an equal footing with his opponent who stands for its defence. I would, however, much prefer having distinct propositions, setting forth, singly and clearly, the points of difference between us; but this I cannot have. I would also like to know how long the discussion is to be continued—how long the fire is to be kept up—but even this is denied me. This, however, I have the satisfaction of knowing: That the debate opens to-day, and that I am to have the liberty of replying to every speech my opponent shall make. I shall try to be ready to say close when he shall say close, and, God willing, to go on as long as he shall say go on. This only I ask of my hearers, that they make some allowance for what may seem to them to be short or abrupt, in my replies, as I shall not know what I am to talk about in any speech I shall make till I have heard the speech to which I shall have to reply. As I am here, I should like to have an opportunity to affirm and try to establish those points of teaching that constitute the peculiarities of my brethren, and upon which many good people esteem them so frightfully heterodox. Though I shall not have an opportunity to do this to my satisfaction, under the present arrangement, I shall try to make the very best of the opportunity. I hope also to have an opportunity to hold my opponent to account for some of his errors— upon the points of difference between his brethren and mine.

The Professor tells us that his first work will be to show "what Campbellism is," and to that work most of his opening speech was devoted. But he will never tell us "what Campbellism is." There is no such thing, sir! "Campbellism is a myth! He speaks of Mr. Campbell as "the founder of the sect." Mr. Campbell never founded any sect. He spent most of his life in both writing and preaching against founding sects. The great work of his life—that for which thousands now hold his memory in such high esteem, and for which the future will rise up and bless him—was earnest and powerful opposition to "sects" among the people of God. Nor are Mr. Campbell's writings at all authoritative among us. That great man never intended his writings to be authoritative anywhere. No one ever laboured more earnestly against all human authority in religion than he. People used to talk so of Mr. Campbell's writings in the States, but that sort of talk has died out pretty generally. No body of people can be found in this country whose members profess to be "Campbellites." We, as a people, have never accepted that name. Mr. Campbell never intended that we should. My opponent can so designate us if he choose. I shall not be offended at it, though I may think it a little discourteous. I deem it of just sufficient importance to say that, hereafter if he calls us by that name he must do it against my protest. I think, however, he did it oftener in his first half-hour speech than he will in the whole of the last day of our discussion.

My opponent says he proposes to show you, first, "What Campbellism is," and, secondly, "That its teachings are false." By "Campbellism," I shall assume that he means Christianity, as understood and propounded by our people, specially those matters wherein we differ from the popular denominations of the day. And he begins with the question of *Spiritual influence in conversion.* On this question he makes copious quotations from Mr. Campbell and others. I am not bound by what Mr. Campbell or Mr. Franklin has said, though I think our people do generally agree with them on this question. Mr. Campbell may have used many expressions that I would not prefer; expressions not the very happiest, and, taken out of their connection, may seem to mean what I do not believe, and even what he himself did not believe. This is true of Mr. Franklin, and other editors among us, as it is also of Baptist scribes. Eminent Baptists have said and written many things that my opponent would not endorse, as we shall see in the future of our discussion. On this question, however, I do, in the main, endorse Mr. Campbell's views, as I understand them. So do my brethren generally. And I am ready to defend them. Mr. Campbell taught that the Holy Spirit converts men, but that it does it always through the instrumentality of the Truth, or by the Gospel; that in conversion the Spirit operates, but not directly or *immediately*, but mediately; not directly, as my hand operates upon this book, when I bring my hand in immediate contact with it; but mediately, and the medium used is the Gospel. That's what Mr. Campbell taught upon this question; that's what our people generally believe; that's what I believe and teach and what I am willing, and, I trust, shall be able to defend. I should like to find a proper gentleman in Canada willing to affirm, in a distinct, logical form, that in the conversion of a sinner, the Holy Spirit operates directly or *immediately* upon his heart. I would like for my opponent to come squarely up to the discussion of that question, for I consider it no unimportant one. I do not think Mr. Franklin was so unfair as my opponent seems to think, in his presentation of the two theories of Spiritual influence. I will quote an author on my friend's side of this question, that you may see what is taught as to immediate spiritual influence. I will read from the book written by the author, and then lay it before my friend, as I should like to have him do, instead of reading scraps, without producing the books from which he reads. I read from *Mission of the Spirit*, by Rev. L. R. Dunn, a work that has received high and extensive endorsement by the orthodox press; pp. 194-95.

"Even where the light of the Gospel does not shine, and the institutions of the Gospel are not enjoyed, there the Spirit acts directly upon man's heart and conscience, writes the law of God upon his mind, gives him the sense of sin and the need of forgiveness. Hence, wherever man, redeemed man, is, there the comforter is at work upon his heart and mind   *   *   *   *   This divine influence is imparted *unconditionally* and *irresistibly*.   *   *   *   *   The Holy Spirit is ever employed to bring man back to God; and *whether he desires it or not*, whether he is willing or unwilling, still the comforter comes to him with his heavenly illumination, his divine influence, convincing him of sin, and his consequent need of the mercy of God. May I not truly say that man really *has no choice* in the matter as to whether he will or will not have this divine influence upon his soul. *He is, he must be* enlightened and convinced *whether he will hear or forbear*, whether he will be saved or damned. He *cannot prevent* the entrance of the Spirit into his heart." "Universal," "unconditional," "immediate," and "irresistible," "even where the light of the Gospel does not shine," upon the hearts of men who would be saved and upon the hearts of such who would prefer to be damned! *Such is the theory we oppose.* "The Gospel is the power of God for salvation;" and I say fearlessly, and proudly—gratefully to God—that it will save every one that receives it. If I repeat it, it is because I believe it most masculinely.

My opponent read something from James

Henshall, I believe, about the Samaritan converts. I am not certain I understood just what it was, but I suppose if it was anything bearing upon the question of spiritual influence in conversion, it was most likely in harmony with what I have said.

Prof. Crawford's language upon the point before us is a little like, he thinks, the doctrines of "Campbellism" are—just a little "evasive and contradictory." So, at least, it strikes me. In his letter, which I have referred to as the ground of our debate, he speaks of "the *direct* operation of the Holy Spirit, by his actual personal agency, on the human soul—opening the heart to the cordial reception of Divine Truth, and enlightening the mind, *through the instrumentality of that Truth*." This would seem to indicate that he believes the sinner is converted, or, at least, enlightened, through the instrumentality of the Truth, but that there is an antecedent work of "opening the heart," done by the Spirit *directly*, in his own person. Will my opponent affirm all this in debate? It is certainly easier to talk about "Campbellism" in a general way, than to prove such a doctrine; but will he try it? I have here also a volume, entitled *The Baptist Pulpit*, containing extracts from sermons by eminent Baptist divines, and their pictures. I will read, on page 44, an extract from a sermon by J. W. Hayhurst, on the "Holy Spirit in Conversion." He says:—"God has given us no means by which the conversion of sinners, or the general revival of religion, can be effected, irrespective of the *direct* agency of the Spirit. The Gospel itself will not do it." This author denies that the Gospel will effect the conversion of the sinner, and says we have no means that will *but the direct agency of the Spirit.* On the contrary, we believe that the Gospel will effect the conversion of the sinner, if he will hear and receive it, and that he can do so if he will; and if he will not, we deny that the Spirit will operate on his heart at all, and call for the proof. Here is a clear issue raised; will my friend undertake to prove the doctrine to which he stands as affirmant? If so, then we may have an interesting and a profitable discussion. There is no good to be effected by his attempting to show that our people are, in teaching, "unsound, evasive and contradictory." I think I could do quite as much for Baptist teachers, and if we are to have that kind of debate, I will do it. It would be useless for me to repeat and notice in detail all the quotations he made from Mr. Campbell, Franklin and others, to show what we teach, on this question, even if I had the books here, and the time to do so. The sum of the matter is, that we believe the Holy Spirit is the Spirit of the Truth; that he is ever present with the Truth—never out of it; that no one can receive the Truth and not be influenced by the Spirit; that no one is converted to Christ by the Spirit without the Truth; that every one who is converted to Christ is converted by the Spirit in the Truth. Not that we believe, as we are sometimes misrepresented, that the Truth is the Holy Spirit, and the Holy Spirit is simply the Truth. But whom the Truth effects, and what the Truth effects, that the Holy Spirit effects; because it is the Spirit of the Truth—ever present in the Truth, and efficient wherever and in whomsoever the Truth is received. In whom the Word of God dwells richly the Holy Spirit dwells also, just as my opponent read from Mr. Campbell. This is what I believe, and this I think our people do generally believe, and this I am willing to defend. You can call it "Campbellism" if you choose—call it what you like—I believe it to be the truth of God, and will defend it. But again he says, in the same letter, that no one is a fit subject of baptism who has not previously been the subject of converting and regenerating Grace, by the operation of the Holy Spirit, through the instrumentality of Divine Truth. This would seem to indicate that the sinner is *converted*, by the operation of the Holy Spirit, *through the Truth;* which is sound and Scriptural. And in his speech he talked of the Spirit "acting *directly* upon the soul, using the Truth as his instrument." Does he mean to say, that, in conversion, the Spirit operates *immediately, through a medium!* That's a contradiction in terms. So is it, also, to say the Spirit acts *directly* upon the soul, *with an instrument!* When the gentleman talks of the influence of the Spirit "through the Truth," affirmatively, as he has done, he thereby consents to our teaching upon the subject; but when he talks of its direct, or immediate, influence, he goes beyond what we teach or believe; and I hope he will, for my sake, be a little more explicit. What does the Spirit do when He acts directly, personally, immediately, upon the sinner's heart? What is the necessity for such operation? He has said the mind is enlightened by the Spirit, through the Truth; now what, if any, antecedent or subsequent work has the Spirit to do in conversion, that must be done by it in its own person, acting *immediately* upon the heart? You can readily see, my friends, that there are two theories upon the question of spiritual influence; and from what I have read, you can see that Mr. Franklin was not so unfair in his statement as Mr. Crawford seems to think.

Mr. Crawford seems to get a little mixed, and needs to explain a little, that we may know just what he does believe upon the subject. Does he believe the Spirit regenerates, or converts, the sinner, by His own personal, direct, immediate act upon the soul ? If not, then I don't see that he need have any dispute with what he calls " Campbellism," upon this subject. But if he does so believe, I deny it, and our work is laid out, and we should go at it, at once. My first, chief, and most comprehensive objection to that theory is, that, so far as the conversion of the world is concerned, it sweeps away the whole Gospel, with Christ, and all that He did and suffered, in it! This I conceive to be a fearfully mischievous error! I believe that God, by the Holy Spirit, approaches men, through Christ; that men are brought to God only through Christ. Jesus said of the Spirit, when He promised to send it to His Disciples, as their Comforter, and through them to act upon the world, " He shall testify of *me* ;" " He shall not speak of *Himself;*" "He shall glorify *me*, for he shall receive of mine and shall show it unto you." The philosophy of conversion is simple, sublimely and beautifully simple ; as simple as that of a mother who would induce her little child to let go an ugly and dangerous knife, by handing it an apple, or something more beautiful than the hurtful thing, knowing that to take hold of the one it must let go the other. Christ is preached, by the Holy Spirit, to the sinner. He is prettier, lovelier, better than sin. To receive Him, one must let go sin. As he enters the heart, sin goes out of it ; and while He remains in it, sin must remain out. There is something far more beautiful in Jesus than there is in sin, and whoever will look can see it. He came down from the beauties and bliss of Heaven, took our nature upon him; our whole nature became more human than any man; lived in a world of sin, want and wretchedness; was hungry, thirsty and weary, often; carried us, with all our wants and woes, upon His great and loving heart; tasted our every cup of bitterness, and carried our griefs; His heart ached; he sighed and wept, suffered and died. He did it all willingly and lovingly, too, for *sinners!* Look at Him in His whole life, so full of cares, anxieties, heaviness, temptations, sadness and sorrows; look at Him among the poor and the suffering; by the grave side, mingling His tears with such as overwhelmed with sorrow, were crying to Heaven for relief. In all His sorrows, conflicts, woes, He only once asked relief. When in the Garden of Gethsemane, made the symbol of sorrows, He saw *death* just before Him, he cried out "O my Father! if it be possible, let this cup pass from me; nevertheless not as I will, but as thou wilt." *This* cup, just this *one;* every other bitterness we taste, he tasted, without a word. And of this terrible one he said—"If this cup may not pass away from me, except I drink it, thy will be done." Then he went out of that Garden.

> "O Garden of Olives! thou dear honour'd spot,
> The fame of thy wonders shall ne'er be forgot;
> The theme most transporting to seraphs above;
> The triumph of sorrow, the triumph of love."

He went out by the Cross, on which He died for sinners. All the shame and suffering of the Cross He endured for sinners. And now He lives, the same loving Jesus, offering pardon and eternal life freely to all who will obey Him. This is God's argument and exhortation to the sinner. This was, and is, the plea of the Spirit, to touch and turn the hearts of men back to God. There is no "unconditional and irresistible" power in this; but it is God's power for salvation.

ADDRESS.

Friday, Sept. 11*th*, 11 *a.m.*,

(PROF. CRAWFORD'S SECOND ADDRESS.)

Prof. Crawford.—My opponent complains that I have acted unfairly in laying down certain propositions which I intend to prove and defend. But I fail to see that there is anything unfair in taking this course. I have laid down one proposition, that I am to show what the prevalent doctrines of the Campbellites are. If I fail in doing so I am beaten on that point; but if I succeed in proving what are the accepted doctrines of Campbellism I have established my first proposition. Secondly, I shall attempt to prove these doctrines to be unsound and untrue. If I fail in doing so, then I am beaten on that point. But if I succeed in proving my propositions then I shall have beaten my opponent. Here, then, there is a definite programme before us. The reason I laid down these propositions is simply this:—I have found in my experience with Campbellites that they can scarcely be tied down; it is hard to get them to say what they are, and what they are not; what they do believe and what they don't. I have examined their current and received writings for the purpose of showing what their real belief is. I consider many of their teachings contrary to the Word of God, and I shall prove them so I hope before this discussion closes. It is my opponent's duty to defend them if he can, and he surely cannot complain of any unfairness in my requiring this. His next complaint is that we call them Campbellites. I would say it was very far from my intention to insult or irritate them by using this designation. I used it because they are very generally known by that name and because it was the one that naturally occurred to my mind in speaking of them. I shall, however, endeavour in future not to speak of them as Campbellites, though if I should make a slip of the tongue, they must not attribute it to any intention of giving offence. They say they are Christians. I say I am a Christian too, and to assume they are the only Christians is to beg the question. They call themselves Disciples of Christ. I claim to be a Disciple of Christ, and I think I have as good a claim as they have to that title. I think it will be seen before the discussion is over that our claim to be called Disciples of Christ is equally as good as theirs. They say they are not a sect. I may be wrong but I consider that when a certain number of people unite in holding certain views, unite in proclaiming these views, and in Church Fellowship they are fully entitled to be called a sect. They say they are not bound by the creed of any man. I know that, but I wish to draw their attention to the fact that Mr. Campbell was cut off from the Baptists for holding these very doctrines I am opposing. He complained that it was not right for us to withdraw from him. We considered many of the doctrines he advocated heresies, and we could not, regarding them as such, act otherwise than we did. Mr. Campbell is the best exponent of their views; he is the founder of the sect, the man who led away the party in that direction. He was, moreover, appointed President of their College, and a teacher in the College. I say then I don't think I have done anything wrong in bringing his arguments forward and saying they are so and so, and that the great bulk of the Campbellites—I beg their pardon—the Disciples, believe in the very same views. Then with regard to Mr. Franklin's book; it is one in wide circulation among them at the present day, and I think if I show what these men advocate, I shall have come pretty near defining what Campbellism really is. More than that I have had a good deal to do with Campbellites, and I think I know what their doctrines are.

My opponent denies that there is anything more than the power of the Truth exercised in the work of conversion—no direct influence of the Spirit acting upon men's souls to bring them to acknowledgement of the Truth. You perceive then that he is a believer in at least one of the views brought out in the quotations I gave from Mr. Campbell's works, so that I cannot see that much fault can be found by my opponent with the quotations given from Mr. Campbell. The difference between my views and those of my opponent on this point is simply this: He says the Gospel and nothing more is necessary to effect a change of heart. I say, and I believe I can establish it, that some other influence is essential.

With regard to their assuming the name of "Christians" and "Disciples," I would just take the liberty of reading an extract from a handbill which has been circulated in his neighborhood. It says that "a discussion on the influence of the Holy Spirit will take place at Springfield between Prof. Crawford, of the Baptist Church, and J. S. Sweeney, a Disciple of Christ," etc. Now, that may do very well in a Campbellite community, but a great many people will think it is just a good big swagger! Remember, Mr. Crawford is not of the Christian Church; he is a Baptist, while his opponent, Mr. Sweeney, is a "Disciple of Christ."

They say there is no salvation out of proper Campbellism; that we are saved by baptism into certain views, therefore I say that this bill is only in keeping with their own doctrine. The Church of Rome says that their's is the only Church of Christ, and our friends the Campbellites have the same opinion of their Church. Then they say that if, according to our views, men are converted by the direct influence of the Spirit, there is no occasion to preach the Gospel to the heathen. I preach nothing of the kind about the souls of the heathen. We are commanded to preach the Gospel to the heathen, and that those who receive that Gospel will be saved; those who reject it will be damned. We are not told, nor do we teach that the heathen will be saved without the Gospel. That is not the point at issue. The real question is, will the Gospel alone, the mere words of Truth without their being accompanied by the Spirit's power, save the sinner? I say not, and that is the doctrine upon which my opponent should take issue with me instead of attributing views to us which we do not hold. Let me proceed with two more quotations and then to the proof of our views.

Franklin—Page 71:—

" Is the power that God exercises in making believers and turning men to God the power of intelligence addressed to the human understanding? Or is it a subtle power of the Spirit, immediately from God, that takes effect on man, as heat, cold, or electricity, not in words addressed to the human understanding that makes believers, and turns men to God?"

Page 75:—

" Do you think there is power in the mere Word to quicken a sinner, dead in trespasses and sins, and turn him to God? Men of faith never say 'the mere Word,' nor the 'bare Word,' when speaking of the Word of God, which is quick and powerful, and sharper than a two-edged sword, but call it the Word of God. The power of God is in it, the power of Christ, and the power of the Holy Spirit is in it. It would be precisely the same power if put forth *immediately*. Men must be deluded beyond description if they cannot see that it is neither more nor less than the power of God for salvation that is put forth in the Gospel. No one argues that sinners can be quickened without the Power of God, but the Gospel is the power of God."

The point at issue between us is surely very plain now. With regard to the irresistible power of the Holy Spirit, I would say that there is a sense in which the Spirit of God may truly be said to be irresistible. For instance, we often find men stubbornly opposed to the Truth, unwilling to receive it, but by the operation of the Holy Spirit in their hearts, making them willing in the day of His power, their stubborn wills are subdued, and an entire change of heart takes place.

Before proceeding to give proofs from the Holy Scriptures, I would say that independently of the fact that the teachings of Mr. Campbell and the Campbellites are opposed to the Word of God, they are also inconsistent with facts and principles admitted on all hands. The denial of the direct influence of the Holy Spirit, and the belief that moral power consists merely in the arguments presented to the mind, is inconsistent in the first place with the creation of man in the moral image of God. The Scriptures say God created man in His own image, fashioned him like himself, morally. And was not this performed, by a direct or immediate operation of His Spirit, without even the instrumentality of Truth? It is also inconsistent with the incarnation of Christ. Our Lord was to be born of a virgin, a weak, fallen woman, like the rest of the human race. But the Spirit of God was to form in, and bring a holy thing from her: "Therefore, also, that holy thing, which shall be born of thee, shall be called the Son of God." Was not this miraculous conception by the direct influence of the Holy Spirit, not only this fashioning of the body, but the forming of the human soul of the Saviour in the womb of the virgin? And is not this doctrine that there is no immediate power of the Spirit of God working through, and by the instrumentality of the Truth, inconsistent with the idea of Satanic influence? Is it by the mere force of argument, or by direct and immediate influence, that Satan captivates and ensnares the souls of men? Does not he act immediately upon the human mind, making evil suggestions, stirring up evil passions and leading men on in rebellion against God. And if Satan acts directly and immediately upon the human soul for evil purposes, shall we deny Almighty God, a similar power for good? Then again the doctrines of the Disciples on this point is inconsistent with a belief in the salvation of infants; because infants, as we hold, are brought forth in sin and shapen in iniquity; they have a moral taint from the very womb. I know that on this point the author from whom I have been quoting, I mean Mr. Franklin, will not agree with me, for he goes right into Pelagianism. But we and the majority of evangelical sects believe that we are sinners from the very womb. And, according to Campbell's belief, how are these infants ever to get into heaven; they must either be changed or go there *in their unregenerate nature.* The latter supposition we cannot entertain for a moment. And if a change is to be made, is it, as Mr. Campbell and his friends would say, by the mere power of argument? It is ridiculous to talk of the power of argument upon an infant, so we must accept the belief that infants are changed and made meet for the inheritance of the saints by the direct, immediate influence of God's Spirit. Mr. Campbell attempts to explain this by saying that man is composed of three parts, soul, body and spirit, and that the *Pneuma*, or spirit, is not contaminated by sin. He says that the *Psyche* only is defiled, and that as infants have not used the *Psyche*, having died before it came into operation, therefore they have died without sin. He denies that there is any sin in the *Pneuma*, or intelligent part. I would like to ask Mr. Campbell where he got hold of that very ingenious theory. He and his followers speak much about restoring a pure speech, Bible language, but they use about as much metaphysics and hair-splitting as any one else.

Whenever you pin a Campbellite down or corner him he will cry out, "Bible language; give me the very words in the Bible." *He* may flourish away as much in metaphysics as he pleases, but he will tie *you* down to the very words of the Bible. You may be sure when a Campbellite talks in this way he is cornered. We must remember that we have only a translation in common use, and that if we must be tied down to the very words of the Bible, we must go to the Greek, the Chaldee, and the Hebrew. I contend that an inference fairly drawn from Scripture has the same weight as Scripture language itself. The Sadducees denied the resurrection of the

dead and they were held accountable for their
unbelief, because God had said, "I am the God
of Abraham and of Isaac and Jacob." There
was no positive declaration of the resurrection
here, but because this sect did not accept the
legitimate inference from the language, they were
held as responsible as if the doctrine was contained in so many words. The Almighty had
not declared "I was the God of Abraham, &c,"
but "I *am* the God," which implies that
although these patriarchs were dead they
still lived to God; and, therefore, that there
must be a future state, or an existence after
death. But the Campbellite says, you must
give me the exact language; I will have none of
your inferences. For my part, I will never find
fault with an argument if it is a fair, legitimate
inference from the language of the Bible, even if
it is not in the exact words. I am not necessarily wrong in my argument, even if I don't quote
the exact language of Scripture, provided I reason
legitimately from it, and do not misrepresent it.

But with respect to this theory of Mr. Campbell, that no moral taint adheres to the *Pneuma*
or spirit, but only to the *Psyche*, or soul, it is contrary to reason. Surely if sin attaches to any
part of our nature, it must be to the *Pneuma* or
rational, and consequently responsible part. Besides, does not the Apostle say to the Corinthians
(II Cor. vii. 1): "Let us cleanse ourselves from
all filthiness of the flesh and 'spirit'" or *Pneuma?*
Moral evil then does adhere to the *Pneuma* which
has to be purged away. Another proof of the
influence of the Spirit in the work of conversion
is the comparatively small success that attended
Christ's labours. No one will say that he did
not preach the truth in all its power and purity,
he that "spake as never man spake," and yet

there were perhaps more conversions on the day of Pentecost than by all the preaching of Christ. Why? Because God had reserved for that day an abundant outpouring of his Holy Spirit. Again, their views on this subject are inconsistent with the idea of prayer for the conversion of souls. If the mere preaching of the Gospel is all that is required to bring sinners to a knowledge of the truth as it is in Jesus, what is the use of praying that men's hearts may be changed? If the power of the Spirit is all spent in giving the mere ideas contained in the Truth, there is no use in praying that conversions may take place. On this hypothesis God has done all that he ever will do for the conversion of the world when he inspired the Scriptures. For what then do we pray? Furthermore, this view of the Campbellites is inconsistent with the views taught by Mr. Campbell himself, that after baptism men receive the Holy Spirit which dwells and operates in them. They admit, then, that after baptism the Spirit of God does dwell and tabernacle in the souls of men. But if after baptism, why not before? Why not in the beginning of the good work as well as in its future progress? But Mr. Campbell says, God has never promised the spirit to any but believers. If we never received more from God than what he has actually promised we would, I fear, fall far short. He gives us all he has promised, and far more. It is true that it is not until man believes that he has an interest in the promises of the covenant, and can plead them at a throne of grace; yet it does not follow from this that God may not, in His Sovereign grace, touch his heart, and bring him into the covenant by inclining him to lay hold of Christ in faith. Mr. Campbell has another argument from analogy. He says it is an easier matter to enlist in the army than to become a good soldier; easier to start in the race than to run and obtain the Crown. I can bring analogy on the other side of the question. Suppose we try.

REPLY.

Friday, Sept. 11th, 11.30 *a.m.*
(MR. SWEENEY'S SECOND REPLY.)

Mr. Sweeney.—My opponent tells us that he has had a good deal to do with "Cambellites," and that he finds them pretty hard to "tie down." No doubt of it! I agree with him that the people whom he calls Campbellites are pretty hard to "tie down." But I do not think they are generally hard to be brought up to the defence of their positions, and that is what he means. In that sense, I should like to see him "tied down." Why would he not agree to affirm in a distinct proposition, that in conversion the Holy Spirit operates immediately upon the human soul? Was it because he was too hard to be tied down? I say the Spirit operates mediately; he will not deny it. He contends that it operates immediately; this I deny, and now let us tie down to the work at once. The brother sitting by him says that's right—that he would meet that single issue—but he is not in the discussion, and Professor Crawford is. And the Professor finds it easier to talk about Campbellism than to meet a plain issue.

My friend says God created man in his own image, and that Campbellism is inconsistent with that fact. Indeed! Does it follow from that fact, that *in conversion* the Holy Spirit operates immediately upon the sinner's heart? If so, I confess my inability to see how it so follows. He says our teaching is inconsistent, also, with the incarnation. How is it so? Was the incarnation the conversion of a sinner?

Surely not. Must the conversion of a sinner necessarily be accomplished, just like the miraculous conception? I think not. Is it a question of *power* we are discussing? Have I said that the Spirit *cannot* operate without the Truth? No, sir! Nor do I intend to say so.

Then he says that our view is inconsistent with belief in the devil's immediate operations upon the souls of men. But, to make an argument of this, for his own or against my position, he must establish two things: First, that the devil does so operate; and, secondly, that in conversion the Spirit must necessarily operate just as the devil does in tempting men. As to the first position, I shall not be very dogmatic, not being positively certain that I know just what is true in the case. And as to the second, I deny squarely that it is true. He thinks that if the devil operates immediately upon the hearts of men, for evil, we ought not to deny God a similar power for good. But is it necessary for God to operate in the same manner for good, that the devil does, for evil? Let me remind you again that we are not discussing a question of power, but rather one of *fact*. Not what can, but what does the Spirit do?—in the conversion of sinners.

Next we are told that the doctrine of the Disciples on this point is inconsistent with a belief in the salvation of infants. Well, what have we in the Bible about the salvation of infants—in the sense of conversion? Let him put his finger on the passage. Jesus "came to save that which was *lost*." Were infants lost? I deny that they were, or that they are. It is not enough, for me, for the gentleman to say that a majority of evangelical sects believe that we are sinners from the very womb. A majority of evangelical sects cannot determine such questions for me. *Jesus* said, to men, "Except ye be converted, and become as little children, ye shall not enter into the Kingdom of Heaven," and that's better authority than that of *all* "the evangelical sects." If my friend is right, that infants are sinners, then we must understand the Saviour as teaching men that they must "be converted, and become as little "—*sinners!* to enter into the Kingdom of Heaven! My friend tells us how Mr. Campbell attempted to evade the force of this argument, and how he would like to ask Mr. Campbell a question about it. I feel no concern about Mr. Campbell's theory; nor would I fear for Professor Crawford to ask him many questions, were he here. No doubt the Professor could profit by the answers. The gentleman tells us that the Bible says, "They go astray from their mother's womb." Yes; it says they do so, "*speaking lies.*" When children can *speak lies* they "*go* astray." Of course, then, they are not *born* astray, as he would have us believe.

My opponent adduces another argument for the direct operation of the Spirit, from what he is pleased to call the comparatively small success that attended Christ's labours. This assumes that the labours of Christ were comparatively a failure. Then, of course, he did not accomplish what he *aimed* to accomplish; and he failed because the Holy Spirit did not co-operate with him! The Second person in the Trinity, for want of the co-operation of the Third person, failing! Was the Godhead divided? Rather fine theology, that! Christ's work was preparatory to the subsequent work of the Spirit, through the Apostles. What success, suppose you, would have attended the labours of the apostles after the coming of the Holy Spirit upon them, but for the previous and preparatory labours of Jusus? What did the apostles preach on the day of Pentecost, when speaking as the Spirit gave them utterance, that reached the hearts of their hearers, and yielded such grand results? Was it not *what Jesus had done?* Did they preach the comparative failure of Jesus? No, indeed! Jesus came to lay the foundation for the future success of the Gospel. The argument here, by the way, turns with tremendous force against my friend's theory. What was it that pricked the people to the heart on the day of Pentecost, and caused them to yield to the claims of Jesus? Evidently, it was what the apostles preached? And what did they preach? *Facts* that Jesus did not declare—that, indeed, had not transpired—during his personal ministry among the people. The grand results of Pentecost, and of subsequent apostolic preaching, are to be attributed to what was preached concerning Jesus—concerning his life, death, burial, resurrection, ascension, and lordship in Heaven. But if the Spirit converts men, as my friend supposes, without the Gospel, without preaching, by his own direct action upon their hearts, then I submit, he might have done his work just as well before these facts transpired as after, and without any reference to them whatever. Again. Where is the proof that the Spirit exerted any influence upon the hearts of the people on the day of Pentecost, other than through what was preached? Nowhere. I will immediately yield the point in controversy, if the gentleman will show, even by a fair inference, that the Holy Spirit did operate immediately upon the heart of one of the thousands that were converted on the day of Pentecost—or ever afterward.

Again, we are informed that our view of the subject in hand is inconsistent with the idea of prayer for the conversion of the sinner. I think not; but I do think my opponent's view is inconsistent with prayer, or anything else man can do, for the conversion of sinners. This, I predict, will be clearly developed as we proceed. But I do pray for the conversion of sinners, whether consistently or inconsistently, without expecting it to be accomplished in the manner my friend thinks it is; just as we both pray, "Give us this day our daily bread," without expecting our bread to come, already baked, *directly* from heaven.

The gentleman thinks my brethren inconsistent in allowing that the Spirit does dwell in and immediately influence the hearts of Christians, while we deny that he so influences the hearts of sinners. I don't know that they are. The relation of Christians to the Holy Spirit, to Christ, to God, and to all the blessings of the Gospel, and that of aliens are not the same. The distinction, however, is one I don't care to spend time on. What does the Spirit do, even in the sanctification of Christians, without means? "Sanctify them through Thy truth," prayed the Saviour; and *through* the truth is mediately. And I suppose that is the way Christian sanctification is carried on.

I was surprised to hear my friend say that we teach that there is no salvation out of proper Campbellism. His mistake here is a most egregious one. It is positively amusing! No, no! We teach that there is salvation in *Christ*; and that persons are saved by being baptized into him.

But the gentleman seems just a little irritated, because we wish to be called simply "Christians," or "Disciples of Christ," and refuse to wear any party name; because we profess to belong to "the Church of Christ," and to no party. He thinks this "just a good big swagger." Well, let us see about that. Does he not claim to be a "Christian," or "Disciple of Christ?" And does he not claim also to belong to "the Church of Christ?" He certainly does; and is that "just a good big swagger?" I certainly do not deny that he is a Christian, or Disciple of Christ; that he belongs to the Church of Christ; neither does the handbill, with which he seems so displeased. But his pretensions, are greater than mine; he pretends to be more than a Christian, and to belong to one Church more than the Church of Christ! He claims to be a Baptist, and to belong to the Baptist Church. This is more than I claim for myself, and yet I award it all to him, and say nothing about it being a bigger swagger than mine? The handbill says nothing but what is true; it says, "Professor Crawford of the Baptist Church," and he will not deny that he is "of the Baptist Church," But, then, he says, "Remember, Mr. Crawford is not of the Christian Church!" But the handbill doesn't say that; nor can the Professor deduce that conclusion from what it does say, unless he can show that being "of the Baptist Church" is entirely inconsistent with one's being at the same time "of the Christian Church." And, by the way, I should like to hear from him on this point. Then, the handbill says, "J. S. Sweeney, a Disciple of Christ," and I see nothing about that, for J. S. Sweeney professes to be "a disciple of Christ"—an humble one. I claim to belong to the "Church of Christ;" and if I do not belong to it, then I belong to *no* Church. The gentleman can say I belong to none if he chooses, though I hardly believe he will.

The question is simply this: Have we the right to refuse to be called anything else than Christians, or Disciples of Christ, or other Scripture name, and to pretend to belong to no other Church than the Church of Christ? That's it. I say we have. I will take no party name upon me; of course you can call me a "Campbellite" if you choose; you could call me Satan if you would, but without my consent, I shall insist that it would be at least just a trifle impolite. My mother's people were called Methodists, and I speak of them as such because they chose that name. My father was once called a Baptist, because he chose to be so designated; but now he, with many others has laid off that party name, and wishes to be called by no other than a Scripture name; and I believe he has that right. I, of course, have no unkind feelings toward people who choose to wear party names; I only refuse to wear one myself. The Master was called Beelzebub without his approval, and I would try patiently to bear even as much myself, for the sake of doing what I conceive to be my right and duty. If my opponent wishes to be called a "Christian" or "Disciple of Christ," and not a Baptist, let him only say so, and I will not call him a Baptist again, unless it should be a slip of the tongue; and I think, that, in this particular, I could control my tongue better than some have done.

The gentleman persists in his effort to make the impression that the writings of Mr. Campbell, and those of Mr. Franklin, are of greater importance among us than we are willing to attach to them. True, Mr. Campbell was President of Bethany College, and editor of a paper

that circulated largely among our people ; but
to neither of these positions was he appointed
by any concerted action of our people, so as to
make us responsible for what he wrote. In the
main, our people do accord with what he wrote
and taught, and now that he is dead we honor
his memory as that of a *man* and a great teacher.
And while I would rather undertake to defend
his writings, as a whole, than the writings of any
other uninspired man ; nevertheless, nothing he
ever wrote is our creed. Nothing he ever wrote
is authoritative with us. And the book Mr.
Franklin wrote and publishes, from which my
friend quotes, Mr. Franklin is alone responsible
for. These remarks I make solely for the benefit
of such persons as may need and desire informa-
tion upon the subject, and not because our people do not in the main believe what those men
have written. Has the gentleman produced anything from Mr. Campbell or Mr. Franklin with
which my position, as I have defined it in this
debate, does not harmonize ? I think not. I
think the point of difference between us is quite
clearly made out. We teach, affirmatively, that
in conversion the Spirit operates through the
truth ; my friend agrees to this. But he goes
further, and says it also operates without the
truth ; that is, by its own immediate personal
presence in the sinner's heart ; and this immediate and unconditional action of the Spirit, he
holds to be necessary to " open the heart " and
" make the sinner willing to receive the truth."
This I deny. Now let us have the Scripture
upon the subject. We have had the gentleman's
inferences ; they have been tried and, I think,
found wanting.

 Will the gentleman plant himself upon the
case of Lydia ? Will he say that her heart was

opened, and that she was made able and willing to receive the truth, by such an interest as he contends for? If so, there I'll meet him.

One word as to the quotation I made from Dunn's book—the "*Mission of the Spirit.*" When I read that quotation, and emphatically denied what it said, the gentleman by my opponent's side, or somebody else in that vicinity, muttered, "infidel." [Here the gentleman referred to, a minister, said, "it was I."] Very well; he thinks I am "infidel" because I deny the teaching of that quotation. Now, I put it to Professor Crawford, will he endorse the doctrine of the quotation? Will he? I say he will not. In fact, he has already repudiated it. Will his brother call him "infidel?" I pause just a moment to listen. I don't hear any one say "infidel."

Upon another point raised by my opponent, I wish to say a few words, and will begin by reading a passage from Dr. Lumkin, in "*The Baptist Pulpit,*" page 83.

"The word of God is that 'sword of the spirit' which God has directed to be used by all his servanes, and on which, under his direction, they are to depend for success in all their labours. 'For the word of God is quick and powerful, and sharper than any two-edged sword, piercing even to the dividing asunder of soul and spirit, and is a discerner of the thoughts and intents of the heart.' But they cannot use this *powerful*, this *efficient* weapon, unless they have a knowledge of the word of God."

I make this quotation from this distinguished Baptist divine because he understands as I do the two passages of Scriptures which he uses in the extract I have read. One of the passages calls the word of God "the sword of the Spirit," and Christians are told to "take" the sword of the

Spirit, which is the word of God, and use it in the Christian warfare. We are not to expect the *Spirit* to take up and use this weapon, as my friend seems to understand the matter; but *we* are to use it. So Dr. Lumkin understands it, for he says, "the word of God is that sword of the Spirit which God has directed to be *used by all his servants*." Then, after quoting the other passage, which says, "the word of God is *living* and *powerful*, and sharper than any two-edged sword, piercing even to the dividing asunder of soul and spirit," the Dr. calls the word of God "this *powerful*, this *efficient* weapon." Certainly it's powerful. The power in it is divine power, "the power of God," "the power of God unto salvation." It is "able to save your souls." Certainly it's "*efficient*" because the power of the Holy Spirit is in it—*always* in it—and not now in it, and then out, as my friend seems to understand the matter. When, therefore, one speaks of the "*mere* word," the word *without the Spirit's power*," he assumes what is never true. The word of God is *never the word without the spirit*, any more than Professor Crawford is himself without his spirit. In the sense of being without the spirit, without the divine and almighty energy, there is no such thing as "the word *alone*," or "the *mere* word." The divine power for conversion and sanctification is *always* in the Gospel. I trust I am understood on this point. If my opponent is prepared to show that the word of God is sometimes dead, as the body without the spirit is dead, let him do it at once; and not persist in using such phrases as assume what he cannot show ever to be true. I do most earnestly protest against Christians ever using such phrases as "the word of God alone," "the mere word," in the sense I understand the Professor to use them. Heaven and earth *may* fail, but that word shall *never* fail. Does my friend believe there is to be a resurrection from the dead? Does he believe there is a heaven? Shall I say he has nothing for these but the word of God *alone*, the *mere* word?

While my opponent will not endorse Dr. Dunn outright he preaches nearly the same thing. He believes in the Gospel, he says, but the sinner will not and cannot receive it till the Spirit goes before and enables him to receive it and makes him willing. The sinner, he thinks, is opposed to God, resists the truth with all his might, prefers to remain in sin rather than be saved; but the spirit, despite his resistance, *breaks* in upon his heart, *crushing* down all resistance, and "*makes* him willing" to receive the Gospel! Well, after all, that looks very much like an irresistible operation. Now, it looks to me, that if God will thus irresistibly break in upon his own image, and crush down man's selfhood, to save him, he might better have thus prevented him from sinning in the first place, and saved the world all the sufferings and sorrows brought in by sin. But where is the Scripture for this divine violence in conversion? We have yet to hear it, I think. *Jesus* says: "Behold, I stand at the door, and knock; if any man hear my voice, and *open the door*, I will come in to him, and will sup with him, and he with me." What is it to "open the door" unto the Lord? Here is the answer: "He that hath an ear let him hear what the spirit *saith* to the churches." But Professor Crawford doesn't believe in knocking and waiting for the door to be opened by him who dwells within. He believes that while the sinner bars the door against the Spirit, resisting his entrance with might and main, the Spirit will *break* in, like "the thief or robber," only more boldly!

ADDRESS.

Thursday, 10th Sept., 2 *o'clock, P.M.*
(PROFESSOR CRAWFORD'S THIRD ADDRESS.)

Professor Crawford—My opponent complains very much at my still employing the term Campbellites, and wishes to have the name of Disciples. Well, I don't want to irritate or hurt the feelings of anybody, and I shall, if my memory serves me, give them that name—though, I must say that I do so under protest, as I think I have as much right to the name as they have.

Mr. Sweeney—Well, I will call you by that name if you desire.

Professor Crawford—I wish my opponent not to make any remarks while I am speaking. He complains also of my saying that Campbell was the founder of the sect. By this I mean that Campbell began to write and advocate what he called the ancient Gospel until others took it up and formed what I think we have the right to call a sect. I regard as a sect any section of a professing church, and I claim that they are entitled to that name. Mr. Campbell was the founder of that sect, and acted as their leader for many years, and was recognized as such by his followers. My opponent asks who appointed him to the presidency of their College? I presume it was the trustees of the College who sustained him, and "paid the piper." It was certainly not the Presbyterians, the Methodists, nor the Baptists who supplied the funds. No, it was the Campbellites—the Disciples—and, therefore, I maintain he was just as much a professor for that body as I am for the Baptists at Woodstock. He may not have been appointed to his professorship directly by the body, but by the trustees acting for them, though it was doubtless the people who supplied the "sinews of war." Though I was not placed in my office by the whole body of Baptists, but by the Trustees of the College acting for them, yet I am recognized by the churches of our denomination as an exponent of doctrines generally held by them. So with Mr. Campbell, and I don't think I have done anything unfair in quoting from Mr. Campbell's works to show what the views of the Campbellites or Disciples are.

Some complaint has been made because some members of this congregation have seen fit to express their feelings by applauding the speakers. I think there has been very little of that; in fact, they have behaved throughout remarkably well. It is my wish, however, that they should not say a single word when either of us is speaking, or manifest their feelings in any way; and I would say further, that I think it scarcely fair for my opponent to ask me questions when he is speaking, and when he knows I have no opportunity of answering them. Then, in his reasoning he seems to speak as though I undervalued the Gospel by saying that something more than the mere preaching of the Word was necessary to the saving of sinners, namely, the influence of the Holy Spirit. I firmly believe that the whole of the Scriptures were dictated to the Prophets and the Apostles by the direct inspiration of the Holy Spirit. We believe that in these Divine Oracles God has revealed His holy will and purpose; that they reveal the only method by which sinful men may find acceptance in the eyes of his Maker—by the Fountain opened in the House of David for sin and uncleanness. Let not my opponent speak as if we set a low value upon God's

Holy Word: we yield not to him in our reverence for, and belief in, its inspired utterances. And then in speaking of the work of the Spirit it seems to me my opponent is just a little disposed to lead us off the track. When I was a foolish young fellow I used to spend a good deal of my time in galloping after a pack of hounds. I used to notice that the young dogs were very apt to get on the wrong track, to get off the scent and get after a herring instead of following up in pursuit of the game. But the old dogs never got off the scent. It seems to me there is a little of this inclination "to get off the scent" on the part of my opponent, when he goes away to the heathen and speaks of the influence of the Spirit in their conversion. I don't know that the heathen are converted without the Gospel: it is not my idea on the subject, and is not taught at Woodstock nor in the Word of God. The question is not what takes place where the Gospel is not preached; it is, does God convert men by the Words of Truth alone or by the influence of His Spirit working along with the Word? I say that the Spirit does act directly and immediately upon the soul, making men willing to receive the Truth, opening their hearts for its reception. The Spirit operates upon the souls of men, and using the Truth as its instrument, converts and sanctifies them. My opponent also misstates my argument with regard to the creation of man in the moral image of God. My argument was, that as God acted directly and immediately in moulding the human soul into His own moral image, so He can in the work of conversion and sanctification. To deny its possibility in one case is to deny it in the other. And I also argue that as Satan acts directly and immediately upon the souls of men for his evil purposes, so the Almighty can and does act in accomplishing the salvation of the sinner. But my opponent says, it is not what God can do; it is, what *does* He do? But Mr. Campbell himself explains this matter: He says "If the Spirit of God has spoken all its arguments; or, if the New and Old Testaments contain all the arguments which can be offered to reconcile man to God, and to purify them who are reconciled, then *all the power* of the Holy Spirit which can operate on the human mind *is spent;* and he that is not sanctified and saved by these, cannot be saved by angels or spirits, human or divine."

You observe it is not what "will" or "does" operate, but what "*can*" operate. His doctrine is that no moral effect can be produced but by moral means, that is, by the Truth: whereas, I have shown by these examples that God has produced moral effects, without any means, that is, directly; and if in these cases, why not in others? Why not in conversion? I think this quotation from his own author is a sufficient answer to that argument.

When I had to leave off in my last speech, I was referring to the arguments used by Mr. Campbell, who, reasoning from analogy, said it was easier to believe than to become sanctified; easier to enlist in the army than to become a good soldier; easier to start in the race than to win the crown. I was just going to say that we could bring arguments, by analogy, from the other side of the question, in fact, such arguments are only the shadow of reasoning. I might ask was it easier for Lazarus to awaken from the sleep of death, than afterwards to walk about in his grave-clothes? And when Christ brought the maiden to life, was it an easier thing for her to rise and sit up in bed, than to eat afterwards? Or was it easier for the son of the widow of Nain to sit up in the bier, than afterwards to speak to the multitude? So you see this arguing from analogy is not worth a straw! The Roman Catholics tell us about St. Dennis, that when his head was cut off, he took it under his arm and walked a thousand miles! It seems a pretty big thing to walk a thousand miles, but it's not quite so big a thing as having his head cut off, to pick it up, and take the first step!

Let us now find what the Word of God has to say on this subject of the Spirit's influence. Ezekiel 36, 26, and 27: "A new heart also will I give you, and a new Spirit will I put within you; and I will take away the stony heart out of your flesh, and I will give you an heart of flesh. And I will put my Spirit within you, and cause you to walk in my statutes, and ye shall keep my judgments and do them." Here then, He is to "put a new Spirit" within them, and to put *His Spirit* within them. What does that mean, but that the Spirit of the living God, would take up its abode in their souls, and being there would work a mighty change in them, causing them to walk in His statutes. Perhaps my opponent will say the Spirit enters by the Word. I admit it. I believe when the Spirit enters into the heart of a man, He uses the Divine Word as His instrument. But it is, nevertheless, the Spirit acting upon the soul, causing it to embrace the Truth, which effects the change of heart. Again II. Cor. 3, 14-16: "But their minds were blinded; for until this day remaineth the same veil untaken away in the reading of the Old Testament; which veil is done away in Christ. But even unto this day, when Moses is read the veil is upon their hearts.

Nevertheless, when it shall turn to the Lord, the veil shall be taken away. Now the Lord is that Spirit," &c. He is here speaking of the Jews. The Truth was presented to them, but still the veil remained before their eyes; they heard the Truth, but they could not know or understand until God would take away the veil; then they would turn to Him. My opponent will say the veil was taken away by the Truth, but the Truth was the very thing they had heard, and read, and rejected, for it was when Moses was read to them that the veil of prejudice was on their hearts. How is the Truth to enter until the Spirit shall take away the veil? Again in Ephesians, 2, 10: "For we are his workmanship, created in Christ Jesus unto good works, which God hath before ordained that we should walk in them." The disciple's idea is that we are His workmanship, inasmuch as God has made the Word, and that Word alone converts the soul. It is just the same as saying that the man who makes the axe, cuts down the tree. They leave out the real agent in the work, and take only the instrument used by that agent. Again, Ephesians 2, 4-5: "But God, who is rich in mercy, for His great love wherewith He loved us, even when we were dead in sins, hath quickened us together with Christ, (by grace ye are saved)." Here then, you see, we were all dead in sins, but God has quickened those who believe together with Him. I ask can a dead man be quickened without Divine power? I say not. My opponent will perhaps say it is a figure. I admit that the language is figurative; but there is a meaning in the figure. There is a moral and spiritual death, and just as the mere words, "Lazarus come forth," would not of themselves, without Divine influence, have brought the dead man to life, so the Truth, without being accompanied by the Spirit's influence will not bring the soul into the newness of spiritual life. Then in I. Cor. 3-6, 7 : "I have planted, Apollos watered; but God gave the increase. So then, neither is he that planteth anything, neither he that watereth ; but God that giveth the increase." Paul planted the good seed of the Word, and by it the Church ; Apollos came after and watered, but without other influence there would be no increase. The farmer may sow his seed ; the dews and rains of Heaven may water the ground, but it is the Almighty power of God that causes it to grow. Is there any innate power in the seed itself ? Certainly not ; we must not confound these two things. We talk of seed growing, but it is only God's way of carrying on his work. God's power is just as necessary to make it grow as it was to create it in the first place. But, according to Mr. Campbell, the power of the Spirit is spent in the planting and watering. Whence then does the increase come ? I. Peter, 1-22 : "Seeing ye have purified your souls in obeying the truth through the Spirit, unto unfeigned love of the brethren, see that ye love one another with a pure heart fervently." Here, you observe, they had obeyed the truth, how ? "Through the Spirit." There would be no meaning to these words if the truth was all that was required, but both are necessary. I will read next, Ezekiel 36, 27 : "And I will put my Spirit within you and cause you to walk in my statutes, and ye shall keep my judgments and do them." A change was to be wrought among them : "they were to walk in his statutes and keep his judgments," but how was this change to be brought about . "I will put my Spirit within you, and *cause* you to do so." The

Spirit was necessary to cause or induce them to obey the Truth. Then in Heb. 8, 10: "For this is the covenant that I will make with the House of Israel after those days, saith the Lord; I will put my laws into their mind and write them in their hearts; and I will be to them a God, and they shall be to me a people." His laws were not only to be put into their mind; they were to be *written* in their hearts; not merely the words of this law to be clearly presented to the mind, something more was required. It does not say that the Truth will write itself in their hearts, or that they themselves were to do this, but "*I* will write it." Romans 8, 9, "But ye are not in the flesh, but in the Spirit, if so be that the Spirit of God dwell in you. Now if any man have not the Spirit of God, he is none of His." Here then the Spirit of God is to dwell in them. My opponent and Mr. Campbell say that all that is meant is that the words of the Spirit dwell in the man, and that to be filled with the Spirit is to have the Word of God dwell richly in them. We say that the Spirit of God dwells in them, and I appeal to common sense if that is not plainly the meaning of the passage. I venture to say that ninety-nine out of every hundred unprejudiced men would say that this is the only interpretation of which the words are susceptible. We must get a new vocabulary if we take any other meaning out of these plain words. I will read next I. Cor. vi. 19: "What! know ye not that your body is the Temple of the Holy Ghost which is in you, which ye have of God, and ye are not your own?" What do we understand by our being the Temples of the Holy Ghost? Does it not mean that the Holy Spirit is in us? Not merely that the words are there, but the actual

Spirit? I will illustrate: Suppose you say Mr. Crawford was at such a house on a certain day. I say, "No, I think I can prove an *alibi*." But says my Disciple brother, "Yes, you were there, for if you were not personally, your *words* were there, for they were reading one of your sermons." I hold that no reasonable person can take any other meaning from the text I have quoted than the one I have given it. It means more than the mere words of the Holy Ghost.

REPLY.

Thursday, Sept. 10th, 2½ p.m.
(MR. SWEENEY'S THIRD REPLY.)

Mr. Sweeney—I trust that we have come together this afternoon prepared to pursue the discussion profitably.

I take occasion, first, to remove an impression that was probably made upon the audience, by a remark that my friend made about the behaviour of the hearers. He said that the audience had behaved remarkably well, and from this it might be inferred that I had complained of the conduct of the audience; but I certainly have not. True, there was a brother, sitting near my friend, who spoke a time or two, and nodded oftener, this forenoon, and some member of the congregation complained of it. That was all. In this connection my friend also complained of my speaking to him while delivering his speech. He should not have begun it. I will try not to speak to him again, however, while he is speaking, as I certainly have no desire to interrupt him. And when I ask him a question, in the course of my speech, I don't wish him to answer it at the time but desire him to bear it in mind and answer it when his time comes. I refer to these little matters merely that no capital may be made out of them.

The gentleman says he will call us Campbellites no more, if his memory serves him well. It seems to me his memory is a little bad. I fear, too, there is something else at fault; for he says that while he shall call us Disciples, he will do so under protest. Now, as I have said already, when we ask to be called Disciples of Christ, we do not mean it to be implied that we are the only Disciples of Christ, or that he is not one. By no means. Yet he will call us Disciples *under protest!* He is something like Galileo, who said the world turned round the sun, when it was a new doctrine, and being pressed he retracted the statement, but it is said that as he turned away from where the retraction was extorted from him, he nodded his head significantly and said, in a low voice, "But it *does* turn, though." I am afraid the professor feels that we "*are* Campbellites, though." I would rather not have him convinced so against his will.

The gentleman tells us that Mr. Campbell founded a sect by going out from among the Baptists. By the way, he has improved his statement as to the separation of Mr. Campbell from the Baptists, since this forenoon. Then, if my memory serves me well, he had it that the Baptists "cut him off." But that is immaterial. He thinks Mr. Campbell went out from the Baptists and formed a sect, while Mr. Campbell claimed that he went out from the Baptists that he might occupy the simple, primitive, unsectarian, apostolic ground. I believe, too, that he was, to say the very least, *less* a sectarian after he laid off the Baptist name and party peculiarities than he was while wearing and maintaining them. In this particular, at any rate, Mr. Campbell became more apostolic.

I would like to hold my friend to one point at a time. Whether we are a sect, in the current sense of that word, has no bearing upon the question between us, as to spiritual influence in conversion. Let us stick to that point for the present.

The gentleman tells us that the question is,

Does God convert men by the Word of Truth alone, or by the Spirit working with the Word? I deny that that is a fair statement of the question. "Word of Truth *alone*" is his language, not mine. I deny that any of my brethren would accept that statement: for, by "alone" he evidently means to exclude from the truth the power thereof. He means by that word to exclude the power that we hold is ever present with it, and essential to it, and, indeed, inseparable from it. Then, he states his side of the question as being, that the Spirit works along with the Word. I thought he believed that the Spirit works *without* the Word—works where the Word *can't* work. To say that the Spirit works *immediately* "along *with the Word*" is to contradict one's self in the very statement, as I have already said. We believe the Spirit is the Spirit of the Truth, is ever present with that Truth, is ever efficient where that Truth is received, and consequently the Truth does nothing without the Spirit—does not even exist without it, any more than my body is J. S. Sweeney without the spirit. Let not our position be misunderstood. Does my friend believe the Spirit does desert the Gospel and leave it powerless?—that it is in the Gospel sometimes, making it efficient, and at other times out of it, rendering it inefficient? If this is his position, I am solicitous that he should say so. It is not mine. I believe in no such Divine inconstancy. I believe that the Gospel, the Word of God, is not occasionally, but *always*, "the power of God," always "quick and powerful."

My notes bring me back to Mr. Campbell again. Now, I have not objected to my friend's quoting from Mr. Campbell, to show what our people generally believe on this question or that, but I have objected to his calling him the founder of what he is pleased to call a sect, and being an authority among us. I believe that Mr. Campbell and others abandoned their respective sects and returned to primitive Christianity. At any rate, they aimed to do so. And if the gentleman thinks they failed to do this, and thinks he can show that they only founded another sect, let him do so. I am certainly not conscious of trying to maintain a mere sect. If I were convinced that I am engaged in such a work, I would abandon it at once. Let the gentleman proceed to show us wherein we have failed and do fail to occupy primitive apostolic ground, and I will consider his effort a friendly one and try to profit by it. I have never claimed perfection. Possibly we have failed to do the thing we have aimed to do, and done the very things we aimed not to do; and when I am convinced this is so, I will try again. If he thinks, now, that he can show that we do not come nearer to primitive Christianity, in our teaching and practice, than others, let him do it. I only ask that we have credit for trying to do so, and for believing that we do.

The gentleman says, very emphatically, that he and his brethren do not undervalue the Word of God. Well, of course, what I said upon that point I said in reference to their *theory* of conversion, and not respecting their intentions. Did I not read from a distinguished Baptist preacher that God has given us "*no* means" for the conversion of sinners, "irrespective of the *direct* influence of the Spirit?" Now, while I do not say that its advocates intend it, I do say that this theory undervalues the Gospel, which Paul calls *the* power of God for salvation. So it seems to me. Suppose some man manufactures a machine for cutting wheat, and sells it to a farmer; and then I say to that farmer, "you have *no* means for cutting wheat, irrespective of *another* machine whose claims I may be advocating." Do I not undervalue the one he has just bought? What would the manufacturer who had furnished the machine the farmer had, think about the force of my remark? As to the conversion of the sinner, my friend's theory says, "the Gospel will not do it"—will not do the very thing it is, in my judgment, intended to do; the very thing it is called "the power of God" to accomplish! That's what I mean to say, and the gentleman can fix it up to suit him.

My friend thinks I wish to get him away from the question—want to get him off the track. He says when he was a foolish boy he used to go hunting. I shouldn't wonder! And he knows that young pups may be drawn off the trail of the game, by herring being drawn across the trail. But he is not to be tricked in that way! No sir; not he! He, I suppose, is "an old dog," and means to keep track. Perhaps, he might better be looking after the "pups," if there are any in the chase, lest they be led astray by my tricks. But more seriously. Have I attempted to shun the discussion of a point of difference between us?

The gentleman says the question is not as to the conversion of heathens, but of people in Gospel lands. Very well; let him show that the Spirit operates, as he says it does, *anywhere*. Leave the heathen out of the question; though I think Rev. Mr. Dunn, from whom I read in my first speech, is more consistent than he. If the Spirit operates anywhere without the Gospel, why not where the light of the Gospel doesn't shine?

I must again remind our hearers that the question between us is not one of power, but one of fact. *Does* the Spirit so act in conversion ? Not, *can* it so act ; I would consent to discuss no question as to the power of the Spirit. My friend thinks Mr. Campbell argued that the Spirit cannot act directly ; I suppose the gentleman does not understand Mr. Campbell's argument. Mr. Campbell never limited the Divine power, I suppose, though his argument may have limited the powers of man as to moral effects. I, however, feel no concern about Mr. Campbell's *arguments*. Professor Crawford is too late to debate with Mr. Campbell, that much abused man. I suppose if he had come along about fifty years ago Campbellism would have been wiped from the earth in its very incipiency!

I care nothing about the question as to whether it was easier to raise Lazarus from the dead or for him to walk after he was raised. The raising of the dead body of Lazarus was one thing and the conversion of a soul to God is another and quite different one. The effect in the one case was purely physical, and in the other as purely moral. If Mr. Crawford was replying to some of Mr. Campbell's analogical arguments, why that's an affair I am clean out of, and about which, consequently, I feel little or no concern.

But I must now give attention to the passages of Scripture quoted in my friend's last speech, in support of his view of the subject. Ezekiel, 36, 26-27 : " A new heart also will I give you, and a new Spirit will I put within you ; and I will take away the stony heart out of your flesh, and I will give you a heart of flesh. And I will put my Spirit within you and cause you to walk in my statutes, and ye shall keep my judgments and do them." Now, I can see nothing in this passage about the kind of influence in question. Granting that the prophet was speaking of conversion, that is of individual conversion, which he certainly was not, he does not say how it was to be accomplished. All that God said he would do could be done in perfect harmony with our view of spiritual influence. My opponent assumes the very point, and the only point, in controversy; he assumes that the work here spoken of was to be done by the Holy Spirit acting *directly* upon the heart, whereas that is the only point in question between us. 2 Cor., 3, 14-16: "But their minds were blinded; for until this day remaineth the same veil untaken away in the reading of the Old Testament; which veil is done away in Christ. But even unto this day, when Moses is read, the veil is upon their heart. Nevertheless, when it shall turn to the Lord, the veil shall be taken away." Just what my friend sees in this Scripture to support his theory is more than I can tell. The apostle is speaking of the Jews, in the passage; and he says that when they read the Old Testament their minds are blinded by what he calls a veil; that veil, doubtless, was, and is, a false theory of interpretation. If the Jews were rightly to interpret the Old Testament they would, of course, all become Christians. When they turn to Christ then they will see clearly what has all along been obscure in their own Scriptures. This veil is done away in Christ; Christ solves the mysteries of the types and prophecies of the Old Testament. But, rejecting Him, the Old Testament is dark, obscure. But does the apostle say this veil will be removed by an immediate operation of the Spirit? Nothing of the kind. "*When they turn to the Lord*," receive him as answering to the types and shadows, as the fulfilment of the prophecies, of their Scriptures, then the obscurity will be gone. Why, my opponent reads this very passage with a veil over his mind! He is looking for a doctrine in it that's not there, and hence it is all obscure to him. The Old Testament is not the only book that is so read, nor are the Jews the only people that read with a veil over their minds. Eph. 2, 10; "For we are his workmanship, created in Christ Jesus unto good works, which God hath before ordained, that we should walk in them." I believe all that is taught in this passage as firmly as my opponent can. Those Ephesian Christians were "created in Christ"—of course they were, but how? That's the question we are discussing; and that's the question about which nothing is said in the verse quoted. It only states the fact. But let us turn back to chapter 1 and verse 10, where we have something to the point: "In whom ye also trusted, after that ye heard the Word of Truth, the Gospel *of your salvation;* in whom also *after that ye believed,* ye were sealed with that Holy Spirit of promise." This touches the point in question. Here we learn that the Ephesians trusted in Christ after they "heard the Word of Truth," which the apostle calls the *Gospel of their salvation.* Then, *after they believed,* they were "sealed with that Holy Spirit of promise." Does this look like the doctrine Professor Crawford preaches, concerning the Holy Spirit? My friend quotes also the 4th and 5th verses of the second chapter, wherein the apostle says the Ephesians "were dead," but had been "quickened together with Christ," and asks if a dead man can be made alive without Divine power? There is, I submit, no question between us as to the necessity for Divine power in conversion; but

4

the question is as to *how* that Divine power is *exerted*. If my friend means to assume that the Ephesians were, or that other unconverted persons are, dead in such a sense as that Divine power could not be exerted upon them through the Gospel, then I deny it and call for the proof. It may not be amiss just now and here to say a word or two about figurative language, as it will not be denied that the apostle here speaks figuratively. When one thing is called by the name of another, in some respects *different* thing, this is a figurative speech. One thing may be called by the name of another when the two are alike in one particular, or more; if the two were alike in *every* particular they would, of course, be the same thing. With these remarks about figures of speech, that will not be called in question by my learned opponent, I raise this question: In what particular is the state, or condition, of an unconverted man like that of a *dead* man? If my friend says they are alike in that, that neither of them can hear, or reason, or believe, or will, or act, I deny it, and am ready for the question. If he cannot make this out, then of what use is this passage in his cause, in this controversy? None whatever. 1 Cor. 3. 6: "I have planted, Apollos watered, but God gave the increase." Here my friend has the veil over his mind again. He understands the "planted," "watered," and "made to grow," (for that is the meaning of "gave the increase") to be predicated of *the Word of God*; that is, he understands Paul to mean, "I have planted the Word of God, Apollos watered the Word of God, but God made the Word to grow." How did Apollos water *the Word of God?* Is that the way the Professor teaches Biblical interpretation at Woodstock? Why, the Word of God that Paul preached at

Corinth took root and grew before ever Apollos went there: for we read that when Paul first went there, "Crispus, the chief ruler of the synagogue, believed on the Lord with all his house; and many of the Corinthians hearing believed and were baptized" (Acts xviii, 8). What, then, was it that Paul planted, Apollos watered, and God made to grow? It was the cause—the Christian community—the Church, in that city. So, it turns out that the Apostle was not talking about *conversion* in the sense we are at all; and even if he were, he says nothing about the kind of influence my friend is contending for. He, of course, is trying to find it in the phrase "God gave the increase." But, allowing his own interpretation or application of the passage, it says nothing as to *how* "God gave the increase."

But now, having confined myself thus far in the discussion to the speeches of my opponent, and having, at least to my own satisfaction, replied to his arguments, in the remainder of my time in this speech I propose to notice a passage of Scripture or two that I believe to be irreconcilably opposed to the theory my friend advocates. Matt. xiii, 15, "For this people's heart is waxed gross, and their ears are dull of hearing, and their eyes they have closed; lest at any time they should see with their eyes, and hear with their ears, and should understand with their heart, and should be converted, and I should heal them." To be healed, one must be converted; to be converted one must understand with the heart; to understand with the heart, one must see and hear: this is the Lord's order. But the people of whom he was speaking were not healed. Why? Because they were not converted. Why were they not converted? Because they had not seen with their eyes and heard with their ears. But, why had they not seen with their eyes and heard with their ears? Let the Lord answer: "Their ears are dull of hearing, and their eyes they have closed; lest at any time they should see with their eyes and hear with their ears." One more question may be asked: Why were their ears dull of hearing and their eyes closed? Were they or were they not responsible for it? If my friend says it was a matter over which they had no control, then he denies all just responsibility and sweeps away all foundation for praise or blame, vice or virtue: and I shall treat him hereafter as a regular Calvinist.

But the Lord says of these people, "Their eyes *they have closed*, lest at any time they should see with their eyes and hear with their ears, and understand with their heart, and should be converted, and I should heal them." This justly throws the responsibility upon them. But when you say the closing of their eyes was a matter over which they had no control, and the opening of them a thing they could no more do than they could open heaven, you relieve them of all just responsibility. This seems to me as clear as a sunbeam. I believe men have the power of choice—that they can hear or they can refuse to hear—that they can see or refuse to see: I believe God has made them so. I believe a man may go down to perdition before God will violate the laws of His happiness and of His being—before He will break down the dignity of His own image to save him. God will never convert a man whether he is willing or not.

ADDRESS.

Thursday, Sept. 10th, 3 p.m.

(PROF. CRAWFORD'S FOURTH ADDRESS.)

Prof. Crawford—We have heard that Mr. Campbell has been very much abused. Now, when I bring forth the arguments used by Mr. Campbell in order to show that they are wrong, I don't think I lay myself open to the charge of having abused him. I do not want to hurt the feelings of, or insult, any one, but I do say that he taught what I regard as heresy. My opponent says that I will not affirm that the Holy Spirit acts directly and immediately upon the soul. Have I not time and again affirmed that it operates directly upon the soul in taking away the veil? In the text in which it speaks of the veil being taken away, who is it that is to take away the veil? God himself, of course. He will fulfil this promise. And is not this by the immediate operation of the Spirit upon the soul, taking away the veil of sinful prejudice, and preparing the heart for the reception of the Truth? Let me not be misunderstood: I say the Holy Spirit does act immediately in preparing for the entrance of the Truth, and in carrying on the work of grace thus begun it uses the Truth as its instrument. My opponent tries to evade the question. He says it is the Holy Spirit operating through the Truth, but when you come to examine his words you find that it is not in the sense of the Holy Spirit using the Truth as its instrument. I think the audience clearly understand my position in this matter without my being obliged to repeat it again and again to satisfy my opponent. There is such a thing as having a knowledge of the Truth merely as a matter of fact or history, without being in possession of a "saving knowledge of the Truth." I may believe the words of the Gospel, but yet my heart may not be opened so as to see its beauty, and accept it as the means of saving my soul. I may look at it through a perverting medium of prejudice, and it requires the influence of God's Spirit to remove this prejudice and to show me the Truth in all its loveliness, and apply it to my heart and conscience so as to convert my soul. It is like viewing a beautiful landscape through crooked glass; there is no beauty thus to be seen in it, no loveliness, nothing to please the eye or the fancy. Everything, however, that is necessary to inspire pleasure and delight is there; I see every tree and every house, I see it all, but everything is twisted and contorted by the crooked medium through which I view it. So it is with the human mind until the Spirit of God operates upon the soul. There is an obscurity, a veil of prejudice before the understanding; but whenever the Spirit of God takes away that veil, removes that prejudice, the soul sees Christ in all his loveliness and beauty. He becomes then for the first time "the chief among ten thousand, the altogether lovely."

Here is where I find the greatest fault with the doctrines of the Disciples: they think if they can by arguing, by using logic with a man, get the Truth to lodge in his mind, the work is done. I believe that is the kind of doctrine that makes stony-ground hearers of the Word; that gives the form of godliness without the power. I doubt very much if that kind of doctrine will have any very great effect; it will not only make the sinner feel self-sufficient, but will puff up the preacher with a sort of self-sufficiency. For if he can only by the dint of reasoning, or by his eloquence, get men to accept the Gospel as dry facts, just as they would believe any other book, they would feel that they had saved their souls, and that their work was done, instead of feeling their dependence upon God and giving him all the glory. But it is only when the veil is taken away by the Spirit of the living God, and when God puts His Spirit into men's hearts, that they see the Truth in all its loveliness. It is then that their hearts become melted into submission to his will. It is then that the sinner is constrained to abandon his evil ways, and consecrate himself, body and soul, to the service of Christ. I think it is now pretty clear what are the views I and my opponent hold respectively on this subject, without our paddling over the same ground again and again. I think, too, you will perceive that when I quote from the works of Mr. Campbell and Mr. Franklin to show their views, I am not very far from the doctrines held by the Disciples, as well as by my opponent. And it is scarcely fair for him to accuse me of not sticking to the propositions I first laid down, for I don't think he can show where I have deviated from them in a single instance. I find no fault with the quotation he gives from a Baptist author (J. W. Hayhurst): "God has given us no means by which sinners can be converted, or a general revival take place, irrespective of the direct agency of the Spirit." Why, instead of finding fault with that doctrine, it is just what I have been trying to make you understand is my position. I hold that without the Spirit of God accompanying the Truth and using it as its instrument, there is no salvation for the sinner.

80   DEBATE.

The Gospel cannot of itself do it; it requires the Spirit of God to apply it. The preacher cannot do it; it is true that the Bible speaks in some passages as if the soul was converted by the preacher, but we all know that the preacher is only the subordinate agent. And so it sometimes speaks as if conversion was effected by the Gospel, but the meaning is that the Gospel is but the instrument in the hands of the Spirit.

With reference to the passages of Scripture he has quoted as, "I will put my Spirit within you," I would ask what is God's Spirit but the Holy Ghost? And when God's Spirit is said to be in a man, there is nothing to show that it is in him, merely by the words of the Spirit being in him, any more than that I am *in* a room if my sermons are read there. I don't deny but a man may at the same time have the Words of the Truth in him or in his heart, but when God says He will put His Spirit *in* them it means not that the words *alone* are there, but the Spirit is there in His actual presence. I again appeal to common sense whether any other meaning can legitimately be drawn from the words.

Then in regard to that passage (2 Cor. 3, 15-16) where it speaks of the veil being taken away, he asks who takes the veil away? He has not explained who takes it away if it is not God. In order to weaken the force of that passage he must explain how the veil is taken away if not by the influence of God's Spirit. It is merely evading the point to ask this question without producing anything to show that my exposition of the text is not the correct one. Why is it that the Apostle gives us the promise of God that the veil shall be taken away by God himself?

With regard to Lydia's case, I don't think he has shown that it conflicts in the least with what

I have been saying. I say that the veil that had hidden the Truth from her heart was taken away by the power of God's Spirit. Speaking of her the Apostle states: "Whose heart the Lord opened, that she attended unto the things which were spoken of Paul." Nothing can be plainer than this language. God had to "open her heart" before the Truth was received by her. Speaking of the passage where it says: "You hath he quickened who were dead in trespasses and sins," my opponent asserts that in using a figure it is not necessary that the figure shall cover every quality on the thing prefigured. I admit this. I do not say that in every respect those who are unconverted, those who are *dead* in trespasses and sins, are the same in every respect as a corpse in the grave; but I do mean to say that there is a moral death, resembling essentially, in many particulars, physical dissolution; and it is death inasmuch as God alone can quicken or bring to life the soul in such a case. I say that a man without any theory or prejudice upon this subject, reading in the passage of which I am speaking, that men "are dead in trespasses and sins," would say it must be a very great depravity indeed when men are said to be *dead* to all that is good. Surely there is something very strong and inveterate where such a figure as this is employed.

My opponent, speaking of I Cor. iii. 6: "I have planted, Apollos watered, but God gave the increase," says the planting and the watering means the planting and taking care of Churches. I think it is more natural to take it as referring to the planting and watering of good seed in individual hearts, and by that seed as the instrument, planting the Church. But whatever view you may take in that respect, the fact remains,

"God gave the increase." Paul says that they had done their share of the work; they had planted and watered, but something else was necessary before the harvest could be reaped. It is our duty to preach the Gospel, to warn sinners, to point out to them the happiness of the Christian's life, and the folly and guilt of unbelief, but the success must come from God. But according to the views of the Disciples, when I have lodged the words of the Gospel in my hearer's hearts that is all that is required—it is the Truth alone working that gives the increase; but the Bible says that the increase comes from God.

I will now refer to a few passages upon which my opponent has not touched. Romans viii. 9: "But ye are not in the flesh, but in the Spirit, if so be that the Spirit of God dwell in you. Now, if any man have not the Spirit of God, he is none of his." I ask if there is anything more in this than that the words of the Truth dwell in the man? The Apostle speaks distinctly of the Spirit of God dwelling in them. I think in this case also we can appeal to common sense as to the meaning of the passage; the language is unmistakable. Again, I Cor. vi. 19: "What! know ye not that your body is the temple of the Holy Ghost, which is in you, which ye have of God, and ye are not your own?" Surely there is here the Holy Spirit abiding and working personally in the soul; it is not merely that the Spirit or meaning of the Truth is there. I think there can be no other explanation given of this passage. Suppose we use an illustration to make it still plainer, though the words are certainly plain enough. If you employ a tailor to make you a coat, and when it is finished he leaves it at your house and retires: could you with any propriety say that because the coat made by the tailor was in your house the tailor himself was in the house ; or, if you put on the coat could you say that the tailor was on your back. So it would be no more proper to say that the Holy Spirit was in your heart as in a temple, if no more was meant than that your words were in your heart.

I would refer you next to Philippians ii. 13 : "For it is God which worketh in you both to will and do of his good pleasure." More than the words of the Truth, or the spirit or meaning of the words, is required ; God himself must work in you even to will and to do. And in II Timothy ii. 25, 26 : "In meekness instructing those that oppose themselves ; if God peradventure will give them repentance to the acknowledging of the Truth ; and that they may recover themselves out of the snare of the devil, who are taken captive by him of his will." Here, then, you observe that it is necessary for "God to give them repentance." It was the duty of the preacher or apostle to instruct the people in meekness, but God had to give them repentance before their hearts could be changed. Here, for instance, I hold that I am contending for the truth to-day, but my opponent will not acknowledge it, without divine help. So strongly do I believe in the doctrine I am advocating that I am fully persuaded that unless the Spirit make him willing, he will not acknowledge the Truth.

REPLY.

Thursday, Sept. 10th, 3½ p.m.
(MR. SWEENEY'S FOURTH REPLY.)

Mr. Sweeney—How the sinner could be justly blamed or held responsible for not receiving the Truth, if he has not the power to do it, is to me profoundly mysterious. But I will go over the gentleman's speech in the order in which it was delivered, as nearly as possible, if order may be used in such connection.

He told us that he had not abused Mr. Campbell. I have not accused him of it. I did not mean to use the word abuse in its worse sense either, in what I did say. A man is abused in one sense, when he is misrepresented, whether it is done intentionally or unintentionally. In the sense of being misrepresented, few men have been more abused than Mr. Campbell, in my judgment. He is not often right fairly represented by those who differ from him. But what we call prejudice is a wonderful something!

My friend still reads the third chapter of second Corinthians with the veil untaken away from his mind. He thinks the veil must be removed from the minds of the Jews by an immediate operation of the Holy Spirit, before they can turn to the Lord, notwithstanding the passage itself says "which veil is done away in Christ," and that "*when it* [Israel] *shall turn to the Lord,* the veil shall be taken away." He is contending that it must be taken away by a *direct* action of the Spirit, *before it can turn* to the Lord." Well, I certainly have no power to remove the veil from the Professor's mind by an immediate operation, and, therefore, I suppose it must remain untaken away. It is certain that Paul did not understand that the veil was to be removed by the Spirit going before the Truth, for he goes right on to say, "But if our Gospel be hid, it is hid to them that are lost; in whom the God of this world hath blinded the minds of them that believe not, lest *the light of the glorious Gospel of Christ*, who is the image of God, should shine unto them." Why, if Paul believed as my friend does, did he not explain that Israel *could* not receive Christ till the Spirit had taken away the veil, by a direct action upon their hearts? I think my opponent is pretty fully committed to one position— that the direct influence of the Spirit, for which he contends, goes before the Truth, and is necessary to enable the sinner to receive the Truth. The sinner, he thinks, is both unable and unwilling to receive the Truth till this direct operation is performed. I suppose, of course, that the professor would not, if he knew it, preach the Gospel to any who had not been enabled and made willing to receive it. This operation for which he contends, goes before all preaching; and, so far as the sinner is concerned, is necessarily both unconditional and irresistible. It comes while the sinner is unable to ask for it, and unwilling to receive it! Is the effect of this influence regeneration? If so, the sinner is unconditionally and irresistibly regenerated. If not, then this influence is not an influence *in* regeneration or conversion, after all; but an influence *before* that change. And as the gentleman seems to believe that after this direct operation, which enables and makes the sinner willing to receive the truth, the Spirit operates through the truth, he is with me at last, that, *in conversion*, the

Spirit operates through the truth. The difference between us, it seems, is simply about this crushing work of the Spirit that he contends for, going before all preaching, all faith, or repentance, or any other condition on the part of the creature. Now, the point on which I wish the professor to be explicit is this: When this immediate act of the Spirit passes upon the heart of a sinner is he not then regenerated or converted? I hope the gentleman will, for my benefit, make himself fully understood on this point.

But again: Is this unconditional and irresistible operation universal? If anyone dies without it he must either be taken into heaven in his sins, or sent to hell for what he could no more do than he could dethrone the God of the universe. If this influence is universal, then all will be saved, for it will make all both willing and able to receive Christ, and, of course, my friend will not allow that any one can fall from grace. So that, it seems to me, my opponent must advocate either universalism, or unconditional election and reprobation. I presume that he will come out a Calvinist.

Now, I deny that the Scriptures teach any such Spiritual influence as that contended for. I deny also that there is any necessity for it. The sinner can receive Christ, when He is preached to him, if he will. There is something sublimely beautiful in Christ, even to the sinner, if he will look at him. I know when I did not profess to be a Christian, and was not a Christian; but I can't say that there ever was a time, since I heard His story, that there was not something lovely and beautiful in Christ. Any man can see it if he will. If he will, the sinner can see something better in Christ than there is in sin, and can receive him. This makes him justly responsible.

But on my friend's theory, men will be damned, if any are damned, for no other reason than that the Spirit did not enable and make them willing to do what they could not do without his unconditional assistance. Now, if this has any justice in it, it takes Calvinism to see it ; with the senses God has given them, common men cannot. If I ever see it I suppose I will have to be perverted in my vision by some such influence as the gentleman contends for. It is certainly useless for him to try to make any one see it by preaching it to him. If I am to be damned for what I could not do, or for what I could not help doing, just because I was made to be damned, I suppose I couldn't more than be damned for saying that the thing is unjust. I should think so in hell forever, unless there I should experience the operation the Professor contends for, and I should say so too ; and I should have the satisfaction, even in hell, of ringing it round the dark walls of my prison, "unjust, unjust."

Let it be borne in mind that my friend's theory places every sinner just where he can do nothing, absolutely nothing, in the matter of his salvation. He must wait for the Holy Spirit to come ; and he can't even pray for that ; can't even desire it ; cannot, indeed, but resist it ; and yet if he dies in that condition he will be sent to hell for ever, because—because—because *what?* I hope the Professor will tell us if he can. Or, will he say that there is something one can do in the case ; that he can seek the needed influence ; that he can put himself in a state of receptivity and invite the Spirit into his heart, as Arminianism teaches? This would, at least, place the sinner in the predicament of the traveller, who wanted to cross the river , and to whom the ferryman sagely announced, that he could'nt cross without the boat, and that he couldn't get the boat without going across! But according to my opponent's theory a man couldn't even *want to cross!*

But, now, I should like to have the passage of Scripture that teaches this doctrine. I only want one passage. Where is it? Where? and only echo answers back, Where?"

The gentleman quotes certain passages that speak of the Spirit's influence in the Church, upon Christians; these I need not notice; for you will remember that he has told you already that we believe the Holy Spirit dwells in the hearts of Christians as it does not in the hearts of aliens. The Saviour, too, made this distinction when he promised the Spirit to his disciples. The passage that says God works in you to will and to do of his good pleasure was spoken to and of Christians. And even if it were spoken to sinners it would afford my friend's theory no support, as it says nothing as to the manner of God's working in persons to will and to do.

As to Lydia's case, I think my friend assumes the very thing to be proven. True, "the Lord opened Lydia's heart that she attended to the things spoken by Paul;" but he did not open her heart *that she might receive* the word, for Paul had preached to her *before* it is said "the Lord opened her heart, that she *attended* to the things spoken to her." Then, *how* did the Lord open her heart? The gentleman assumes that it was by Holy Spirit, and that the Spirit acted immediately upon her heart. Now, I will admit that it was done by the Spirit, but I deny that it was in the manner contended for. Let that be proven, not assumed. There is a man in Lexington, Ky., representing the University there, who came into Bourbon county and raised one hundred thousand dollars for that institution; and I remember hearing him say that "the Lord opened the hearts of the people of that county," that they responded thus liberally to his plea; but I don't suppose he ever dreamt that it was done by an immediate act of the Spirit upon their hearts. My friend reads this passage, too, with a veil upon his mind! He overlooks what is in it, and sees, or thinks he sees, what is not in it. He overlooks that important fact, that Paul had spoken to Lydia and she had heard the Gospel—which is the means through which God opens people's hearts—before it is said the Lord opened her heart. Then he thinks he sees the immediate operation of the Spirit in the passage, when in fact it does not even so much as mention the Holy Spirit itself.

The gentlemen comes back to his lame argument drawn from the passage that speaks of the unconverted as "dead in trespasses and sins." He admits that the language is figurative, and does not deny what I said as to the interpretation of such language. The point, therefore, to be settled is this: In what respect, or respects, is the conversion of a sinner like the resurrection of the dead? He admits that the conversion of a sinner is a moral change, and I hardly think he will deny that the literal resurrection of the dead is a physical one. In this important respect therefore the two things are different. He thinks the use of the figure certainly indicates great depravity. I admit it. He claims that the unconverted man is dead to all that's good. This I do not believe. It would be hard to convince me that there is a man in all the Queen's dominions who is, both in fact and conception, dead to *all* that is good. You may take the hardened sinner on examination, and you will find that in the depths of his sinful heart he cherishes the thought of some things that are good. Can any man hear of Christ's sufferings through his life and on the cross and remain unmoved? There are unregenerate persons who love their wives, their children, their friends and their homes, and for them would shed their heart's blood: and is there not something good in even these unregenerate ones? Christians are, in Scripture, represented as "dead in sin," "dead from the rudiments of the world;" but are they *as* dead, in conception and in fact, to these, as the body of Lazarus was to the things on the earth? I think not. True, the alien is not living to God, not an heir of God in Christ, as the Christian is, not having been born again, or adopted into the family of God, as the Christian has been. But that he is dead in such a sense as to be beyond the reach of the Gospel is the thing I deny, and this is the very thing my opponent needs to prove. I believe the alien is "dead in sins;" but I believe the Gospel is God's means of quickening him. I believe he needs to be born again; but I believe he is to be "born of incorruptible seed, by the Word of God which lives and abides for ever."

My opponent thinks the preaching of my brethren very dangerous preaching; he thinks its effect will be to make both preacher and people feel self-sufficient and proud—the preacher, because he has the power by his logic to convert the people: and the people, because they have the intelligence and understanding to receive the truth. Well, I don't know but poor humanity deserves and needs a little encouragement; it has been long and soundly berated, and traduced; and I am inclined to speak just a word or two in its favor, poor, and sinful, and wretched as it is. The preacher should preach Jesus, and not his logic. The people can and should *save themselves*, by accepting Jesus. We should all feel humbled in view of our sins, feel proud and sufficient in Christ. Poor, and sinful, and wretched, and dead, as unregenerated men are, God loves them, and Jesus died for them. And it was not a mass of seething putridity, or pile of dead men's bones, that thus worked the love of heaven! No, indeed! There is something in a *man*, though he be not regenerated, more than was in the grave of Lazarus! True, he is lost, and in one sense dead; but he is a man, endowed with reason and volition; he is the image of Almighty God, and is capable of enjoying God and Heaven forever; hence Jesus died to reclaim him. And by preaching this stupendous display of love to him his heart may be reached and touched and turned back to God and Heaven.

Just here I desire to call attention to the language of our Saviour, bearing directly upon the point of difference between us. John xiv, 16-17: "And I will pray the Father, and He shall give you another Comforter, that He may abide with you forever; even the Spirit of Truth, whom the world cannot receive." Now, I hold that the Professor's theory is in direct conflict with this teaching. Here the Lord says of the Spirit, "whom the world can*not* receive;" while my friend says the world *can* and *must* receive it, before it can receive the Truth! This is a flat contradiction. The Saviour teaches that the world *can* receive His Word, but can*not* receive the Spirit; while Professor Crawford says the world can*not* receive the Word, but *can* and *must* receive the Spirit! Choose ye, my friends, this day, whom you will believe. I say to you, my friends, and to my opponent, that when any theory I hold throws me upon such desperate courses, I shall very seriously fall out with it, to say the least. Candidly, my friends, the point of difference between us seems so plainly made out, and my opponent's effort to make out his case seems so clearly a failure, that I feel that I might just as well quit. To argue the question further upon what my friend has adduced in favor of his theory looks like presuming a want of Scripture intelligence upon your part that I am sure is not just to you.

My notes upon the gentleman's speech bring me back to Lydia's case, "whose heart the Lord opened that she attended to the things spoken by Paul." But what need I further say upon that point? Have I not already shown that there is nothing in it to support my friend's heterodox notion of spiritual influence in conversion?

But the gentleman quotes Rom viii., 9, and calls upon me to reply to what he calls his argument thence derived, and as I have nothing else to do I will turn and read the passage at any rate, that you may see its entire want of pertinence to the question in hand. "But ye are not in the flesh, but in the Spirit, if so be that the Spirit of God dwell in you. Now if any man have not the Spirit of Christ he is none of His." Now, what, pray you, is there here bearing upon the point of difference between us? I believe the Spirit of God dwells *in the hearts of His children.* In another letter this same apostle says, "*Because ye are* sons God hath sent forth the Spirit of His Son into your hearts, crying Abba Father." I believe also, that "if any man have not the Spirit of Christ he is none of his." There is no controversy about this. Professor Crawford needs a passage that will say, if any man be *not* Christ's he has His Spirit, *nevertheless!* Why, if the gentleman's theory is correct how would one's having the Spirit of Christ in his heart be evidence of his sonship? When we differ about spiritual influence *in conversion,* why does the gentleman bring forward passages speaking of the Spirit in Christians? Is this logic? It's a burlesque of it.

My friend seems to think there is about the same intimacy of relationship between a tailor and the coat he makes, that there is between the Spirit and the Truth, and that the dwelling of the Holy Spirit in the heart of a Christian is just like the dwelling of a tailor in the house! Is that so? Let us see. How many houses can a tailor be in at the same time? One. How many hearts can the Spirit work in at the same time? To ask these two questions shows the pointlessness of my friend's tailor-illustration. By all means let us have the tailor's *goose* in the next. God, Christ, and the Spirit, are said to be in Christians, but they are not there like a tailor is in a house. They can be in the Gospel, too, wherever it is preached, but a tailor can not be with every coat he makes wherever it goes. Illustrations are good things when fairly and skillfully used. Working upon minds and hearts and wills, is different from working on coats! A tailor can be in but one shop at a time, and can work on but one coat at a time; but even a man can work upon thousands of hearts at once. God works in Christians, and sinners too, to will and to do. But He does it by means, and not by a personal presence, as a tailor works on a coat. God works in us to will and to do, much as we work in one another to will and to do; by using motives. I presume that if I were to assure my opponent that he would receive five thousand dollars for going with me to Kentucky, that would work in him to will and to do —to will and to go. The Spirit, on the day of Pentecost worked upon at least three thousand hearts at once, and worked effectually, worked in them to will and to do.

ADDRESS.

Thursday, 10th Sept., 4 *o'clock*, **P.M.**

(PROFESSOR CRAWFORD'S FIFTH ADDRESS.)

Professor Crawford.—My opponent wants to make you believe that a man, according to my doctrine, is not guilty if he rejects the Truth ; because the Spirit of God has not operated upon his heart. Now, while it is true that a man cannot be converted unless the Spirit of God makes him willing to receive the truth, it is also true that the Truth is what we ought to receive without any Divine aid. We ought to receive it ; and the reason why we don't is because of the opposition and sin of our hearts. The Truth itself ought to be received, and it would be received if the carnal mind were not enmity against God. Therefore, I hold that a man is guilty if the Truth is set before him and he rejects it, for it is worthy of our acceptance. But man will not have the Truth, and therefore we say the Spirit of God is necessary to make him willing to receive it. My opponent says every man hearing the Gospel must be affected by it in the right way. He asks, can any man hear of Christ's sufferings, of the blood flowing from his wounded side and hands, of all the pain he endured for mankind during his life and while on the Cross ; can he hear this story unmoved? I say yes. I hold that men have heard the Gospel story in all its beauty and pathos, have heard its truths expounded with fidelity and love, and yet have gone away scoffing, abandoned to sin and unbelief. I appeal to those who have heard the **Gospel** preached and witnessed its effects. Some have fallen in with the offers of mercy, others have gone their way blaspheming. Who made them to differ? God in the one case has given repentance to the acknowledgment of the truth, and in the other he has left them to follow the promptings of their own rebellious hearts. But yet man must be held accountable if he fails to receive the Truth, for it is worthy of his reception, and it is because of his enmity that he does not accept it. We have no power in ourselves; it is "by grace we are saved through faith, and that not of ourselves; it is the gift of God, not of works lest any man should boast." (Eph. 2, 8-9.) If God saves a man by Christ, it is a free, unmerited favour, just as it was a free, unmerited favour on His part to send His Son to this lower world that he might obey and suffer and die in our room and stead. Then, with respect to the freedom of the will. In one sense man is free to accept or reject; in another he is not. His heart is evil and because it is so prejudice is there, and he is swayed by that prejudice. But man's inability is, after all, a *moral*, not a physical, inability, and, being so, it leaves him responsible if he does not accept the offers of mercy which are freely tendered to him. Some will say that there is no distinction between moral and physical inability, but a simple illustration will show the difference. A man is in prison because he has been a rebel against his country. His sovereign comes to him and says, "I will give you a free, unconditional pardon, I will allow you to go"; but at the same time he leaves the prison doors closed and bolted, so that the man cannot depart, no matter how willing he may be to leave his cell. This is physical inability. But suppose the king says, "I will allow you to go, if you will only acknowledge your offences, and beg your sovereign's pardon. But if the man, being a rebel at heart, and holding relentless and bitter enmity to the king, refuses to acknowledge his offences or to ask forgiveness, but would rather die than thus submit. Such is the man's inveterate enmity to his sovereign that you may say he cannot humble himself to ask his forgiveness or acknowledge his offence. This is moral inability. There is inability in both cases, but there is this vast difference, that in the second case, the man *could* have regained his freedom but for the inherent enmity of his own wicked heart. We say, then, our doctrine is not an unreasonable one in this respect. The exceeding sinfulness of the sinner's heart leaves him so entirely unable to do anything for himself, that he can be saved by nothing short of God's Holy Spirit working in that wicked heart. God alone can overcome his reluctance or inability, and if God does so, it is purely and solely an act of grace. It would have been no injustice on the Almighty's part if he had left us in our rebellion; man could not justly have found any fault with his Maker if he had never sent his Son to suffer and die for us. There would have been nothing unjust in this, so that it was a pure act of grace on God's part to provide a means of saving sinners; there was no obligation on his part to do so. This is our doctrine on this subject, and I do not wish to have it misrepresented.

My opponent says every man must and does see a beauty in the Gospel and in Christ. What does the Word of God say on this subject? Isaiah liii. 2 : "He hath no form nor comeliness; and when we shall see him, there is no beauty that we should desire him." This throws us back on the question, How does this desire for him come? Why cannot man in his natural state see any beauty in him? Simply because his heart is enmity against God. Romans viii. 7. My opponent says our doctrine amounts to this that God will repent for the sinner. We never dream of such a thing. The sinner repents, and it is God gives him that repentance—gives him that state of mind in which his sins appear in their true colours. Repentance to what? To the acknowledgment of the Truth. Here is the Truth laid before the sinner, but he will not receive it until God, through His Spirit, works upon the heart, bringing repentance, and preparing it for the reception of that Truth. Let us now proceed to the consideration of some more passages of Scripture. I Cor. ii. 14: "But the natural man receiveth not the things of the Spirit of God: for they are foolishness unto him; neither can he know them, because they are spiritually discerned." He "receiveth not the things of the Spirit of God." All will admit that the "things of the Spirit" means the Truth that the Spirit has handed unto us in the Holy Scriptures; yet the natural man "will not receive it." Now, he cannot be converted by the Truth if he will not receive it. If it is foolishness to him how can it convert him? Surely he must receive it, it must have a lodgment in his heart before it can operate to conversion. And how does he receive it? By the Spirit of God, because these things "are spiritually discerned." I will read next Acts v. 31: "Him hath God exalted with his right hand to be a Prince and a Saviour, for to give repentance to Israel, and forgiveness of sins." It was not *merely* the Truth that was to be instrumental in working this repentance. The Truth had already been laid before them, but I apprehend that it was the

Spirit of God that was to prick them to their hearts, and thus prepare them to receive the Truth. Then in Acts xi. 17, 18: "Forasmuch then as God gave them the like gift as he did unto us, who believed on the Lord Jesus Christ, what was I, that I could withstand God? When they heard these things they held their peace, and glorified God saying: "Then hath God also to the Gentiles granted repentance unto life." Here the passage refers to the occasion when Peter was preaching to Cornelius, telling him that through Christ there was remission of sins; and while he was expounding the Truth the Holy Ghost fell upon them and they glorified God. Zechariah iv. 6: "Then he answered and spake unto me, saying, This is the Word of the Lord unto Zerubbabel, saying, Not by might, nor by power, but by my Spirit, says the Lord of Hosts." The meaning and intention of this passage is made doubly clear from the illustration which accompanies it. There was seen in the accompanying vision the candlestick of gold, with a bowl upon the top of it, seven lamps thereon, and seven pipes to the seven lamps. There were two olive trees, one on each side, supplying oil to the lamps. The angel explaining the vision says, "Not by might, nor by power, but by my Spirit." More is evidently meant by this representation than the mere power of Truth. It is the power of the Spirit employing the Truth. The wick of the lamp is necessary, which may represent the Divine Truth, but without the oil, or the Holy Spirit, it would be of no avail. The Spirit of God must work with that Truth, applying it to the soul, or there can be no conversion or sanctification. Matt. 28: 18, 19, 20, "All power is given unto Me in Heaven and in earth. Go ye, therefore, and teach all nations, baptizing them in the name of the Father, and of the Son, and of the Holy Ghost; teaching them to observe all things, whatsoever I have commanded you; and lo I am with you alway, even unto the end of the world." The Apostles were commissioned to go and preach the Gospel, but He was to be with them alway. His Divine power had to accompany the Word to give its effect in the conversion of soul's. Rom. 8, 26: "Likewise the Spirit also helpeth our infirmities; for we know not what we should pray for, as we ought; but the Spirit also maketh intercession for us with groanings that cannot be uttered." Here then you see the Spirit maketh intercession with groanings that cannot be uttered. The Spirit operating upon the man's soul prompts him to prayer; while he cannot adequately express his feelings, but by "groanings that cannot be uttered." This is the effect produced upon the man by the Spirit. If this does not prove that some other power than the Word itself is present, then I don't understand the English language. If it was the mere Word, it is a language that might be uttered; but when the Spirit operates it is with groanings that *cannot* be uttered. I appeal again to common sense, if this passage does not prove plainly the presence and power of the Holy Spirit. Psalm 110: 1, 2, 3: "The Lord said unto my Lord, sit thou at My right hand, until I make thine enemies thy footstool. The Lord shall send the rod of thy strength out of Zion; rule thou in the midst of thine enemies. Thy people shall be willing in the day of thy power, in the beauty of holiness from the womb of the morning; thou hast the dew of thy youth." Men are naturally unwilling to receive the Gospel; oftentimes they repel it with blasphemies; but they shall be willing that is made willing in the day of His power. Willing to do what? To receive the Gospel.

I think these passages we have quoted clearly show that it is God's Holy Spirit that opens the heart to the reception of the Truth, and employs that Truth in the sanctification of the soul.

Let us now look at some passages upon which my opponent evidently relies in attempting to establish his case. Rom. I: 16, 17: "For I am not ashamed of the Gospel of Christ; for it is the power of God unto salvation, to everyone that believeth; to the Jew first, and also to the Greek. For therein is the righteousness of God revealed from faith to faith; as it is written, the just shall live by faith." Here the Gospel is said to be the power of God unto salvation, because in it the righteousness of God is revealed. That is the righteousness which God has provided for man's justification; that is the obedience unto death of Jesus Christ, man's divine surety. Man of himself has no justifying righteousness; he is shapen in sin and brought forth in iniquity; but by Christ's righteousness His obedience is imputed to the believer, and so he finds acceptance with God. And it is in the Gospel that God reveals his righteousness. But the part of the passage that my opponent dwells upon is this: "it (the Gospel) is the *power* of God unto salvation," and he attempts to prove from this that the Word alone can do the work. It does not say that the Gospel is "the power unto salvation." It is the "*power of God.*" We often speak figuratively of the power of the tongue, but does that mean the mere physical power of the tongue itself? Certainly not; it means the power of the mind finding utterance through the organ of speech. We talk of the power of the press, but we do not mean by that the mere power of the actual machine used in printing; We mean the intellectual and moral power which finds expression by means of the printing-press. So with the Gospel; It is not the power itself; the power is of God, and the Gospel is the instrument he employs in applying that power. Another illustration suggests itself: we frequently hear of the "power of the sword"; but there is no power in the sword itself, it is merely the instrument in the hands of those who wield it. The figure used in the passage I have quoted is one of great beauty and effect, and the man who cannot see its beauty and effect cannot see very far. Acts ii. 11, 13, 14: "And he showed us how he had seen an angel in his house which stood and said unto him, Send men to Joppa, and call for Simon, whose surname is Peter, who shall tell thee words whereby thou and all thy house shall be saved." There is nothing in this passage conflicting with the doctrine I am advocating, namely that the Word is the instrument in the hands of the Spirit, whereby men are saved. Let us illustrate: a man is in the water in danger of drowning; I throw him a rope, which by his taking hold of it—by my pulling him to land, he is saved. There would be nothing wrong in saying that the rope had saved the man, though in reality it was I who rescued him, the rope being merely the instrument used. The very same figure is employed in the passage which I have quoted. We hold as well as my opponent that a man is saved by the Word, just as the man was saved by taking hold of the rope. But the Word is the instrument in the hands of the Spirit as the rope was the instrument in my hands by which I saved the man. The question is this, Is the Word all that is necessary to man's salvation? We say not.

REPLY.

Thursday 10*th Sept.*, 4.30 *p. m.*

MR. SWEENEY'S FIFTH REPLY.

Mr. Sweeney—My friend has gotten into the mysteries of Calvinism. He is fully committed to it, and it is Calvinism—regular old angular Calvinism—that we are to discuss now, instead of Campbellism. Well, this will certainly be refreshing.

He tells us that the unregenerated man cannot receive the truth; that he can neither understand it or love it; that he can never be converted till the Spirit of God makes him willing to receive the truth; that all this is because of the essential and necessary opposition of his heart to the truth; and yet he says, he ought to receive the truth; that he is responsible for rejecting it; that he is justly guilty before God. In other words, the sinner ought to do what he can't do! that he is responsible, justly, for not doing what he is utterly unable to do! that is, guilty for not doing what God will not permit him to do! That's it. That is what my friend offers you in opposition to what he calls "Campbellism." I would rather have "Campbellism"—and that's a myth—than Calvinism.

The gentlemen can see nothing in the cross of Christ to affect the unconverted man. The story may be told to him, over and over; but, plainly, because God does not do his work the man goes away from the preaching of the gospel, blaspheming and gnashing his teeth, with rage and devilish fury. While another man, upon whose heart the Spirit does his work, hears the same story at the same time, and he goes his way "praising God." And the gentlemen tells us, "it was God who made them to differ." God made one to blaspheme and the other to praise Him! Well, perhaps blasphemy is just as good as praise, after all; and we have only been wrongly taught to suppose that there was a great difference in favor of praise! If man has no power of choice, and can only be, and do, evil, till the Holy Spirit is sent directly from heaven to enable him, and "make him willing," to be and to do otherwise, then what we call evil is the divine choice! and, I submit, that we have no right to murmur or complain about it, or even to wish it were otherwise than as it is. We should accept blasphemy and cursing as of divine appointment. If, therefore, I understand my opponent correctly, he is inconsistent in finding fault with "Campbellism," or any other "ism" under the sun. Still, my friend says the sinner is to "blame," is "guilty," and "will be responsible for not receiving the truth, because it is worthy of acceptance." But *can* he receive it? No. Must he not necessarily resist it, till the Spirit "makes him willing" to receive it? Yes. Then, plainly, my friend believes that God will punish a man in hell for ever for not seeing what he refused to let him see, and for not receiving what he would not let him receive! He thinks God has a right to do this. Well, of course, I would not be found disputing with God about his right to do this or that thing; but this I will say, and do say, that if it is right for God to punish a man for not doing what he of his own choice withheld from him the power of doing, then I am utterly unable to decide that anything is wrong. If that is just, will the learned gentleman please to name one thing that he conceives to be unjust

I should consider a *man* little better, if any, than a brute that would treat his child in that manner. I remember once stepping into a news-depot to get a paper, and about the time I called for my paper the dealer directed his little boy to bring in a stick of wood, that he pointed out, lying in the back yard; and, casting my eye in that direction, I decided at a glance that the stick would be too much for the boy, unless he was an extraordinarily stout one. So not being in a hurry, I lingered a moment to see if I had missed my guess. The little boy worked manfully for a considerable time at the log, but honestly failed. It was too much for him. Meanwhile, the dealer was busy with his customers. But when he had a little leisure he turned to his boy, and asked, Why did you not bring in that stick of wood, as I told you? The little boy looked up innocently, and honestly, into his father's face, and said—"Father, I *couldn't.*" Then his father, cruelly—I will say, at a venture—smote him on the face, and with angry words, ordered him out of his presence. Now, I felt indignant at the brutal conduct of the news-dealer, and after that got my papers elsewhere, I quit him. If I should be convinced that the conduct of that man toward his child was godlike, then all my conceptions of God would be utterly confounded; and my notions of right and wrong, of justice and injustice, completely upset; and I should be prepared to call anything right and anything wrong; everything just, and everything equally unjust. But, my friends, the worthy gentleman is wrong. I think he feels that he is trying to manage a tough case. What one *cannot* do, that he ought to do! What he cannot do, that he *must* do! Good heavens! Does God require us to do, or be eternally damned, what he knows we cannot do; what he witholds from us intentionally the power to do; what he knows we cannot but resist with our whole nature? It cannot be true. It's false! It's from beneath, and not from the Word of God. Doubtless my friend very sincerely believes it, but he is mistaken. He has read God's Word with a false philosophy in his mind; with a "veil" over his understanding, as the Jews read Moses.

We are told that the Holy Spirit "makes the sinner willing." *Makes* him *willing?* That seems to me a contradiction in itself. The *will compelled?* That's not according to my notion of volition. The will can't be compelled, and that's the ground of man's just accountability. True, God works in us "to [induce us to] will and to do," but *we* do the willing and the doing ourselves, when it's done at all. Nor do I believe that he works in us otherwise than by offering incentives to the right and laying restraints upon the wrong, leaving us free to act or not act, as we may freely choose. To induce repentance and obedience, God offers the sinner pardon. To induce him to persevere in his begun confidence he offers him a home in Heaven, where there shall be no more sin, nor sorrow, nor tears, nor death. A home without tears! Oh, yes! God has written over the gate to Heaven, in letters of golden light, "There shall be no more tears." And for that blissful abode of the faithful and the true, I will dare and do what I can in life. Here we weep bitter tears of sorrow. Here our mothers weep on our breasts. Our dearest ones weep; but *there* "there shall be no more tears." Thus, dear, sinning, sorrowing, dying man, God would "work in you to will and to do"; thus he would work in you to induce you to "strive to enter in at the strait gate"; to "do his commandments, that you may have a right to the tree of life, and may enter through the gates into the city."

The gentleman infers that man does not and cannot repent of his sins, from the language of Peter, Acts xi. 18: "Then hath God also to the Gentiles *granted* repentance unto life." Now, Peter meant no more than that God had extended to the Gentiles the privileges and blessings of the Gospel; that he had offered to them as well as to the Jews, life, *upon* the condition of their repentance. "Repentance" in the passage is used metonymically, the means, or condition, is put for the end. The meaning is obviously that God hath extended the offer of life and salvation to the Gentiles, as well as to the Jews, upon the condition of their repentance. It's a monstrous perversion of this Scripture to use it to prove that one cannot repent, who has heard the Gospel, until God sends the Spirit to make him do it!

To prove that the unregenerate man cannot receive Christ, my opponent quotes Isaiah liii, 1, "And when we shall see him there is no beauty in him that we should desire him." But the prophet here speaks of Christ, as he appeared to the Jews, before his death, burial, resurrection and and ascension to Heaven. He does not speak of Him as He is presented to men in the Gospel. The prophet does not say that there is no beauty in Him that we should desire Him, *since* "he hath borne our griefs and carried our sorrows"; *since* "he was wounded for our transgressions," and "bruised for our iniquities"; *since* "he was brought as a lamb to the slaughter; and as the sheep before her shearers is dumb, so he opened not his mouth." No, no! It was by all this that he was made to us the chief among all the tens of thousands, and the one altogether lovely. I say that the sinner *can*, if he *will*, see this beauty in Him. But he can also shut his eyes to it all.

Grave as is the subject we are discussing, I confess to having been amused at my friend's effort to relieve his doctrine of some of its hardest features. He admits that he teaches the sinner's utter inability to do anything to prevent his damnation, and yet contends that his damnation is just; and he attempts to relieve the case by drawing a fine distinction between "moral" and "physical inability"—as if it would make any difference to a man in hell whether he was there on account of the one or the other kind of inability to prevent it! Did any sinner make his moral condition what it is? My friend says no. Has he not told us that even infants are in this moral condition, out of which only the direct operation of the Holy Spirit can bring them from their new birth? Then the fact is that according to his teaching the sinner comes into this world with this "moral inability"; he didn't make it, nor can he remedy it. If, therefore, the Spirit doesn't "make him able and willing to receive the truth" he can't do it, and he will be eternally damned for not doing what he was, by no fault of his own, utterly unable to do. Now, it may do very well, as a mere intellectual exercise, for my friend up at Woodstock, before his class of young divinity students, so draw out and illustrate such distinctions between the "moral" and the "physical," but really it would be of little consequence to me if I were to be condemned without the ability to accept the means of salvation, whether my inability were moral or physical. I hold that accountability can be justly grounded only in ability. If, therefore, one is morally unable, he is not justly morally accountable. But my opponent says the sinner is morally unable to receive the truth, and yet morally accountable for not doing it.

The gentleman quotes 1 Cor. ii., 14: "The natural man receiveth not the things of the Spirit." But, when the Apostle uses this language, is he talking about conversion? And does he mean to say that the unconverted man can not receive the truth? I deny that conversion is the subject of which the Apostle is speaking, and that he means to teach that unconverted men cannot receive the truth. He is speaking of *inspiration*. The spiritual men of the passage are inspired men, and the "natural man" is the uninspired man. "The things of the Spirit" are the *revelations* of the Spirit, which, of course, the natural, or uninspired man, does not receive. But, if the Apostle is talking of conversion, and means to say that the unconverted receiveth not the Spirit's influences, then, I submit, that the passage is as much against my friend's theory as mine. Is not the immediate influence of the Spirit, for which he contends, as much one of "the things of the Spirit" as the mediate influence for which I contend? Certainly it is. Indeed, it is more "immediately" so. Whatever the passage means, therefore, it has no bearing against my view of the Spirit's influence that it does not have equally against my friend's.

I believe as firmly as my opponent does that the "carnal mind [the mind of the *flesh*] is enmity against God"; that "it is not subject to the law of God, neither indeed can be." But this affords no ground for the doctrine he preaches. The Apostle does not say that what he calls "the carnal mind" will be subjected to the law of

God by an immediate operation of the Holy Spirit. Christians will have to contend with the "carnal mind" as long as they are in the flesh. Paul himself had to do it. Christians must be led by the Spirit, and "keep the body under"; but they will find the flesh lusting against the Spirit, as long as they live in the flesh. "It's the Spirit that's born of the Spirit" that's regenerated; the flesh is not. "Flesh and blood cannot inherit the kingdom of God." The resurrection will put an end to the war between the "carnal mind" and "the mind of the Spirit." So this passage contains nothing to the Professor's purpose.

My friend quotes Acts v. 31 : "Him hath God exalted with his right hand, a Prince and a Saviour, to give repentance to Israel, and forgiveness of sins." He quotes this because it speaks of Christ as *giving* repentance. I suppose that repentance is used here for the *end it always looks to*. Repentance looks to pardon and peace; and this Jesus gives to those who repent. This is not an uncommon form of expression. We often meet with it in Holy Scripture, as well as in other writings. But please to notice, my friends, that nothing is said as to *how* Jesus gives repentance, in the passage. The goodness of God leads men to repentance, we are taught; and, I think, his goodness is displayed in the Gospel of his Son. If my friend had read the next verse in this passage he would have learned to whom God gives the Holy Spirit : "The Holy Ghost whom God hath given *to them that obey him*."

I presume few of you failed to see Prof. Crawford's trouble with the case of Cornelius. He quoted Acts xi. 17, 18. "Forasmuch then as God gave them the like gift as he did unto us, who believed on the Lord Jesus Christ, what was I that I could withstand God?" This is the language of Peter, after he had preached to the Gentiles in the house of Cornelius. He refers to the bestowment of the Spirit upon the Gentiles. He says, "God gave them the like gift as he did unto us (Jews) *who believed* on the Lord Jesus Christ." This tells us whom among the Jews God gave the Spirit to. It was to them "who *believed* on the Lord Jesus Christ." But my friend is trying to prove that God bestows the Spirit directly upon *unbelievers*! This passage is not his witness! The Professor told you correctly I think, that Peter referred to the occasion when he was preaching to Cornelius and those assembled in his house. Let us therefore turn back to the tenth chapter, where that preaching and its circumstances are recorded. In the 44th verse we learn the fact of the bestowment of the Spirit upon the Gentiles. It is given in these words: "While Peter yet spake these words, the Holy Ghost fell on all them which *heard the word*. Upon whom? "Upon all them which *heard the word*." Then by reading a few of the preceding verses, we learn that Peter preached to them Jesus, before the Holy Spirit "fell on them." But my friend thinks it utterly useless to preach the Gospel to a man upon whom the Holy Spirit has not *already* come; as it must go before "and open the heart," and "*make* persons willing to receive the word," he thinks.

But again. This case is altogether against the Professor's theory. Before Peter had come to his house, and after he came, and *before the Holy Spirit was given*, Cornelius was willing, anxious, and waiting to hear and receive the Word which God had sent unto the children of

Israel, preaching peace by Jesus Christ. But my friend tells us the unregenerate man is neither able or willing to receive the Truth till the Spirit comes and *makes* him so. There is no comfort in this case for the gentleman's theory.

In this connection the gentleman quoted at some length from the fourth chapter of the prophecy of Zechariah. The quotation contained this expression: "Not by might, nor by power, but by my Spirit saith the Lord of hosts." Does Professor Crawford really believe there is anything in this passage that supports his view of spiritual influence in conversion? *What is it* that is "not by might, nor by power," but by the Spirit of God? Is it conversion? And if so, *how* is it by the Spirit of God? If I were denying that God does *anything in any manner*, by His Spirit, then this passage would be pertinent. The gentleman had something to say about the seven lamps the Prophet saw. He thinks the wick represents the Word, and the oil the Holy Spirit; and concludes that as without the oil the wick would be of no avail, "so without the Spirit the Word would be of no avail." Well, that's spinning the prophecy out pretty fine. I don't think there is any authority for saying that the Word and Spirit of God are represented by the wick and oil of a lamp. At any rate such fanciful interpretations are not admissable in a *debate*. By the way, though, if the wick does represent the Word of God, and the oil His Spirit, what sort of a light would my friend have without any wick? Were he to touch off the oil "*immediately*," without any wick, he would, if he survived this "immediate operation" long, very soon conclude that he had better always have wick in his lamp.

The worthy gentleman quotes the promise of the Saviour to His Apostles, following the Great commission, given in Matthew. 28th chapter— "Lo I am with you alway, even unto the end of the world." But if he sees anything in this about any immediate operation of the Spirit in the conversion of sinners, I should like to know what it is. It seems to me there would have been more propriety in my bringing this passage into the discussion as against his position. Christ says, "Lo, I am with you alway," but he is not personally and immediately present always with his disciples. Well, if he can be with his disciples ever, without being personally and immediately present, then why may not the Holy Spirit work also without being personally and immediately present? The only pertinent inference to be made from the passage is against my opponent.

The gentleman quotes Rom. viii. 26, "Likewise the Spirit also helpeth our infirmities." This is spoken to Christians, and of them; and therefore has no reference to the question of Spiritual influence in conversion.

Psalm cx. 3, "Thy people shall be willing in the day of Thy power." This speaks of the *Lord's people*, and not of the unregenerate, and says nothing about the Spirit, by direct, personal influence, compelling any one's will. "Shall be" is not in the original, and therefore—

ADDRESS.

Friday, Sept. 11th, 10 a.m.

(PROF. CRAWFORD'S SIXTH ADDRESS.)

Prof. Crawford—I would just say with respect to the arrangements for this meeting, as to time, &c., they were made by the mutual agreement of both sides, and we are now carrying them out. My opponent still goes on to speak of the sinner being irresponsible when he does not receive the Truth, since we say the Spirit of God is necessary to make him willing to receive that Truth. I don't think it is necessary to spend much more time on that point, as I think it was made plain enough, and proven clearly enough in my last address. He argues if a sinner, according to our doctrine, is not saved, it is not his fault, but God's. We say it is not so. As I said before, his inability springs from his corrupt heart; it is a moral, not a physical inability. God is under no obligation to save the sinner; it is purely an act of grace if he does so. But I do say that without the Divine power of His Spirit the sinner cannot be saved, even with the Word, owing to his enmity to Divine Truth through the sin of his rebellious heart; but the giving of that Spirit is an act of grace—nothing more. It was grace that contrived the plan of salvation in the councils of eternity; it was purely an act of grace for God, in due time, to send His Son to suffer and die for sinners, and if a single soul is saved from everlasting damnation, it is only through God's sovereign grace. My opponent has said a good deal about the passage where it refers to men being made "willing in the day of his power." Here I contend that it is Christ's power that is referred to, and that it is by the exertion of that power that they shall be made willing. I find that the Greek word *psuchikos* employed in 1 Cor. ii. 14, and rendered "*natural*," "the natural man received not the things of the Spirit of God; for they are foolishness to him; neither can he know them, because they are spiritually discerned," is employed in the New Testament to signify man in his natural state by virtue of his union with Adam. The 45th and 46th verses of the 15th chapter of this very epistle shows the meaning which the apostle attaches to this word. The first man, Adam, was made a living soul (*psuche*); the last Adam was made a quickening spirit (*pneuma*). Howbeit that was not first that was spiritual (*pneumatikon*), but that which was natural (*psuchikon*), and afterwards that which was spiritual. The first word is here used in speaking of man in his natural state, as he is in Adam; the second is applied to the man whose nature has been quickened and renewed by his union with Christ. He says in the preceding verse, that God revealed his truth to the apostles; he goes on to say that a man in his natural state receives not this very truth thus revealed, for it is foolishness to him. And the reason he does not receive it is because it is spiritually discerned. We hold that unless it is received and "discerned" by the influence of the Spirit, conversion and sanctification cannot follow. My opponent quotes a passage in which it speaks of the sinner closing his eyes against the Truth. He asks if there is a sense in which the sinner can be spoken of as denying the truth. Certainly there is; but does that prove that God cannot open his eyes? He next refers to the case of Lydia, and asks if she did not hear the words first? Certainly she did; but the passage reads, "A certain woman named Lydia, heard us; *whose heart the Lord opened* that she attended unto the things which were spoken of Paul." She had listened to Paul's preaching, but before the Gospel he preached could be of any avail, the Lord had to open her heart for its reception. This is just what I have been contending for all along, and no power on earth can explain away the meaning of that passage. Let us read Isaiah liii. 2, "For he shall grow up before him as a tender plant, and as a root out of a dry ground; he hath no form nor comeliness; and when we shall see him there is no beauty that we should desire him." He is before them, but when they behold him they see no beauty in him that they should desire him. Their understandings are so darkened that his loveliness is not apparent until the Spirit shows him to them in all his beauty. I say then that I did not misquote or pervert the passage, but gave what I considered to be its true meaning. This exposition of the passage is supported by the Saviour's own words in John iii. 19; "And this is the condemnation that light is come into the world, and men loved darkness rather than light because their deeds were evil." The light of the Gospel which reveals Christ in his beauty is shining around them, but by the natural tendencies of their wicked hearts men love the darkness; they cannot endure the light. Is not this the case? Men hear the Truth, and hearing, hate it. And what overcomes this hatred of the Truth? I hold—and I think I have already shown from the Bible that my view is the correct one—that nothing can do it but the Divine power of God's Spirit, acting upon the soul through the medium of the Truth. Turn next to John vi. 43-44: "Jesus therefore answered and said unto them, murmur not among yourselves. No man can come to me, except the Father which hath sent me draw him: and I will raise him up at the last day?" Here you see Christ was preaching to these people; but they murmured and rejected him. But he says, do not murmur; no man can come unto me except the Father draw him. My opponent will perhaps quote the remainder of the passage but he cannot make very much of that. Christ goes on to say, "It is written in the Prophets, And they shall be all taught of God. Every man therefore that hath heard *and hath learned of the Father*, cometh unto me." Christ does not say that those who hear the word shall come unto him. It it those "that have heard the word and *have learned of the Father*." What further testimony can any man require that the power of God's Spirit must accompany the hearing of the Word? Bear in mind that they were not only to hear of the Father, they were to be taught of *Him*. Another passage much relied on by the Disciples is, John vi. 63: "It is the Spirit that quickeneth; the flesh profiteth nothing: the words that I speak unto you they are Spirit, and they are life. But there are some of you that believe not." I ask does the word "Spirit," here mean the Holy Ghost? Grant for the sake of argument that it does. The word in this case cannot be taken literally. It would be evidently absurd to say that the words of Christ could be literally spirit, words are not spirit in any literal sense. If the word here means the Holy Spirit, Christ's words are only said, in a figure, to be spirit inasmuch as they are the instrument by which the Spirit of God works. Something is said of the instrument which is meant in reality of the agent, whose instrument the truth which Christ preached is. I would make a similar remark respecting the word *life*. It would be evidently more absurd to say that our Lord's words were literally life. I might explain the figure here employed by the language of every day life or by quotations from authors in every age. Take for example this passage: Deut. 24, 6, " No man shall take the nether or the upper millstone to pledge; for he taketh a man's life to pledge." Does that mean that the nether or the upper millstone is literally a man's life? Certainly not; no one will claim this interpretation of the passage. It means that as the Jew according to the custom of the country, required to grind his own corn and by hand, if you took away his millstones you took away that which was a means of sustaining life; hence, in a figure, the millstone is said to be his life. Now, in like manner, as the truth which Christ preached is the only instrument by which eternal life is conveyed to perishing men, these words are said by metonymy to be life. But I contend that the word " Spirit " in the text does not signify the Holy Spirit but the spirit of the law as contrasted with the letter of the law. We frequently in conversation speak of the spirit and the letter of the law. We sometimes say the law is kept in the spirit if not in the letter. Our Lord, as you may see from the context, was controverting with the cavilling Jews, who contended for the letter of the law but who could not see that that law pointed to Christ who wast he spirit of that law. When Christ, therefore, says to these cavillers and sticklers for the letter of the law who yet rejected Christ who was the substance of it, " The words that I speak unto you they are

Spirit;" He evidently means that the words
which He taught respecting himself and His
kingdom were the very spirit or soul of that law
for which they were so zealously contending.
Our Lord here speaks of the law under a figure,
as though it was made up of two parts, the body
or flesh, and spirit; hence the meaning of the
words in the text, "It is the Spirit that quickeneth, the flesh profiteth nothing." In order that
I may explain this somewhat more fully, turn to
2 Cor., 3, 6: Who also hath made us able ministers of the New Testament, not of the letter,
but of the spirit; for the letter killeth, but the
spirit giveth light." You see the very same idea
is brought out in this passage. The letter of the
law is here contrasted with the spirit of the law.
It was not by the blood of bulls or goats, but by
the spirit of all the ceremonial observances—the
truth that was embodied in that law, that God
would work in this dispensation. The law given
from Mount Sinai was engraven on tables of
stone, but the spirit of the law, the Truths of the
Gospel, must be written and engraved on the
fleshly tables of the heart. The giving of God's
law was accompanied by great glory. When
Moses came down from the Mount, the children
of Israel could not behold his face for the glory
of his countenance; "which glory was to be
done away, and to be succeeded by that which
was still more glorious." Paul goes on to ask,
"If the ministration of death was glorious, how
shall not the ministration of the Spirit be rather
glorious?" Here the letter of the law was glorious, but "the flesh or body of the law profiteth
nothing in the salvation of the soul. If the
body had no power, the spirit of the law had the
power. The Apostle goes on to say, "For if the
ministration of condemnation be glory, much

more doth the ministration of righteousness exceed in glory. The ministration of righteousness here means the Gospel, for in it is the righteousness which God has provided for the sinner revealed. For even that which was made glorious had no glory in this respect, by reason of the glory that excelleth. For if that which is done away was glorious, much more that which remaineth is glorious." The fourteenth and following verses bring out the idea still more clearly: "But their minds were blinded; for until this day remaineth the same veil, untaken away in the reading of the Old Testament: which veil is done away in Christ. But even unto this day, when Moses is read, the veil is upon their hearts. Nevertheless, when it shall turn to the Lord the veil shall be taken away. Now *the Lord is that Spirit*, or *the Spirit (pneuma)*; and where the Spirit of the Lord is, there is liberty." The term Lord is here undoubtedly applied to the Lord Jesus Christ, therefore Christ is the Spirit of the Law. Now let us look at the passage referred to by my opponent, and on which we are commenting. John vi. 63: "It is the Spirit that quickeneth; the flesh profiteth nothing; the words that I speak unto you, they are spirit and they are life." The meaning is that the words of Christ concerning himself and his kingdom are the true spirit of the law for the body or letter of which these Jews were so fiercely contending; and that these words of truth are the only instrument which God has appointed for conveying eternal life to perishing sinners. Now I ask does this passage teach according to my opponent that the truth alone, without the accompanying power of the Holy Spirit, can and does impart spiritual life? If my interpretation be the correct one it only teaches that the words of the Gospel which is the spirit of the law, become the medium through which life is imparted to perishing sinners.

The next passage is Heb. iv. 12: "For the Word of God is quick and powerful, and sharper than a two-edged sword, piercing even to the dividing asunder of soul and spirit, and of the joints and marrow, and is a discerner of the thoughts and intents of the heart." Now their argument is this, that because the Word is declared to be quick and powerful, therefore there is nothing more than this Word necessary to the conversion of the sinner. What does it mean by saying the Word is "quick and powerful, sharper than any two-edged sword?" Now I ask him can a sword be truly called " quick (or live), and powerful " in itself? Is there any life or power in a sword itself? Must it not be used as an instrument in the hands of an agent? We say a sword is "quick" and "powerful," but we use the figure of metonymy, and mean that the sword possesses those qualities only when used as an instrument in the hands of him who wields it. Then I. Peter, 1, 23; Being born again, not of corruptible seed, but of incorruptible, by the Word of God, which liveth and abideth forever." The Apostle here, in carrying out the figure, says the change effected in conversion—the second birth—is not of corruptible seed, as was the first, but of incorruptible seed, the Word of God. He likens the Word of God to seed, but as I said in a previous address, the seed may be planted in the ground, but *of itself* it will not germinate; a Divine influence is required. There is nothing more in this passage than what I have contended for all along, i.e., that the Word is the instrument by which the Spirit works. We believe as well as our opponent that the Word is required. The difference in our doctrine is this: we say that the Spirit uses the Word as the instrument, just as a soldier uses the sword, but the Divine Power lies in the Spirit, as the sword of itself is not the power, but the man who uses it. Our opponents say that the Word is the Power. This is just where we differ. Mr. Campbell says that we are "begotten of the Word, but born in baptism," but this curious distinction between begotten and born is not in the original, as the same word (*gennao*) is used to express both. We must look into the original, for the whole argument here depends on it.

REPLY.

Friday. Sept. 11*th,* 10.30 *a.m.*

MR. SWEENEY'S SIXTH REPLY.

Mr. Sweeney.—My opponent is inclined to complain of my still going on to speak of the same things. He is in the lead. He has been in the lead all the time. He has had his own way about almost everything connected with the debate. I have simply submitted to what he has dictated. I claim the right to reply to his speeches in my own way. If he "repeats himself, I shall follow him round and round." I am following him. I am a little like the old servant who was told by his master to plough a furrow across the field in the direction of a red cow; he ploughed toward the cow; the cow got up and moved, and he kept on ploughing toward the cow. The cow kept going "round and round," and he kept ploughing toward her. Of course he made a pretty crooked furrow, but he ploughed toward the cow. So I am following, and I mean to follow my opponent. If he goes "round and round" why, I shall go "round and round," too. I wanted to affirm my belief on the points of difference between us where I am logically in the affirmative, in clear and distinct form; and I wanted my opponent to affirm his belief in distinct propositions. He refused, preferring such a debate as we now have. I reluctantly consented; but now we are in for it. My friend must allow me to plough around after him; where he goes there will I go also. I must hold him to his doctrine. He says that one man blasphemes and gnashes his teeth in rage and fury on hearing the Gospel, because the Spirit does not do for him that which he alone can do, and without which the man cannot but blaspheme and rage; while another man gives praises to God because the Spirit did for him unconditionally what he would not do for the other. Without the Spirit's aid both men were utterly unable to receive the Truth, and bound to resist it. They were both born so; neither of them desired to be otherwise. The Spirit "enables" and "makes one willing" to praise God, and leaves the other to blaspheme and gnash his teeth with rage and bitterness. If this be true it must be the will of God that the one should blaspheme and rage, as much as that the other should praise Him; and if it be the Divine choice, it must be better that he should blaspheme than that he should praise. A doctor finds two men alike diseased; neither wishes to be healed; he unconditionally heals one and leaves the other, when it would have cost him no more to heal both. Would we not conclude that he only wanted one healed? This is the gentleman's notion of regeneration and salvation. This, too, is just where the doctrine of immediate spiritual influence in conversion will land any man who undertakes to defend it. My friend has done about as well with it as any one man can, I suppose.

The Professor came down here from Woodstock to demolish what he calls "Campbellism," and at the close of the first day he finds himself crowded into his own works, and back into the last ditch, trying in vain to maintain his position there! Where is "Campbellism" now? We hear nothing of it. The gentleman is manfully labouring to make his own "ism" look respectable.

My opponent sometimes astonishes me. I

confess it. I thought the point of difference between us was clearly made out, and fully understood. I was, therefore, astonished to hear him say in his last speech that his position is that the natural hatred of the Truth in the sinner's heart can only be overcome by the Divine Power of God's Spirit, acting upon the soul, *through the medium of the Truth*. I say this astonishes me. I thought he was contending for an *immediate* action of the Spirit upon the soul. If he does really believe that the enmity of the human heart can be overcome by the Spirit, acting through the medium of the Truth, why has he been contending for a previous direct operation of the Spirit "to open the heart," and "enable and make the sinner willing to receive the Truth?" The gentleman ought not to take both sides of the question in the same speech. Let it be borne in mind that *I* believe the Divine Power of the Spirit overcomes the enmity of the human heart, by acting upon it through the medium of Divine Truth. That's my position. I contend for the sufficiency, therefore, of the Truth, of which the Holy Spirit is always the spirit, to accomplish the conversion and sanctification of sinners. And I deny that the moral condition of men is such that they cannot receive it. They can receive it, but are not compelled to, and are, therefore, justly responsible. I believe in salvation by grace, as much, I think, as my opponent does, and more. I believe the grace of God brings salvation for, and offers it alike unto, *all* men. Christ died for all. God has concluded all under sin, and offers mercy unto all.

My friend still contends that in the second chapter of I Cor. "the natural man" means the unregenerate, and the "spiritual" means the regenerate; that the contrast there is between the regenerate and the unregenerate; and that the Apostle means to teach, therefore, that those who are unregenerate cannot receive the truth. Here, as I have said, he is wrong. The subject of which the Apostle treats is *inspiration*, and the contrast is between the *inspired* and the *uninspired;* and "the things of the Spirit" are *revelations*. The inspired man knows the things which hitherto eye had not seen, nor ear heard, the uninspired cannot know them. That is what the Apostle means to teach. Let us read—"But the natural man receiveth not the things of the Spirit of God, for they are foolishness unto him; neither can he know them, because they are spiritually discerned. But he that is spiritual [that is inspired] judgeth all things." Do Christians—all Christians, discern all things hitherto unrevealed? I think not. But in the first verse of the next chapter the Apostle says, "And I, brethren, could not speak unto *you as unto spiritual*, but as unto carnal." Certainly, the Corinthian Church members were regenerated persons; yet they were not "spiritual." This shows that the gentleman is wrong in saying that the subject is conversion, and the contrast between the converted and unconverted. The Apostle meant to say here, I think, that uninspired men could not know what the apostles and prophets of Christ knew; for those things were "spiritually discerned"—that is discerned by inspiration of the Holy Spirit. But, as I have said before, if the Apostle was talking of conversion, and meant by "the things of the Spirit" the Spirit's influences in conversion, then the direct influence for which my friend contends being as much one of "the things of the Spirit" as his mediate influence, the passage is as much opposed to his theory as it is to mine. Why does not my opponent give attention to this?

He comes back to the case of Lydia. Now, bear in mind that his position is that Lydia was an unregenerate person, and "blind to all that is good," until the Spirit opened her heart. But the Scripture says of her before anything is said about her heart being opened, that she "worshipped God; and that she "heard" Paul. After this it is said, "whose heart the Lord opened, that she *attended* unto things that were spoken of Paul." Now, certainly I have as much right to assume that her heart was opened through what she heard, as my friend has to assume that it was by an immediate operation of the Spirit, when the Holy Spirit is not named at all in connection with the effect. So my friend fails here, manifestly. And here he is before us, at the close of a whole day's debate, with his cause pitifully, and vainly, and I think, hopelessly, crying out for a single passage of Scripture to support it. Where is the passage that says the Holy Spirit ever did operate immediately in the conversion of a sinner? Where is the passage that says it ever will so operate? Where the passage that teaches the necessity for such an operation? Where is the Scripture fact from which such necessity can be fairly inferred?

He still hangs on the passage in Isaiah—"But when we shall see Him there is no beauty in Him that we should desire Him." Now, as I have said, there is spoken of Jesus, as to the humble manner in which He came into the world, falling so far beneath the high expectations of the Jews, as to power, grandeur, and glory; that they would not desire Him. It is not spoken of Him *as He is now preached* to sinners in the Gospel. In fact, even in His first appearance in the world the publicans and sinners saw more beauty in Him, and desired Him more than the Jews. But the passage does not say what the Professor says, by any means. He wants a passage to say that there is beauty in Jesus, but sinners can't see it, till regenerated. Whereas this passage says, "When we *shall see Him* there *is no beauty in Him*, that we should desire Him." The beauty that there is in Jesus did not appear, until his life and death and resurrection, were accomplished, and hence Jesus was not preached to sinners till all this was finished.

The gentleman also quotes that "Men love darkness rather than light, because their deeds are evil." Why do men whose deeds are evil love darkness rather than light? My friend says it is because they are naturally and necessarily blind to all that is good. Then why should they shun the light? Why prefer darkness? If their evil deeds appear good to them, and in what is beautiful and true they can see no beauty, why do they shun the light and seek the darkness? The very fact that men whose deeds are evil do prefer darkness to light, upsets my friend's theory and proves the just responsibility of the evil-doers. Why do they hide—hide from their fellows, hide from themselves, attempt to hide from God? Why, if they are utterly blind? Think of a man, "blind as a bat," and knowing no difference between good and evil, seeking the darkness in which to hide, because his deeds are evil! I am glad my opponent has appealed to this passage. Why do evil-doers seek the darkness.? It is because their deeds are evil! But why seek darkness because their deeds are evil if they don't know it? Ah! they do know it, and that's why they love darkness; "This is the condemnation of the world, that light has come into the world, and men love darkness rather than light because their deeds are evil"—*and they know it.* But my friend apologizes for the sinner; he says he cannot see the light; he says he does not know his deeds are evil; cannot see what is good, cannot repent of his sins, cannot ask for mercy and pardon; that the whole matter rests upon God; and that if He chooses to save one and leave another to damnation he will do it; in fact, he says God does so do. Why, then, should he preach to a sinner? Why exhort him? Why blame him? Why should anybody blame him or punish him for anything he does, if my friend's doctrine be true? I cannot see how the gentleman should consent to the punishment of an unregenerate man for anything, unless it should be for doing right? He might, with some show of consistency, blame a sinner for doing right, as he thinks he is naturally opposed to all that is right—and for him to do right would be sinning against nature.

I would like for the learned gentleman to tell us what all the invitations of the Gospel mean. Why are sinners invited, exhorted, entreated? Does the Gospel mock men in their wretchedness and misery? I read a touching account several years ago of the falling and burning of the Pemberton Mills, in the Eastern part of the United States. In the fall and wreck scores of young women, who were employed there, were caught in the nooks and corners of the ruins; many were killed, and many were penned up alive. The wreck took fire; the alarm reached the ears of those poor girls who were penned up and helpless; brave men, with axes and all other available implements, ran into the smoke and heat and cut a way for their escape, and then called upon them to come out: "Fire! fire! Escape now with your lives! Run from this burning wreck!" and many escaped. The conduct of those men was heroic and deserving of the highest praise; but let us suppose that, without any effort whatever to remove the obstructions which those poor women could never have overcome, those men had stood back and cried, "Fire! fire! Come out and live, for why will you die? Save yourselves." How would most people have looked upon their conduct? Would they not have called it cowardly, misanthropic, mean, dastardly, devilish? Would Professor Crawford have said that was just and *Godlike?* Would he have said that if any one of those poor girls was saved it would be solely a matter of grace, and therefore any one left to perish would have no right to complain? Or will he say that in this case the inability of the women was of the "*physical*" kind?

My friends, I do most candidly look upon the theory of my opponent as infinitely worse than heterodox. It seems to me that it scandalizes the Gospel; that it is a scandal on the character of God, as revealed in Christ. I may not understand it. I may have no right conception of justice and goodness. It may not be God's will that I should have. Anyhow, my opponent cannot complain that I thus express myself. If my whole nature is opposed to the Truth, I can't, in his view of the subject, help myself; and, of course, he will not complain at me. What I say can make me no worse than I am by nature, according to his theory.

John vi, 44: "No man can come unto me except the Father which hath sent me draw him; and I will raise him up at the last day." But how does the Father draw people to Christ? My friend, of course, thinks he does it unconditionally and irresistibly. But the passage says nothing of the kind. He rightly anticipated that I would read the connection to show how persons are drawn to Christ. The next verse tells it, I think, plainly enough. "It is written in the prophets, and they shall all be taught of God; every man, therefore, that hath learned of the Father cometh to me." God draws men to Christ by *teaching*. This is just what I have been contending for all the time. When, therefore, Jesus had finished the work of his personal ministry, when he had risen from the dead, claiming all authority in heaven and earth, he said to his apostles, "Go"—not to a select few—not to any kindred—not to Jews and Samaritans—"Go" —wherever man is found—where kings sit on thrones in regal splendour, and where slaves toil in chains. "Go," said He, breathing the spirit of universal benevolence—the Spirit of Christianity—"Go, preach the Gospel to *every creature;* he [or whoever] that believes and is baptized shall be saved." "Go, teach all nations." That's it. That's God's method of drawing men to him.

My friend's error is not a harmless one. Many honest souls who have imbibed it—notwithstanding my friend teaches that the unregenerate cannot receive the truth—have been kept waiting, waiting, waiting, for this irresistible drawing. Some have died waiting for it. Some have gone to lunatic asylums waiting for it. Of the last, I have an instance in mind now. No, it is not harmless. It's a pernicious error. I know, my friends, as some have said, that 1 am at times almost "vehement" in my style. My apology is that I am in earnest. If I talk "loudly" it is because I feel deeply. I ought to talk louder, much louder, than my opponent; because I believe much more in talking than he does. Indeed, if I believed as he does, I don't know that I should talk on religion at all. I know I should not attempt to preach to the unregenerate. It would be a waste of breath and time.

Failing to find any Scripture in support of his own theory, my opponent spent a portion of his last half hour reading some passages of Scripture that, he tells you, I rely upon as supporting my view of the Spirit's influence in conversion. Well, I do rely on the passages he quoted, and more too. He takes the pains to give you my construction of the passages, as if I were not competent to do that myself. I am much obliged to him. But if it becomes necessary for me to comment upon any passages of Scripture I chose to use in the discussion of this question, or any other, I feel competent to do so for myself. I am here to represent myself and my brethren. But our teaching upon the question of the Spirit's influence is not under discussion. How many times has my opponent told you the "the Spirit operates through the medium of Truth?" Does he not believe this? Certainly he does. He believes more. He believes "the Spirit goes before the Truth," and operates without it "to enable and make the sinner willing to receive it." This I deny. This is the matter under discussion. My affirmative teaching upon the subject is unquestioned. To the extent that we differ, I am in the negative. I simply deny my friend's unscriptural theory and ask for the proof. And he would make you believe, I suppose, by examining certain Scriptures which he tells you I rely upon, that I am advocating some questionable theory of Spiritual influence. No, indeed! Nobody questions the correctness and Scripturalness of my affirmative teaching upon this subject.

A large portion of the gentleman's speech, specially that portion wherein he was commenting upon certain passages that he says I rely on, needs no reply.

In commenting upon that passage which speaks of the Word of God as "the sword of the Spirit," the gentleman informs us that the "Word is only the instrument," while the "Spirit is the agent that must wield it," in the work of conversion. I deny that the Word of God is called the sword of the Spirit, *because the Spirit itself wields it.* As I have already shown, the Apostle, in the only passage in which this figure is used, tells *Christians* to "take the sword of the Spirit," and use it. It is the duty of Christians to wield this sword. True, the Holy Spirit is ever in the truth and ever in the church, and may thus mediately be said to use the word of truth as a sword. But independently of the ministry of the church, and of the church itself, I deny that the Holy Spirit even uses the truth in converting sinners.

In the few minutes of time left me I wish to call attention to a case of conversion recorded in Scripture, not as confirming my view of Spiritual influence, as that needs no confirmation, but as precluding the proof of my opponent's theory. The case is recorded in the eighth chapter of Acts of Apostles. To begin, I'll read the 29th verse: "Then the Spirit said unto Philip, 'Go near and join thyself to this chariot.'" Philip, to whom the Spirit thus spoke, was a preacher of the Gospel. He had come to the place where he now was, by the direction of an angel. In the chariot was an Ethiopian, servant to Candace, queen of the Ethiopians, who was reading a prophecy concerning Jesus, as he rode along in his chariot. "And Philip ran thither to Him, and heard Him read the prophet Esaias, and said, 'Understandest thou what thou readest?' And he said how can I except some man should guide me? And he desired Philip that he would come up and sit with him." Here the passage that he was reading is given, and the narrative proceeds: "Then Philip opened his mouth, and began at the same Scripture, and preached unto him Jesus. And as they went on their way they came unto a certain water; and the eunuch said, 'See water; what doth hinder me to be baptized?' And Philip said, 'If thou believest with all thine heart thou mayest.' And he answered and said, I believe that Jesus Christ is the Son of God. And he commanded the chariot to stand still; and they went down both into the water, both Philip and the eunuch; and he baptized him. And when they were come up out of the water, the Spirit of the Lord caught away Philip, that the eunuch saw him no more; and he went on his way rejoicing." Here we have the New Testament secret of a case of conversion. What was the work done by the Spirit by his own personal presence? "Then the Spirit said to Philip [the preacher], Go near, and join thyself to this chariot." Philip did so, and asked the unconverted man, who was reading a prophecy concerning Jesus, "Understandest thou what thou readest?" The man answered, "How can I, except some man should guide?" If Professor Crawford had been the preacher, doubtless, he would have said, "You cannot at all; neither can any *man* guide you; you must wait for the Holy Spirit to come in his own person, and by a direct act upon your heart, to open it and prepare the way for instruction." But what did Philip do? He "opened his mouth and began at the same Scripture, and *preached to him Jesus."* The man was converted. *Then,* the Holy Spirit said to the preacher, "Go," to the man to be converted; *now*, my friend would say to the Spirit, *you* must go and open his heart. In New Testament times men were converted by preaching; they were not told to wait for the Spirit to come and open their hearts. The preachers did not preach to the people that they could not understand peaching; did not teach the people that they could not be taught.

ADDRESS.

Friday, Sept. 11th, 11 *a.m.*
(PROF. CRAWFORD'S SEVENTH ADDRESS.)

Professor Crawford.—In my last address I distinguished between moral and physical inability, and showed that the sinner's inability to receive the Truth being a moral and not a physical one, springing from the enmity and wickedness of his own heart, he is fully responsible if he fails to accept that Truth. My opponent endeavoured to show that, according to Calvinism, the sinner is entirely exonerated from blame, if he does not become a converted man. He brings forward a number of illustrations in his attempts to show this; but you will please observe that every one of these illustrations bears on *physical* and not on *moral* inability. For instance, when he speaks of a number of persons being in a fire, they are told to escape but cannot. Anyone can see that that is a case of physical, not of moral, inability. Yet he dwells on this case with wonderful eloquence, as if it were a very powerful argument for his side of the question. I say, without the least hesitation, that they were not responsible in that case. And when he speaks of the boy who was attempting to roll a large stick—one that was beyond his strength to move—that does not bear on the point at issue; that was purely a case of physical inability, and I hold, as well as my opponent, that the boy was not responsible. But Mr. Sweeney should bring forward a case of *moral* inability, and then let him show from this, if he can, that man is not responsible. He would then hit the nail on the head; but going on as he is now, he is merely fighting a man of straw. He was trying to show what Calvinism is, but he only succeeded in presenting a caricature of the system. Mr. Sweeney says, if he were a believer in that doctrine, he would sit perfectly still, for he would not be blameable if he did go on in his evil course. But in what, I would ask, does man's inability consist? It lies in the sinful state of his own heart. He says, "I will not receive the truth,' ' I will not have this man Christ Jesus to rule over me,' yet, I am not responsible because the Spirit has not made me willing." Is our doctrine as my opponent has represented it the Calvinism we believe and teach, the Calvinism of the Word of God? We say the individual is responsible. Why does he reject the truth? Why does he not accept Jesus Christ as his Saviour? The inability, I admit, is a strong one, but at the same time, he is held responsible, simply because his own evil heart prevents him from accepting the truth. There is no physical impossibility preventing his reception of the truth and therefore, he is held guilty in God's sight, if he rejects it. But if he is ever delivered from his inability, it is solely by the grace of God, operating in his heart, disposing him to accept the truth, making him willing in the day of his power.

I would like to dwell on some of the passages of Scripture bearing on this point, but it will be almost impossible, unless we prolong this debate for six weeks or so, to get over all our ground. Let us take an example or two: He dwells for a long time on the case of Lydia; his argument was that she was a worshipper of God before "the Lord opened her heart, that she attended

unto the things which were spoken of Paul."
True; but it remains for him to show whether
she was a worshipper of God in the same sense
in which Simon Magus was said to believe. But,
granting that she was a true worshipper of God,
there is nothing in the passage regarding her
which goes in the least against our side of the argument. We say that even believers must have
their hearts opened by Divine influence before
they can receive the truth. The passage says
that "whose heart the Lord opened, so that she
attended unto the things which were spoken of
Paul." What could be plainer? The ingenuity
of Satan himself cannot explain this passage
away. This passage asserts a direct Divine
operation upon the human heart, resulting in
the reception of truth; which doctrine my
opponent denies. Then, again, he refers
to the passage where it speaks of the veil
being taken away; God promises to take
this veil away. He gets over this by re-
minding us that the veil was taken away in
Christ. Very true. The veil that was on the truth
concerning the promised Messiah during the
past dispensation was done away in the death of
Christ. Then this veil was rent; but the latter
part of the verse, and the part to which my arguments applied, speaks of another veil, the veil
which was upon the heart of the Jewish people
when the truth of Moses was read to them in
the Synagogue. This is the veil which God
promises to take away; not the veil which was
upon the truth which was already done away in
the death of Christ. I contend, indeed, that this
promise is to be fulfilled by the operation of
God's Spirit opening their hearts, as in the case
of Lydia. Mr. Sweeney, in trying to rebut this,
quotes the words "When it shall turn to the

Lord the veil shall be taken away," and from them he contends that it is not the Holy Spirit but their own turning to the Lord that is to take away the veil. To this I would reply that neither our word "when" nor the original word necessarily has the meaning which my opponent claims for it in this passage. It is commonly a mere adverb of time, as in the preceding verse, "*When* Moses is read." Let me illustrate this by an example or two. Suppose I should say "The stable door was thrown open *when* the horses escaped." Do I mean by this that the escape of the horses was the cause of the stable door being thrown open? Or suppose I should say "The shutters were thrown open, *when* the light entered the apartment," would this mean that the entrance of the light was the cause of the shutters being opened? Certainly not. In like manner the words "When, it shall turn to the Lord the veil shall be taken away," does not necessarily signify that their turning to the Lord is the cause of the veil being taken from their hearts. On the contrary the whole reasoning of the Apostle as well as the circumstances of the case prove just the reverse. The word "when" is here merely an adverb of time.

I will give one more passage upon which to exercise his ingenuity:—1 Thess. 1-5: "For our Gospel came not unto you in *word only*, but also in power, and in the Holy Ghost, and in much assurance." The last clause is exegetical of the one coming before; no ingenuity or sophistry can explain away the force of that passage. Then with reference to another passage; it was John 14, 16-17: "And I will pray the Father, and he shall give you another Comforter that He may abide with you forever; even the Spirit of Truth, whom the world cannot receive, because it seeth Him not, neither knoweth Him; but ye know Him, for He dwelleth with you and shall be in you." That is, the people of the world, in their natural state, cannot receive the Spirit of Truth; there is a moral inability on their part, they resist its influence. But it is an entirely different question whether or not that Spirit *can* force a passage into the human mind by causing the obdurate heart to relent. That is God's work, the other is man's. The one is a question of moral ability on the part of men in their sinful state; the other is a question of ability on the part of God's Holy Spirit; and who will deny the power of Almighty God? That my interpretation of the passage is the correct one, and that while the world cannot receive the Holy Spirit, those whose hearts God opens can, is evident from the remainder of the verse, viz: "But ye know Him, for He dwelleth in you."

Let us look at Ezekiel 36, 27: "And *I will put my Spirit within you*, and cause you to walk in my statutes, and ye shall keep my judgments and do them." Here it is said that "God will put His Spirit within them." But according to my opponent's version of the other passage, the world *cannot* receive the Spirit. Either my view is correct, that though man in his natural state is morally unable to receive the Spirit, that Spirit can force its way into his heart; I say either this view is correct or there is a flat contradiction in the two passages. Whatever my opponent may believe, I believe that the Word of God, never, if we read it aright, contradicts itself.

He has tried very hard to bring me into the doctrine of the Divine Decrees or Election. I have tried to avoid it, simply because I don't think it is necessary in conducting this controversy; but as the matter now stands, I cannot omit it without doing injustice to myself and to my argument. I don't want you to imagine that I am afraid or ashamed of this doctrine, though I thought it would be as well to leave it out, because we had plenty of ground to go over without it. But he has forced it upon me, and I must take it up in justice to my cause, though it must be very briefly. This being the case I cannot follow my antagonist in every remark and insinuation he throws out; I am content to let the people judge of the respective merits of our arguments when they come out in print. There will not then be quite so much noise to draw them off the real points at issue; they will be enabled to study the matter calmly and dispassionately.

In entering upon this point I would commence by saying that man is by nature a sinner; he is "shapen in sin and brought forth in iniquity." When a child is born, it is not the *creation* of a spirit, for this would make God create an unclean spirit. We hold there is a connection with Adam, both as regards the soul and the body. You ask me, do you understand this? I do not understand it. There are things revealed in the Word of God that we are not competent to understand. I was in the loins of my father Adam the covenant-head. When he sinned, and I sinned in him. Here then is a direct issue with the views brought forth by my opponent. He says a child is not shapen in sin and brought forth in iniquity; but that it is holy at its birth. I would ask him why does a child suffer and die then, for do not suffering and death of intelligent responsible creatures both come by sin? When children arrive in heaven according to his view, they cannot join in the grand chorus, "Thou has redeemed us to God by Thy blood," for they never sinned, and were never redeemed by the blood of Christ. We say let those hold this view who please, but it seems rather strange that there will be in heaven some of the human family who were never redeemed by Christ, and who had no interest in his atoning work. We hold, too, that man is a transgressor in his own person. The Apostle thus sums up this argument by which he would prove the universal guilt of mankind. "Now, we know that what things soever the law saith, it saith to them who are under the law, that every mouth may be stopped, and all the world may become guilty before God." The question is, Is God under obligation to provide salvation for these transgressors? He might have left us to the operation of His justice, but grace comes in. The provisions of the covenant of grace interpose. God, in accordance with that covenant, sends His Son to make an atonement for sin. He commissions His Apostles to "preach the gospel to every creature." It was an infinite atonement, because nothing short of an infinite atonement—an atonement made by a divine person—could save even one man. Shall man, then, receive the benefit of that atonement? It is a *fact* that all men do not receive the gospel. The question is, Could God make all men receive that gospel? Surely no one will deny that. But if he has not done so, it was his purpose to bring some to the reception of that gospel, because His grace would have it so; and to allow others to be lost because infinite justice would have it so. See how our Lord reasons upon this in the parable of the laborers in the vineyard. The man who worked all day, and the man who worked an hour, each received a *denarius*. Some complained that this was not just. What is the reply? Have I done thee any harm? Did I not agree with you for a penny? Take it, then. If I choose to make him equal with you have I not a right to do what I will with my own? Let us read some passages of Holy Writ that bear upon this question. Romans viii, 28, 29-30, "And we know that all things work together for good to them who are called according to his purpose. For whom he did foreknow, he also did predestinate to be conformed to the image of his Son, that he might be the first-born among many brethren. Moreover, whom he did predestinate, them he also called, and whom he called, them he also justified, and whom he justified, them he also glorified." He foreknew them, predestinated them, called, justified and glorified them "according to his purpose." I would refer you next to 1 Cor. i, 26-27, for we have time to do little more than read the passages. "For ye see your calling brethren, how that not many wise men after the flesh, not many mighty, not many noble, are called; but God hath chosen the foolish things of the world to confound the things which are mighty." Here you see God has chosen, and this gracious choice was not determined by anything in man; rather the other way, he chose the "weak things" that the glory might be his. Matt. xxiv, 24: "For there shall arise false Christs, and false prophets, and shall show great signs and wonders; insomuch, that if it were possible, they shall deceive the very elect." He says "if it were possible," but it is not possible, for he has chosen them. 1 Peter i, 2: "Elect according to the foreknowledge of God the Father, through sanctification of the spirit unto obedience and sprinkling of the blood of Jesus Christ: grace unto you and peace be multiplied." Then Romans xi, 7: "What then?

Israel hath not obtained that which he seeketh for; but the election hath obtained it, and the rest were blinded." We shall not spend time at present in arguing *how* this can be in harmony with the divine perfections, but the *fact* is there. Eph. i 3-6: "Blessed be the God and Father of our Lord Jesus Christ, who hath blessed us with all spiritual blessings in heavenly places in Christ: According as he hath chosen us in Him before the foundation of the world, that we should be holy and without blame before Him in love: Having predestinated us unto the adoption of children by Jesus Christ himself, according to the good pleasure of His will to the praise of the glory of His grace wherein he hath made us accepted in the beloved." There is no uncertain sound in these words. They were chosen not because he foresaw that they would be holy, but in order that they might be holy. Eph. i, 11: "In whom also we have obtained an inheritance, being predestinated according to the purpose of him who worketh all things after the counsel of his own will." This also requires no explanation to make it plain. II Thess. 2, 13: "But we are bound to give thanks alway to God for you, brethren beloved of the Lord, because God hath from the beginning chosen you to salvation through sanctification of the Spirit and the belief of the Truth." They were chosen to salvation from the beginning, even before they had an existence. And how was this salvation to be effected? Through sanctification of the Spirit and belief of the Truth, John xvii, 2. "As thou hast given Him power over all flesh, that he should give eternal life to as many as thou hast given Him." Not all but as many as God in His eternal purpose had given Him. Acts xiii, 48: "And when the Gentiles heard this they were glad and glorified the Word of the Lord; and as many as were ordained to eternal life believed."It was not because they believed that they were ordained to eternal life, but "as many as were ordained to eternal life believed." I know they will try to explain away the necessity of the word "ordained," but I will quote all the passages in which the same word in the original, which is here translated "ordained," occurs, so as to show its meaning. Matt. xxviii, 16, "Then the eleven disciples went away into Galilee, into a mountain where Jesus had *appointed* them." Luke vii, 8, "For I also am a man *set under* authority." Acts xv, 2, "They *determined* that Paul and Barnabas should go up to Jerusalem." Acts xxii, 10, "There it shall be told thee of all things which are *appointed* for thee to do." Acts xxviii, 23, "And when they had *appointed* Him a day there came to Him, into His lodging," &c. Rom. xiii, 1, "The powers that He *ordained* of God." I Cor., xvi, 15, "They have *addicted* themselves to the ministry of the Saints." These and the passage I first read (Acts xiii, 48) are the only passages in which this word is used in the original. You see from these the true meaning of the word, and, therefore, that it is properly translated "ordained" in the text I quoted, "As many as were ordained to eternal life believed." The next passage is II Timothy 1, 9: "Who hath saved us, and called us with an holy calling, not according to our works, but according to His own purpose and grace, which was given us in Christ Jesus before the world began." Here you observe we were called not according to our works, but according to his own *purpose* and *grace* which he had given *before the world began.* The last passage I shall quote in this connection is Rom. 9, from verse

11 : " For the children being not yet born, neither having done any good or evil, that the purpose of God according to election might stand, not of works, but of him that calleth. It was said unto her, the elder shall serve the younger. As it is written, Jacob have I loved and Esau have I hated. What shall we say then? Is there unrighteousness with God? God forbid. For he saith to Moses, I will have mercy on whom I will have mercy, and I will have compassion on whom I will have compassion. So then it is not of him that willeth, nor of him that runneth, but of God that sheweth mercy." Both Jacob and Esau were sinners, but God saw Jacob in Christ and had chosen him, in him viewed in Christ, clothed in his righteousness and washed in his atoning blood, Jacob was worthy of God's love; whereas Esau, viewed as he was in himself, a sinful creature, was a fit object of God's disapprobation. It was God's electing love, therefore, according to the Apostle, and not anything originally good in Jacob that made them to differ.

REPLY.

Friday, Sept. 11*th,* 11.30 *a.m.*

(MR. SWEENEY'S SEVENTH REPLY.)

Mr. Sweeney.—I congratulate you this morning, friends, as recipients of the Divine favour. We are, I trust, becomingly grateful that we have been preserved through the night and permitted to come together this morning to resume the discussion. I feel somewhat disposed also to congratulate myself; I came here, you know, to defend what my opponent calls "Campbellism," as he had come to show what that thing is in the first place, and prove it false in the second. We have been here now but one day, and instead of making headway with his proposed work of exposition and destruction, the worthy gentleman has been thrown back upon the defence of his own works; instead of demolishing "Campbellism" he is making an almost desperate struggle to make his own doctrine look respectable. You remember, of course, the programme upon which he set out: he was going to show us just what this thing called "Campbellism" is, and then, secondly, he was going to attack it—was going to attack it all along its front line; but he has been driven back, and back, and back, until he is now desperately trying to defend his own doctrine concerning the Divine decrees. Well, I shall follow him up, and show that that position cannot be maintained. I only ask you to note the fact that it is not "Campbellism" that is on trial, but Calvinism.

The gentleman saw fit in his last to indicate

that I quibble and swagger, rather than meet his arguments fairly. Now, I respectfully submit that he might better let the people judge and decide as to such matters; I think they are less partial if not better qualified than he. The people will hear us both, if he is a professor in Woodstock University, and I, as he would have you believe, a mere quibbler and swaggerer. I am willing for our speeches to go to the world, and we shall see whether his brethren or mine are better satisfied when it comes to the matter of publishing our debate in a book.

The gentleman stoutly contends, that while the sinner is utterly unable to turn to Christ, his inability is "moral and not physical," and that because his inability is moral he is justly responsible. But I am utterly unable to see what difference it makes as to what kind of inability it is, so long as the sinner is utterly unable to turn to Christ. Call it moral inability if you please. Does that relieve the sinner? Is he not unable to believe, to repent, to pray, to do anything, according to my friend's theory? Yes. Is he not as unable to turn to Christ as he is to create a planet? Yes. Then why is he responsible in the one case and not in the other, because the one may be called a moral affair, and the other a physical one? Does not all responsibility grow out of ability? Moral responsibility grows out of moral ability, and physical responsibility out of physical ability, if we make the finest distinctions. But such abstruse and metaphysical distinctions are not to the purpose in the matter in hand. I hold that no being on earth, or anywhere else, can justly be held accountable and punished for not being or doing what he was wholly unable to be or do. Will my opponent take issue with me here right squarely, or will he proceed further to inform us that there is a difference between moral and physical inability?

Now, if I understand the position of my opponent, it is briefly about like this: Every one is born utterly depraved, and is conseqently from his birth exposed to the wrath of God. No one can be saved without regeneration. But regeneration is effected by an immediate operation of the Holy Spirit upon the heart. No one can do anything whatever, to superinduce, or invite, such an operation. Neither can any one resist it. If any one is regenerated, therefore, it is not because he wants to be, but because he can't help himself. And, further, every such regenerated one must go to Heaven, willing or unwilling; for no regenerated person, according to Calvinism, can by any possibility, ever be lost. So that no person in Heaven will ever be able to say, "I am here partly because I desired to come;" but every one will have to say, "I am here because I could not go elsewhere. I am here in spite of all the resistance I could make to the Divine violence by which I was overcome." That's it! No man is to be regenerated because he desires to be. No man whom God regenerates can ever be lost. The matter of being saved is a good deal like picking up sticks. Men have no more will or voice in the matter than the sticks that are picked up or those that are passed by. And my opponent thinks that is the Gospel of Christ! But, now, if this be true, what does it matter what one does or refuses to do? Might not one as well, if he feels like it, defy as to implore Heaven? Might not one as well curse as pray? I, for one, can't believe any such thing. Will my friend blame me for it? Yes: He says I am justly blameable because my inability is of the moral and not of the physical kind ! I could more easily be a Universalist. Indeed, Universalism, is almost infinitely more reasonable than the theory my friend advocates. For if the whole matter of salvation depends upon God alone, then in my humble judgment it does Him more honor to say He will save us all finally, than to say He will damn a portion just for His glory ! Grim glory, indeed; so it seems to me.

The gentleman comes back to the case of Lydia ; he admits she was a devout woman and a worshipper of God. Then she was not so depraved as to need the operation of the Spirit for which he contends before she could believe ; but he says everybody—even Christians, if I didn't misunderstand him—must have this direct operation upon the heart, to enable them to receive the truth. But did he show that there was any such operation upon Lydia's heart? I deny that he did; he assumed the very identical thing he should have tried to prove. He assumes that Lydia's heart was opened by an immediate operation of the Spirit, when, in fact, there is nothing said about the Holy Spirit in the whole record of the case ! The passage certainly teaches that Paul preached to Lydia and that she "heard"—and "heard" is evidently used here in the sense of heeded or hearkened— and that the Lord opened her heart, "that she *attended* to the things spoken by Paul." It is not said that her heart was opened so that she could receive the truth, so that she could believe. No, no ! The Word was spoken to her and she heeded, or hearkened to, it, and after this her heart was opened, so that she attended to—or obeyed—what was spoken by Paul. *How* did the Lord open her heart ? It is *assumed* that it was done by an immediate interposition of the Holy

Spirit. But that is the very thing that ought to be proved, because it is the very thing I deny. Indeed, it is the very point in dispute. Now, it was certainly possible for the Lord to open her heart by means of what she saw in the Gospel which she had heard, and I shall claim that it was actually done in that way. I am not out of the record, either. We know that the Gospel is "Quick and powerful;" we know it was preached to her, and that she heard it; and when I assume that her heart was opened by means of what she saw in the Gospel, I do not travel out of the record as the professor has to do in order to press the passage into the unreasonable service of his cause.

The passage in 2 Corinthians, 3rd chapter, wherein the Apostle speaks of the "veil" over the hearts of the Jews when they read Moses has really no bearing whatever upon the point of difference between us, there being no reference in it to any operation of the Spirit whatever. My friend reads with a veil over his heart, just as the Jews read Moses. He reads it with a false theory in his mind; reads it to see what is not in it, and not to see what is in it. So the Jews read Moses; they had a false theory of interpretation. Hence, when the Christ came they could not see him. The whole dispensation of Moses was but a grave mystery, without Christ; it was like a great shadow that could be traced to no substance, or a type answering to no antetype. The Jews came down the shadow looking for a substance so different from the meek and lowly Jesus that they could not see Him when they came to Him. When Israel shall look at Jesus as the fulfilment of all the types, as the substance of all the shadows of the former dispensation, then the veil will disappear and they will see meaning in their Scriptures, that without Christ must remain a mystery. Jesus is a solution of the mysteries of Mosaism, as well as many of the mysteries of nature itself. What is there in the passage about the kind of Spiritual influences Professor Crawford is contending for? Just nothing! Was the Apostle discussing the question of Spiritual influence in this passage? Of course not.

The gentleman's criticism of "when," and his horse and stable illustration need to be labored further, before an answer can be reasonably called for.

Next, the gentleman cites the words of Paul, 1 Thess., i, 5. "For our Gospel came not unto you in word only, but also in power, and in the Holy Ghost, and in much assurance," etc. I suppose the Apostle means nothing more than he says, here. He simply reminds the Thessalonians that the Gospel, when it was preached to them was confirmed by manifestations of Divine power; by manifestations of the Holy Spirit. The Apostles did not simply preach the Gospel in the beginning, at Thessalonica, nor anywhere else, expecting the people to receive it simply upon their word; but they spoke it, "God also bearing them witness both with signs and wonders, and with divers miracles and gifts of the Holy Ghost, according to His own will." There is, in this passage also, nothing about the Spiritual influence my friend contends for; and it is, in this respect, just like all the others he has quoted. Nor do I claim to have exercised much ingenuity in discovering the fact.

The gentleman admits that the world cannot receive the Spirit of Truth; but he thinks "the Spirit can force a passage into the heart," and cause man's obdurate opposition to relent. *"Force a passage!"* Of course the Holy Spirit *could* break in upon any human heart, and violently crush out its opposition. I should not question the Spirit's power to do so; but to call such an operation *conversion*, in the New Testament sense, would be, in my judgment, a monstrous burlesque on conversion. What was the use of Christ dying for the world? What's the use of the Gospel? What is the use of anything but the Divine crushing, violence of the Spirit, if that is the way regeneration is effected? In the light of such teaching how would it sound to say, "We love him *because* he first loved us?" Why? According to my friend's notion it would be better to say we love Him because the Holy Spirit forced a passage into our hearts and crushed them into love for Him.

The gentleman seems to think that when God said by Ezekiel, "I will put my Spirit within you, and cause you to walk in my statutes," He meant He would do so *forcibly*. What sort of obedience would that be, thus compelled? Would it be the obedience of the Gospel? Surely not. The passage in Ezekiel is a promise; not a *threat*. And the passage in John simply means that the world God opposed—that is, sinners—cannot, *as such*, receive the Holy Spirit, which was sent to be a comforter in the Church, and through the Church, by means of the Gospel, to convert the world.

But if God "forces a passage" into one heart why not into another? Why not into all? Here we see the gentleman runs right into the old, hard, angular doctrine of unconditional election and reprobation. There is no avoiding it; he should not scold me about it, I can't help it. That's where his own doctrine lands him, and he would do quite as well to keep cool over it. So he starts out on the doctrine of the Divine Decrees, as he mildly puts it, by asserting the doctrine of hereditary total depravity. With him all are born sinners; God elected some from all eternity to eternal life, others He left to be tormented forever in hell. Wonder if any non-elect infants die? They used to die, and go off to become small fire-brands in hell; but of late we are told none of that class passed by in Divine mercy ever die in infancy! But what is the difference? According to the gentleman's teaching, an infant is as much a sinner as an adult person, and no more innocent or helpless; and if an adult person is to be damned simply because he is of the non-elect why not an infant as well? He tells you that I say infants are holy; well, Paul said so, and I believe it. Just what Paul meant I may not certainly know; but of this I am quite certain, I do not believe that infants are in any sense *guilty* of sin, or in any danger of being lost. There is no Scripture support for this horrid notion—a conception of the darkest ages, and of Africa. I do not believe in a God whose wrath burns with furnace heat against an infant for the nature with which it was born, or who brought one such little one into being to burn it forever in hell. No, no! My friend misunderstands the passages that he supposes teach such a doctrine; he reads them with a veil over his heart, that's the trouble. He tells us that infants are, souls and bodies, in the loins of their parents, and thus partakers of their sins. Well, if this be so, why not allow that they partake also of the justification and sanctification of their parents, and so have it that the infants of justified persons are born justified. He argues further that infants are sinners, from the fact that they suffer and die; but that proves too much. Horses and sheep die; are they sinners? God said, "Cursed is the earth for thy sake," and that smote with death everything that is of the earth; but there is a vast difference between that and sending immortal souls to hell forever for His own pleasure, as Calvinism represents God as doing.

The gentleman's doctrine of fatalism, or "Divine Decrees," as he calls it, ignores all differences between matter and mind, as respects the government of God. It has God operating upon mind precisely as he does upon matter, governing it by sheer force! The doctrine is as absurd as it is destitute of Scripture support; it is dishonorable to God, in that it destroys the chief difference between his image and a stone; and degrading to man, in that it annihilates the law of his happiness, which is the consciousness of doing what he believes to be right from choice. In denying to man the power of choice it robs him of any happiness higher, less selfish, or less animal, than that of a brute. And surely Scriptures supposed to give support to such a theory must be wrongly interpreted—must be read with a veil upon the heart—by him who so reads them.

The gentleman made the leap—plunged headlong into the doctrine of unconditional election and reprobation. He quoted the same old passages that have been quoted since the time of Augustine. Of course, he will not expect me to take up each passage separately and show that it does not teach his doctrine, as he himself did not have time to try to show that any one passage he read does not teach the doctrine he adduced it to prove; he only had time to read the passages. Well, I shall not waste the time to read them all; it would be useless.

The Bible certainly teaches the doctrine of election. Yes, I will go further; it teaches unconditional election—in the ordinary acceptation of the word unconditional. Such election is no doubt taught in some of the passages he read to us. The Bible also teaches conditional election; this will not be denied, it need not be. I repeat, then, that the Bible teaches both conditional and unconditional election. But the Bible is not self-contradictory; how, then, is it to be interpreted in this subject? I submit this as a pretty good rule to be governed by when reading the Bible, upon the subject of election: Whenever we come to a case of election recorded in the Bible let us ask ourselves this question, *To what were the persons named elected?* I apprehend that if we would observe this rule strictly it would aid us much in understanding the subject. Now, that my friend may go to work under this rule, I demand of him the passage of Scripture that teaches the unconditional election of any one to *personal salvation* or *everlasting life*. Will he produce it? Let him try.

I know that in laying the foundation and developing the great scheme of human redemption, there were many elections that God made, and many of them were, in the ordinary sense, unconditional. But when it comes to *personal* election to *salvation*, to individual happiness, in this scheme, no one is so elected unconditionally. Just as a parent may *provide* for the happiness of his children—that is, lay his plans looking to that end—irrespective of their choice—without consulting them—before they are born, it may be—yet when it comes to the *personal enjoyment* of each child in the parental scheme, each child has the power of choice, as many parents proudly know; and, alas! many painfully know it. Men are not *crushed* into personal happiness, though the *means* of being happy may be unconditionally *provided* for us. Now, in the light of these remarks, let us notice a single case of unconditional election, one much relied upon by my opponent; that of Jacob and Esau, recorded in the 9th of Romans. I admit that Jacob was, without respect to conditions in him that we can see, preferred over Esau. This preference was made known, too, before the children were born. Jacob was elected and Esau was not. But now, *to what* was Jacob elected? To personal salvation? To eternal life? I deny that he was. He was elected to a place in the scheme God was developing, which scheme looked to the salvation of the world—looked to, and provided for the descendants of Esau as well as those of Jacob. In this sense Jacob was the elect. In this sense Israel was God's elect. In this sense Christ was the elect of God. In this sense there were the elect angels. In this sense the Apostles were elected and predestined. My friend's mistake is, in seeing Heaven and Hell in all these cases. He reads them with that veil untaken away.

Now when we come to *personal* election to *everlasting life*, we find it always conditional, as for instance, in this passage: "Wherefore the other brethren give diligence to make your calling and election sure; for if you do these things [things above enumerated] ye shall never fall; for so an entrance shall be ministered unto you abundantly into the everlasting kingdom of our Lord and Saviour Jesus Christ."—II. Peter, i., 10, 11.

This passage speaks of election, personal election, to everlasting life; and does it not make that election depend upon the persons elected, in part at least? What mean the phrases, "*make* your calling and election *sure*"—"*if ye* do these things"—"*So* an entrance shall be ministered to you," etc.; I say, what mean these phrases if they do not make this election conditional?

But, my friends, where is "Campbellism," that my friend came here to demolish? It is left out of the fight, is it not? I have driven the gentleman back to the "last ditch." I hope he will rally and make another aggressive movement. This people didn't come here to hear a discussion of election and reprobation.

ADDRESS.

Friday, Sept. 11*th,* 2 *p.m.*

(PROF. CRAWFORD'S EIGHTH ADDRESS.)

Professor Crawford.—My opponent still overlooks the difference between moral and physical inability; or rather he makes none. With him, the man who is in gaol and cannot come out, is, as it regards responsibility, the same as the man whose heart is so wicked and rebellious against his sovereign that he will not submit or consent to do that which would bring him out. The whole of the argument hinges upon this, but he overlooks it entirely. Let him show me a single example of moral inability where there is not responsibility, and he will have proved something. He has hardly looked the passage in the face which I gave on the Divine Decrees. My opponent must meet my arguments on every passage. Any one of these Scriptures is able to sustain the whole weight of this doctrine, for it is the words of the God of Truth. On speaking of the passage with reference to Jacob and Esau, he says the choice was to temporal blessings and not to eternal life. Now I don't think so, but whether this is so or not does not make very much difference as far as my argument is concerned, for Paul, in speaking of the case, undoubtedly uses it in illustration of the blessings of eternal life. Let us grant, for argument's sake, that temporal blessings instead of eternal life were meant, yet in Jacob's case, according to the Apostle, we have at least an illustration of eternal election. First, I will read the passage: "For the children being not yet born, neither having done any good or evil, that the purpose of God according to election, might stand, not of works, but of him that calleth." Now, if it was, as Mr. Sweeny contends, unjust for God, before the children were born, to ordain one to eternal life and not the other, I cannot see how the case is materially altered, if we suppose that temporal blessings alone were meant. If there is injustice in one case there is injustice in the other. "It was said unto her, The elder shall serve the younger: As it is written, Jacob have I loved but Esau have I hated." None of us have any claim upon God; if we had all been eternally lost, no blame could have been thrown upon the Almighty. "What shall we say then? Is their unrighteousness with God? God forbid. For he saith to Moses, I will have mercy on whom I will have mercy, and I will have compassion on whom I will have compassion. So it is not of him that willeth nor of him that runneth, but of God that showeth mercy. For the Scripture saith unto Pharoah, Even for this same purpose have I raised thee up, that I might show my power in thee, and that my name might be declared throughout all the earth. Therefore hath he mercy on whom he will have mercy, and whom he will he hardeneth. Thou wilt say then unto him, "Why doth he yet find fault; for who hath resisted his will?" This is the objection my opponent raises to God's plan, and it has been the objection of the carnal mind in every age. Mark the Apostle's reply: "Nay, but, O man, who art thou that repliest against God? Shall the thing formed say to him that formed it, Why hast thou made me thus? Hath not the potter power over the clay, of the same lumps to make one vessel unto honour, and another unto dishonour? What if God, willing to show his wrath, and to make his power known, endured with much long suffering the vessels of wrath fitted to destruction; And that he might make known the riches of his glory on the vessels of mercy, which he had afore prepared unto glory, even us, whom he hath called, not of the Jews only, but also of the Gentiles?" I have given my interpretations of these passages; it remains for my opponent to upset it if he can, for if one passage stands, it carries the whole thing with it. If the doctrine I have laid down be true, it carries the whole of our controversy. For if, as I contend, the carrying out of God's eternal purpose is that which brings salvation, how is it to be carried out? God's power must be exercised in bringing it to pass, therefore I am right in my views on election, I am right in saying there is a Divine power exercised in the work of conversion. Now with regard to the subject of Baptism. We believe that no person is a fit and proper subject for Christian baptism, who has not previously become a subject of the converting and saving grace through the influence of the Holy Spirit; and that therefore baptism is in no way a regeneration, although it represents in a figure the change effected by Divine grace; nor do we receive the remission of sins through baptism only in a figure. I will give the disciples' views upon this subject, as shown in Mr. Campbell's writings. In his Christian system page 193 he says:—" Whatever the act of faith may be it necessarily becomes the line of discrimination between the two states before described. On the one side they are pardoned, justified, sanctified, reconciled, adopted and saved; on the other they are in a state of condemnation. This act is sometimes called immersion, regeneration, conversion."

Here we have the boundary line separating those who are, and those who are not pardoned, justified, reconciled, adopted and saved, and this boundary according to Mr. Campbell is not faith, but what he calls the act of faith, that is, immersion; and the immersion is, in the language of the Bethany reformation the same as conversion or regeneration. This passage gives no uncertain sound. If any man be not baptised, he is neither pardoned, justified, sanctified, reconciled, adopted, regenerated nor saved.

Then on page 203:
"These expressions" (immersed, converted, regenerated) "in the Apostles' style denote the same act."

According to this quotation, conversion, regeneration and immersion are one and the same thing.

And on page 200:
"For if immersion be equivalent to regeneration, and regeneration be of the same import with being born again, then being born again and being immersed are the same thing."

The meaning here cannot be mistaken. The new birth and baptism are one and the same according to the "ancient Gospel." This looks to me like "another Gospel which is not another."

Page 202 of the same book:
"The Holy Spirit calls nothing personal regeneration except the act of immersion."

Here it is again. Nothing is personal regeneration but baptism!

Then in the "Millennial Harbinger," Vol. I., page 136:
"The sprinkling of a speechless and faithless

babe never moved it one inch in the way to Heaven, and never did change its heart, character, or relation to God and the Kingdom of Heaven. But not so a believer immersed as a volunteer in obedience of the Gospel. He has put on Christ."

The act of "faith," or baptism, according to Mr. Campbell can change the heart and character of a man, and that without the Spirit of God; for, according to him, the Spirit of God never operates on a man's heart in conversion."

"Christian System," page 233:

"There are three births, three kingdoms, and three salvations; one from the womb, one from the water, and one from the grave. We enter a new world on, and not before each birth: the present animal life at the first birth; the spiritual, or the life of God in our souls, at the second birth; and the life eternal in the presence of God at the third birth. And he who dreams of entering the second kingdom, or coming under the dominion of Jesus without the second birth, may, to complete his error, dream of entering the kingdom of glory without a resurrection from the dead."

According to this passage, baptism is the second birth; and without this birth or baptism it is as vain to expect "spiritual life, or the life of God in the soul," as it would be to expect an entrance into the kingdom of glory without a resurrection from the dead!

And "Christianity Restored," page 206:

"Persons are begotten by the Spirit of God impregnated by the Word, and born of the water. In one sense, a person is born of his father, but not until he is first born of his mother; so in every place where water and the Spirit, or water and the Word, are spoken of, the *water stands first.* Every child is born of its father when it is born of its mother. Hence the Saviour put the mother first, and the apostles follow Him. * * * * Now, as soon as, and not before, a disciple who has been begotten of God is born of water, he is born of God or of the Spirit. *Regeneration is, therefore, the " act of being born."*

It was the boast of the Bethany reformation that it was to restore to Christianity a pure speech. To use this quotation, and a very large portion of Mr. Campbell's teachings, do not appear to be in the pure dialect of Canaan. It sounds more like the speech of Ashdod. This figment about the distinction of the *begetting* and *birth* I have already refuted, by showing that for both the same word (*Gennas*) is employed in the original.

And in the " Debate with Rice," page 509 :

" The Apostles never supposes such a case as is often before our minds—a believing unbaptized man. Such a being could not have been found in the whole apostolic age."

Did not the Eunuch believe before Philip would baptize him ? See here is water, what doth hinder me to be baptized ? And Philip said, "if though believest with all thy heart thou mayest." Acts, viii., 36, &c. Did not the dying thief believe, and that with the faith of God's elect, although he never was baptized ? Did not Cornelius and his household believe and receive the gift of the Holy Ghost before Peter ordered their baptism. The Apostle said, " Can any man forbid water that these should not be baptized which have received the Holy Ghost as well as we ? "

" Christian Baptist," pages 416, 417 :

" Peter, to whom was committed the keys, opened the Kingdom of Heaven in this manner, and made *repentance* or *reformation* and *immersion* EQUALLY *necessary to forgiveness.* * * When a person is immersed for the remission of sins it is just the same as if expressed *in order to obtain the remission of sins.* * * I am bold, therefore, to affirm that every one of them who, in the belief of what the Apostles spake, was immersed, did in the very instant in which he was put under water, receive the forgiveness of his sins and the gift of the Holy Spirit."

This is plain speaking. Repentance or reformation, and immersion, are equally necessary to forgiveness. If there be no forgiveness without immersion, of course there can be no salvation without it. In the moment that the candidate is put under the water, but only then does he receive the pardon of his sins and the gift of the Holy Ghost! This is pretty strong doctrine for a Pedobaptist. These are not the views held by Mr. Campbell alone; they are held by the whole body. Only the other evening in making arrangements for this meeting they were avowed by a Campbellite who is now present.

I will quote next from "Christianity Restored," page 198:

"It is not faith, but an act resulting from faith, which changes our state, we shall now attempt to prove."

It would seem that the Apostle was wrong when he taught the Roman Christians that "a man is justified by faith without the deeds of the law." Rom. 3. 28. Perhaps he had not found the ancient Gospel discovered by Mr. Campbell and the Bethany reformers.

"Christian Baptist," page 520:

"I assert that there is but one action ordained or commanded in the New Testament to which God has promised or testified, that he will forgive our sins. This action is Christian immersion."

That is, God has given no promise nor held out any ground of hope of salvation to any unbaptized man. This is plain talking.

"Christian System," page 233:

"Infants, idiots, deaf and dumb persons, innocent Pagans, wherever they can be found, with all pious Pœdobaptists, we commend to the mercy of God."

Here, my Pœdobaptist brethren, are some crumbs of consolation for you from the Campbellites' table. You may come in for your share of the uncovenanted mercy of God with "infants, idiots, deaf and dumb persons, and innocent Pagans wherever they can be found." It seems that you ought to be devoutly thankful for small mercies. There is, however, no uncertain sound here. There is no salvation according to Mr. Campbell, for the unbaptized, however pious, unless it be in the unconvenanted mercies of God. We have not a scrap of evidence, however, in the Word of God, that he will ever save a single soul but according to his revealed plan.

"Chistian Baptist," vol. vi, page 160:

"If men are conscious that their sins are forgiven, and that they are pardoned before they are immersed, I advise them not to go into the water, for they have no need of it."

Are we, then, to do nothing for God but what is essential to salvation? If not essential to salvation may the thing not be essential to loving obedience? Is it not enough for every child of God to know that the Heavenly Father has commanded it? Cornelius was a saved man before his baptism. His prayers and almsdeeds were accepted; but "without faith it is impossible to please God." He had, moreover, received the gift of the Holy Ghost before Peter had ordered his baptism. Mr. Campbell would have advised the centurian and his pious friends "not to go into the water, for they had no need of it."

Let us now see what Mr. Franklin has to say upon this subject: Sermon 4, pages 88 and 89.

"Peter says 1 Peter iii. 21. Baptism doth also now save us. This is a general statement, not of a special few but of *all saved or justified.* They are saved by baptism. It is present in the justification of every person. It is never omitted."

This is a very sweeping assertion. *All* who are saved and justified are baptized. In the case of the saved this ordinance "is never omitted." This is plain enough. On the meaning of the passage here quoted I shall speak when I come to examine the Scripture evidence. My object at present is only to show what the Disciples' doctrine really is. There is no doubt about the meaning of this. It is honest at all events. Then in Sermon iv., page 90.

"Do they say that persons may be pardoned, and the Lord receive them without baptism? Then they differ from the Lord and require something more than the Lord does before they will receive them. But who is received of the Lord? Every justified or pardoned person. His terms of justification or remission of sins are precisely the same as his terms of admission into his body or kingdom. He receives into his kingdom every justified person and no other."

This also is plain enough. It is simply this: There is neither pardon nor justification without baptism; and Christ will receive none but the pardoned and justified. Therefore there is no salvation without baptism.

And in the same Sermon page 95:

"Baptism performs no such part as this at all,

produces no change in the heart or life; but changes the relation, initiates the man previously changed in heart and life into a new state or relation, into the body of Christ. It transfers the man into a new state or relation. In this new state he comes to the blood of Christ which performs another part of the work, without which he would be lost. It takes away his sin, cleanses or washes him from the guilt of sin. The Holy Spirit, his advocate in the Church announces him justified."

Here, then, baptism does not change the heart; that takes place previously. A man is changed in heart and life, yet because he is not baptized he has no access to the blood of Christ, no pardon or justification. Surely this is a strange doctrine, that a man is changed in heart and life before baptism, yet has no access to the blood of Christ, no share in the justification which comes by faith. A man changed in heart and life, and yet lost?

Then in Sermon VI, page 149:

"There will be no difficulty in seeing that the remission of sins and sins blotted out amount to the same. But some will be troubled to see how 'be immersed' and 'be converted' or 'turn' amount to the same; yet this is the case."

Then Sermon XII, page 292:

"The sum of it is then that the Lord taught by the figurative expression, 'Except a man be born of water and of the Spirit he cannot enter the kingdom of God.' The same he did afterwards literally in the words, 'He who believes and is immersed shall be saved,'—or except a man shall believe and be immersed he cannot be saved."

That is, no salvation without baptism. You now know exactly where they stand upon this subject. Let us now proceed to find how these views and interpretations tally with the Word of God: John, 1, 12, "But as many as received Him to them gave He power to become the sons of God." Here, you see, there is salvation to those that believe, and I think we are safe in calling a believer a saved man; but, according to their views, he is not a saved man though he is a believer until he is baptized. 1 John, 2, 29: "If ye know that he is righteous, ye know that every one that doeth righteousness is born of Him." You observe there is a different birth from the birth of baptism; he is born again if he is a righteous man, if his heart is changed. But the Disciples say he has no access to the blood of Christ unless he is baptized.

1 John, 1, 9: "If we confess our sins, he is faithful and just to forgive us our sins, and to cleanse us from all unrighteousness." 1 John' 4, 7: "Beloved, let us love one another, for love is of God; and every one that loveth is born of God and knoweth God." Here, you see, if we love God it is a proof that we have received His Truth in its love and power. The promise is inseparable from love of God and faith in Him; it is not inseparable from baptism. 1 John, 5, 1: "Whosoever believeth that Jesus is the Christ is born of God; and so every one that loveth Him that begat loveth Him also that is begotten of Him." Take the case of the dying thief. He was not baptized; he appeared on the cross a hardened criminal, but when he expressed his belief in the Saviour, Christ said, "To-day shalt thou be with me in Paradise." He was saved, justified, sanctified and admitted to Paradise, yet he was not baptized. Either the Saviour's promise that the thief should be with him in Paradise was not fulfilled, or, if the Camp-

bellite doctrine be true, an unsaved and unconverted, unpardoned, unjustified man was admitted to Heaven. James i, 18 :—Of his own will begat he us of the word of Truth, that we should be a kind of first fruits of his creatures." Titus iii, 5 : "Not by works of righteousness which we have done, but according to his mercy he saved us, by the washings of regeneration and renewing of the Holy Ghost." This is one of the favourite passages with the Disciples. The question is what is meant by the washing of regeneration and the renewing of the Holy Ghost? We contend that the washing refers to the cleansing of the soul from sin by the influence of the Holy Spirit leading the sinner to the blood of Christ and to the fountain opened for sin and uncleanliness. But if it means, according to their view, simple baptism, then all I have to say is, it is directly opposed to all the teachings of the word of God upon this subject; but God's word cannot contradict itself. It is consistent. Truth is one.

REPLY.

Friday. Sept. 11th, 2.30 p.m.

MR. SWEENEY'S EIGHTH REPLY.

Mr. Sweeney.—My opponent says that I must examine every text he adduces and show that it does not mean what he claims it does, or I shall be defeated in the discussion. Well, really, I hadn't understood the matter just that way before. I think he started out to prove that my brethren are wrong on the question of spiritual influence in conversion, in that we deny that "the Spirit operates immediately upon the sinner's heart." He undertook to show that we are thus wrong by proving that the Spirit *does* so operate. Now, I submit that when he adduces a passage to prove this doctrine, he must show that it does it instead of calling upon me to show that it does not. Suppose my friend were to go into court as plaintiff in a cause, and were to call in a dozen witnesses, and then claim that the jury must find for him unless the defendant should show that the witnesses do not prove what plaintiff introduced them for! What would the court think? Would not plaintiff be required to show that the witnessas do prove what he had brought them forward to prove? He has been trying in his last two or three speeches to prove the doctrine of unconditional election to salvation, and reprobation to damnation; but he has introduced no Scripture that, fairly interpreted, comes within a thousand miles of it. This I showed in my last speech, I think. Did he show that the elections spoken of in the passages he adduced were to personal salvation or eternal life? What did he do with the case of Jacob? Did he show that he was elected to eternal life, and that Esau was reprobated to eternal damnation? Can he do it? I think not. He says that if Jacob's election was only to temporal blessings—which he doubts—that the principle is the same. But he did not show that Jacob was unconditionally elected even to any temporal blessings. Jacob's unconditional election was as much for my happiness and salvation as for his own. As to personal salvation and eternal life, Jacob and Esau will have to meet at the judgment where every man will be rewarded according as his works shall have been.

As the gentleman seemed to rely very confidently upon the passage in the first chapter of Ephesians, I will notice that briefly. Take your Bibles at leisure, my friends, and begin at the first of the chapter and read to the 13th verse; and you will find that before you come to the 13th verse, the Apostle speaks of the choosing and predestination, using the pronouns of the first person, "we" and "us." Then at the 13th verse he addresses the Ephesian Christians directly, using the pronoun of the *second* person, thus—"In whom *ye* also trusted, after that *ye* heard the word of Truth, the Gospel of your salvation; in whom also after that ye believed, *ye* were sealed with that Holy Spirit of promise." Now this change from the first person to the second, and then the manner in which the Apostle speaks of the salvation of the Ephesian Christians shows quite conclusively that he was not speaking of election and predestination merely to personal salvation in the former part of the chapter; and that quite upsets the gentleman's interpretation of the passage. Possibly the "we" and "us" in the former part of this chapter include only the Apostles and their predestination to the Apostleship, is particularly emphasized here. They filled their place in the scheme, which looked to the world as much as to them.

My friend quoted other Scriptures that he supposes teach his doctrine. I remember, now, a passage, and it is often used by Calvinists: "It is not of him that willeth, nor of him that runneth, but of God that showeth mercy."—Rom. ix. 16. *What*, I ask, "is not of him that willeth?" Personal salvation? Eternal life? I deny it. I think, if I had the time, and it were necessary, I could show by an analysis of the Apostle's argument in this portion of the Roman letter, that he was arguing *against* a sort of Jewish Calvinism, and vindicating the justice of God in offering mercy to the Gentiles who were considered the non-elect, as well as to the Jews, who were considered the elect people of God. But such a work is not logically required, and will not be expected of me in a discussion of this kind. It is not quite sufficient for the Professor to simply read such passages of Scripture as have long been used by some persons as he uses them, and then claim that I must show that they do not teach what he supposes they do. When he introduces a passage, for instance, to prove *his doctrine* of election, he must show that it teaches it. It will not answer for him to read a passage that simply teaches election, or one that teaches unconditional election. No, no! He must find one that teaches unconditional election to personal, or individual, salvation, or eternal life. This he will not be able to do. I call for the passage. One will do me. Let him point it out, and I promise to give it respectful attention.

The gentleman comes to *baptism*. He tells us first what he believes and what he doesn't believe about it, very briefly, and then proceeds to give you the Disciple's view, as he finds it in the writings of Mr. Campbell, and of some of his co-adjutors.

I should like it if he would produce the books he reads from; not that I now question the correctness of any of his quotations; but I should like to have them for cross examination. Perhaps I might be able to explain some of the scraps he has given us, by reading them in their proper connection. Great injustice may be done to an author without misquoting him. You know the old illustration from Scripture: "Judas went and hanged himself. Go thou likewise; now is the accepted time." Now, I might apply this to my opponent, and claim to have proved that he ought to go right now and hang himself. But you would say my scripture is made of scraps, and misrepresents the Bible. So it does. And so Mr. Campbell has been misrepresented, time and again, and time out of mind. It seemed to me that it was the Professor's purpose in his last speech, when he came to *baptism* to make the impression that Mr. Campbell taught that baptism is regeneration; that the two things are exactly equivalent. Also that baptism is conversion. This was the impression doubtless that some of you received. I will, therefore, read an extract or two from Mr. Campbell that will throw some light upon the matter. In his "*Christian System*," page 273, and speaking of *Regeneration*, he says, "Regeneration literally indicates the whole process of renovating or new-creating man. This process may consist of numerous distinct acts; but also in accordance with general usage to give to the beginning, or consummating act, the name of the whole process. For the most part, however, the name of the whole process is given to the consummating act, because the process is always supposed incomplete until that act is performed." Then after giving some illustrations of the truth stated, he proceeds: "By '*the bath of regeneration*' [baptism] is not meant the first, second or third act; but the *last* act of regeneration, and is, therefore, used to denote the new birth." So Mr. Campbell, by what he calls "a figure of speech, justified on all well established principles of rhetoric," uses baptism to express regeneration, or the new birth, simply because it is the last act of the process. He never taught that regeneration, so far as it is an internal work, a moral change, a purification of the heart, is accomplished by baptism, or in baptism. Far from it. Hear him on this point: "All that is done *in* us before regeneration [using regeneration to express the consummation] God our Father affects by the Word, or the Gospel as dictated and confirmed by the Holy Spirit." *Christian System*, page 278. Then again on page 282, he expressly rebukes such as charge him with "aiming at nothing but the mere immersion of persons as alone necessary to the whole process of conversion or regeneration, in their acceptance of these words."

I read once more, page 283:

"For, as often before stated, our opponents deceive themselves, and their hearers, by representing us as ascribing to the word immersion, and the act of immersion, all that *they call* regeneration. While, therefore, we contend that being born again, and being immersed, are, in the Apostle's style, two names for the same action, we are far from supposing or teaching, that in forming the new man *there is nothing necessary but to be born.*" This shall suffice. Anything read from Mr. Campbell, in which he uses the words regeneration, conversion, and baptism, in some sort interchangably, must be interpreted in the light of his own explanations that I have read you. To this every fair minded person will agree. Mr. Campbell believed that the "whole process" of renewal, or conversion, is essential to the enjoyment of remission of sins. He believed that baptism is the "last act of that process;" and, therefore, that is for the remission of sins. He did not believe that it in any sense procures remission, but that it is a means of enjoyment of remission, procured by the death of Christ. It may not be amiss, and as all love to do justice to the dead, I will read a few lines from that great man upon this point, also: "*All the means of salvation are means of enjoyment, not of procurement.* Birth itself is not for procuring, but for enjoying the life possessed before the birth. So in the analogy—no one is to be baptized, or to be buried with Christ; no one is to be put under the water of regeneration for the purpose of *procuring* life, but for the purpose of *enjoying* the life of which he is possessed." *Christian System*, page 277.

Mr. Campbell, as appears from this reading, did not believe that baptism does in any sense procure pardon; nor do my brethren. We believe that *as an act of faith*, it is a means of appropriation and enjoyment. Nor do we believe that it is even a means of appropriation enjoyment *in the very nature of things;* but it is made so by divine appointment in the Gospel of Jesus Christ.

Now if the gentleman wishes to meet me more fairly and squarely upon this position, I am ready for its defense. I hold that the enjoyment of salvation is conditional; that we appropriate to ourselves and enjoy the salvation of the Gospel by faith; and that baptism is an act of faith for the remission of sins; that according to the Gospel, and in the Gospel Scheme, it is the ordained *expression* of faith, and, therefore, the place where faith takes hold of the promise of remission. Just here I am reminded of the Professor's little whim for pedo-baptist sympathy. He says we turn all the honest and pious unimmersed persons over to the uncovenanted mercies of God; and then reminds them that a "half loaf" is better than no bread at all. Well, if it comes to "*bread*," no bread is just what he gives the unimmersed. He will give them fair promises, but no *bread*. But I stand not here angling for sympathy. I believe that baptism is for the remission of sins, as I have defined the matter, and am willing to be held responsible for the position, and whatever legitimately flows out of it. I want, before proceeding farther, to notice my friend's speech, to make one matter a little plainer. When I say baptism is for remission of sins, I mean that that is the Gospel rule simply, and that is all I mean. We have to do with the Divine law in the case. How many cases properly fall into the Divine equity I don't pretend to say, neither do I profess to practice in that court. Now, to justify the distinction I here make, I will read two or three distinguished authorities, Baptist and Pedo-baptist. *Dr. John Gale*, that great English Baptist, in his Reflections on Walls History of Infant Baptism, says:

"Baptism, I grant, is of great necessity; and though I dare fix no limits to the infinite goodness and mercy of God, which I am confident He will give mighty proofs in great instances of kindness toward all sincere, though mistaken men; however, the Gospel rule is, according to the doctrine of the Apostle, *to repent and be baptised for the remission of sins.* We should be very cautious, therefore, of making any change of these things, lest we deprive ourselves, through our presumption of that title to pardon, without which there is no salvation." *Walls' History of Infant Baptism,* vol. iii, page 83. Dr. Wall says: "If they fear from hence [*i.e.* that John iii., 5, refers to water baptism,] will follow a ground of absolute despair for any new convert for himself, and for any parent in respect of his child dying before he can be baptised; is it not natural to admit of the same *epieikeia* [a Greek word meaning about what we mean by *equity,*] and allowance in these words, as we do, and must do, in many other rules of Holy Scripture? Namely, to understand them thus, that *this is God's ordinary rule,* or the ordinary condition of salvation, but that in extraordinary cases, (where his providence cuts off all opportunity of using it,) he has also extraordinary mercy to save without it." *Ibid*, vol. ii, page 187.

John Wesley said: "It is true, the Second Adam has found a remedy for the disease which came upon all by the offence of the first. But the benefit of this is to be received through the means which He hath appointed; through baptism in particular, which is the ordinary means He hath appointed for that purpose; and to which *He hath tied us,* though he may not have tied himself. Indeed, where it cannot be had, the case is different; but extraordinary cases *do not make void a standing rule.*" *Treatise on Baptism,* c. vi., sec. 2.

I might read to the same purport from many other distinguished authorities, but it would be useless to do so. I think that Mr. Campbell did several times in his life give expression to the same sentiment. I think our people generally accord with these great men upon this point. I do. We believe that baptism is for remission of sins, as a rule, in the Gospel Scheme. If the gentleman thinks we are in error here, let him proceed to show it. Let him meet the question squarely, however, and not go off hunting for some exceptions to the rule. Does the Gospel require believing penitent aliens to be baptised for the remission of sins? That's the question. Is this the rule? I should not think of discussing any questions as to exceptions. That would be puerile. The gentleman thinks it "a strange thing" that persons should be changed in mind, and heart, and will, and yet not pardoned, as some of my brethren have taught. Well, it doesn't seem so very strange to me. Such a thing is not at all shocking to reason, after all. Suppose for illustration, that a number of the subjects of the Queen in this Province were to rebel against Her Majesty's Government, and were to join its enemies in making war upon it, and then suppose Her Majesty's Government were to issue a proclamation to the effect that all such as would lay down their arms, and return to her realms, and there subscribe a certain oath of loyalty, should be pardoned; and then suppose that some of said rebels undergo a change of mind, heart, and will, but have not yet subscribed the required oath: Do they yet enjoy pardon? Certainly not. Well, is there anything remarkably "strange" about the case? I think not. My friend looks even at this matter with that "veil" over his mind.

Then my friend proceeded to quote certain passages of Scripture to show that we are wrong.

Some few of them have a slight bearing upon the question, and others have none whatever, that I can see. I shall notice all such as in my judgment have any relevancy to the question; others I shall certainly not consume time even in reading over.

John i. 12. This passage simply says that Jesus gave to such as believed on him the power, or privilege, to become the sons of God. This I believe, of course, as stoutly as my opponent does. The passage does not say that anybody did, or that anybody can, become a child of God, simply by believing, in the sense in which my friend uses the word faith. No, no. It simply teaches that the believer, of whatever nationality or blood, has the power or the privilege of becoming a child of God.

Now it is useless, as it appears to me, for Professor Crawford to quote such passages as predicate justification, pardon, salvation, eternal life, of faith, without naming anything but faith. In such passages faith is given as the *principles upon which* persons are justified and saved; but it certainly never was intended by the speakers or writers that their language should be used to exclude everything but mere belief, as a conviction, or a psycological condition. Surely not! For instance, when justification, or the new birth, is predicated by faith—and both are—are we to understand that it is by faith without *repentance*, without *confession*, without *prayer*—without any sort of profession of faith? Surely not. Such a method of interpretation would ruin the Bible; and surely a "Professor of Biblical Interpretation" ought to see it.

"The thief on the cross. *The thief on the cross.* THE THIEF ON THE CROSS. The gentleman says he was not baptised, and yet he was saved.

What of it? Grant that he was never baptised—though he might have been—grant that he was saved—though he might not have been—Then what? "*Therefore.*" Well, therefore *what?* Why, therefore, Judas did not mean what he said, when, after he had risen from the dead, he *said*, "Go preach the Gospel to every creature; he that believes and is baptised shall be saved." Why is that thief on the cross always and everywhere brought into the discussion of this question? I have discussed it a good many times in a good many portions of the country with a good many men; and I have yet to discuss it with one without having "the thief on the cross" brought in. I think if I were on the other side of the question I would discuss it once without naming the thief on the cross, for the sake of *originality.* Just for the novelty of the thing. What bearing has the case upon the question? In the first place, the thief lived and died before the Christian Dispensation began. Nothing is clearer than this. And in the second place, if he had lived and died in the Christian Dispensation his case would not have fallen under the rule, but under the head of exceptions.

Whenever, in a discussion as to a rule, you see a party back out of the fight, and begin to hunt up exceptions, you may pretty safely set him down as consciously defeated.

ADDRESS.

(PROF. CRAWFORD'S NINTH ADDRESS.)

Friday, 11th Sept., 3 o'clock, P.M.

Prof. Crawford.—Mr. Sweeney says that I have quoted a number of passages of Scripture to prove the doctrine of the Divine Decrees or Election, and that he flatly denies that they contain such views as I have drawn from them. He says, therefore, that he has little to do with them, and nothing to prove regarding them. I did quote a number of passages, and I gave them the only interpretation of which their language will admit, and it is now his duty to show that interpretation to be wrong. It's all very well for him to deny an interpretation flatly; it is an entirely different thing to disprove it. It is his place, I maintain fully, to confute my interpretation, for if one of these passages stands unconfuted the doctrine for which I contend to prove. Nor do I ask him to do anything here which I will not do myself, for I shall follow the rule of not flatly denying any interpretation which he may put upon certain passages, without producing the proof.

He has brought forth a number of passages to prove that we are saved in baptism, and I shall proceed to prove that this interpretation of these passages is wrong; but in return I hope he will bring forward his disproofs of my interpretation of God's Word in relation to election. Let him take up one text after another, and show wherein I have misinterpreted them, for as I observed before, if but one of these passages stands unconfuted my side of the question is established. Moreover, if I have established the doctrine of the Divine decrees, I have proved the necessity of the direct operation of the Holy Spirit in the work both of regeneration and sanctification. If there be a Divine decree to be executed, its execution cannot be left to mere human contingency; but must be accomplished by Divine power. If I thought at first of omitting the discussion of this question, it was simply on the ground that most of those present, who in the main sympathise with me in this discussion, do not agree with me on this doctrine; and I thought I would conduct the debate without entering upon its discussion. But this doctrine bears with great weight upon our controversy concerning the necessity of the Holy Spirit's operation in the work of conversion. In fact the two doctrines stand or fall together; and now that this point has been introduced, my opponent cannot excuse himself from fairly grappling with it. If he fails here he has virtually given up the controversy concerning the Spirit's operation.

In referring to one of the passages which I quoted, he seems to have misunderstood my argument, and he endeavoured to impress upon the congregation a version of my remarks which is far from correct. I refer to John, i, 12 : " But as many as received Him, to them gave He the power to become the sons of God, even to them that believe on his name." Here he says they have the power or "privilege" (for I have no objection to accept his translation of it) to become the sons of God. That is, as I understand it, by believing they have this privilege, *without baptism*. That was my argument, and what I wish him to consider, instead of putting arguments into my mouth which I never used. It is his place to show, if he can, that we have not the privilege of becoming the sons of God unless we are baptized, or that we are not regenerated until we receive that ordinance.

He refers also to I. John, 4, 7: "Beloved, let us love one another; for love is of God; and every one that loveth is born of God, and knoweth God." My opponent uses the argument that we can all love. But can all love in the sense in which the word is used in the passage? If all can, then all are believers and born of God? He must take the real meaning of the passage, or his argument is of no value. Love, as I understand its meaning in the passage, springs from a right perception of God's character, for he who thus loves "knoweth God." When we have his image impressed upon our hearts, we pass from death unto life. If we can all love in this way, then are we all born of God, according to this text, and that even before baptism.

My opponent gives a little twit upon the matter of close communion. But does not he as well as myself hold close communion? Does he receive unbaptised persons to the Lord's Supper? He does not, therefore he should not twit me about the matter. We think that according to the right construction of Christ's command, no one should be received to the Lord's Supper who has not submitted to the ordinances of baptism, but we don't say as my opponent that there can be no salvation without baptism. We are not alone in holding this view; almost all the leading Protestant denominations do the very same thing, although they differ from us in regard to what baptism is.

He takes up the question of the dying thief—rather a stiff one for the Disciples to get over—and we are told, forsooth, that the thief was saved without babtism because it was before the command to baptize was given. Was it before the time our Lord had said to Nicodemus that unless a man be born of water and of the Spirit, he should not enter into the kingdom of God. And was not baptism instituted by the Lord himself, before the commission. That conference with Nicodemus took place long before the death on the cross.

My opponent says baptism by water is indispensably necessary to salvation. I would like him to explain how, if baptism is *indispensably necessary* to salvation, how or why the dying thief was saved *without* this baptism? He must, to argue consistently, either say the thief was not saved or give up his interpretation of the Gospel on the subject.

He says that I have charged Mr. Campbell with teaching baptismal regeneration. I did not do so; for I know Mr. Campbell's doctrines better than that. Mr. Campbell does not say we are regenerated by baptism, but he says baptism *is* regeneration; that's the difference. Listen to his own words on this subject: "Christian System," page 193—"This act is sometimes called immersion, regeneration, conversion." Page 203: "These expressions (immersed, converted, regenerated) in the apostle's style, denote the same act." Page 200: "For if immersion be equivalent to regeneration, be of the same import with being born again, then being born again and being immersed are the same thing." Page 202: "The Holy Spirit calls nothing personal regeneration except the act of immersion." Now, I hardly know which is the most unscriptural baptismal regeneration, or to teach that baptism and regeneration are one and the same thing. Can we take any other meaning than the one I have given from these words? We are bound to take his words as they stand; I know that he speaks inconsistently with his own views as given in other places, but I say the whole system is a contradiction from beginning to end. But the quotations I have given show that I have made no false charges against Mr. Campbell.

My opponent also accuses me of garbling quotations from Mr. Campbell's works. He says I do it on the same principle as he proved that this audience ought to go and hang themselves, viz., by quoting "Judas went out and hanged himself," and then "Go thou and do likewise!" I would appeal to the audience if I have quoted unfairly from Campbell's works, or garbled his remarks. I have given the name of the books and the page on which my quotations are to be found. Nor have I quoted mere detached clauses and parts of sentences, but whole sentences and paragraphs, in which there can be no mistake about his meaning. And why does my opponent complain, or charge me with garbling the quotations, when he himself defends these very views as taught by Mr. Campbell? If I have garbled these quotations it's a very easy matter to prove it, and that's what my opponent should do before he makes such a charge.

He then gives a quotation from Dr. Gale, and tries to make it appear that the Doctor teaches the same as Mr. Campbell about the necessity of baptism. Dr. Gale says: "Baptism, I grant is of great necessity; and though I dare fix no limits to the infinite goodness and mercy of God, which I am confident he will give mighty proofs of, in great instances of kindness towards all sincere, though mistaken men; however the Gospel rule is, according to the doctrine of the Apostle, *to repent, and be baptised, for the remission of sins.*

We should be very cautious, therefore, of making any change in these things, lest we deprive ourselves, through our presumption, of that title to pardon, without which there is no salvation." Here you see the whole amount of this quotation is that God requires us to be baptized; it is His rule and He requires it if we would be fully obedient to that rule. We, as Baptists, believe that, but we don't think that no man can be saved without it. We say that a man can be savingly converted without observing this ordinance; that God overlooks the omission.

Now I say that every disobedience to God's commands endangers our salvation. I say it is no trifling thing to omit obedience to any ordinance or command that Christ has given. That is just what this writer says, and he puts it strongly. But the view my friend wants to force upon us is not legitimately in the passage. It is not believed by respectable Baptist authors, and though he may pick out some who hold it, or who have employed an unguarded expression, it is not believed by the denomination. But even if the writer did believe in that view, that is not the question. I am not bound, nor is the Baptist denomination bound to defend, any extra vagrant or inconsistent expression which may perchance be discovered in the works of Dr. Gale, or any other writer. The Baptists as a body repudiate such a doctrine as no salvation without baptism, whereas Mr. Campbell and his followers distinctly teach it. Does not my opponent as well as Mr. Campbell and Mr. Franklin take this ground? Does not Mr. Campbell tell us plainly in the "Christian Baptist," page 416, that the apostle Peter to whom was committed the keys of the kingdom of Heaven, has "made repentance or reformation, and immersion equally necessary to forgiveness"? Again as he not said on page 520, "That there is but one action ordained or commanded in the New Testament to which God has promised, or testified, that he will forgive our sins. This action is Christian immersion." Mr. Franklin is equally explicit. "They are saved by baptism" says he. *It is present in the justification of every person.* It is *never* omitted. Sermon iv. p. 89. And in his 12th Sermon p. 292 does he not interpret the commission to be tantamount to, "except a man shall believe, *and be immersed he cannot be saved*"? Very evidently the teaching of the Campbellites is that we cannot be converted, justified or saved without baptism, and that is the point upon which we take issue with them. We say that if a man believes on the Lord Jesus Christ, he shall be saved.

Let us now consider some passages of scripture bearing on this point. I may state that I am glad my opponent has gone before me over this ground, for, on the other points in dispute he had the advantage of me in that respect. We now see exactly what he teaches, and I know exactly what I have to rebut. I shall first go on to give proof for our doctrine, namely, that we are justified by faith. John iii. 18: "He that believeth on him is not condemned, but he that believth not is condemned already, because he hath not believed in the name of the only begotton Son of God." Now I ask if salvation is not here promised by faith: "he that believeth in him is not condemned," therefore we say if we believe in him even if we should not be baptized we are saved. Acts 10: 43: "To Him give all the prophets witness, that through His name whosoever believeth on Him, shall receive remission of sins." Here you observe remission of sins is promised through his name, to all who believe on him. But my opponent says that a man's sins are not remitted until he is baptized. He says that Baptism is implied in faith, just as love, repentance, and other virtues are included in faith. But there is a vast difference. Love and other virtues are *inseparably connected* with faith, there can be no true faith without them; they are so spoken of in various passages in Scripture. But I say that Baptism, being an external ordinance, and not in itself a Chrisitan grace or virtue, is not *essentially* connected with faith. It is his part to show that baptism *is inseparably connected* with, and included in faith, else I have gained the point. This is the very point which he has to establish. Acts 13 : 38, 39 : "Be it known unto you, therefore, men and brethren, that through this man is preached unto you the forgiveness of sins; and by him all that believe are justified from all things from which ye could not be justified by the law of Moses." Here the promise is made to Faith. Romans 4 : 2 : "For if Abraham were justified by works he hath wherof to glory. But not before God. For what saith the Scripture? Abraham believed God, and it was counted unto him for righteousness. Now to him that worketh is the reward not reckoned of grace, but of debt. But to him that worketh not, but believeth on Him that justified the ungodly, his faith is counted for righteousness." You see, "his faith is counted for righteousness;" there is not a word of baptism. Gal. v., 6 : "For in Jesus Christ neither circumcision availeth anything, nor uncircumcision; but faith which worketh by love." It is not works; not baptism, but "faith which worketh by love." Rom. iii, 28. "Therefore, we conclude that a man is justified by faith without the deeds of the law." Surely if baptism were essentially necessary it would have been mentioned, but the Apostle tells us that "a man is justified by faith without the deeds of the law." Acts xvi., 30, 31, "And brought them out, and said, 'Sirs, what must I do to be saved?' And they said, 'Believe on the Lord Jesus Christ, and thou shalt be saved, and thy house.'" They are not told that they cannot be saved unless they are baptized. "Believe, and thou shalt be saved." John iii., 14, 15, 16, "And as Moses lifted up the serpent in the wilderness, even so must the son of man be lifted up; that whosoever believeth in Him shall not perish, but have eternal life. For God so loved the world, that He gave His only begotten Son, that whosoever believeth on Him should not perish but have everlasting life." Just as the simple looking at the brazen serpent in faith saved the Israelites, so he that looks in faith upon the Saviour, is saved by that look. John vi., 47, "Verily, verily I say unto you, he that believeth on Me hath everlasting life." He does not say that after he is baptized he shall have everlasting life, but "he that believeth on Me *hath* everlasting life." I might quote a great many other passages to prove this point, but I think those which I have given make it sufficiently clear.

Let us now consider some of the disputed passages. John 3, 3-8: "Jesus answered and said unto him, Verily, verily, I say unto thee, except a man be born again he cannot see the kingdom of God. Nicodemus saith unto Him, How can a man be born when he is old? Can he enter the second time into his mother's womb and be born? Jesus answered, Verily, verily, I say unto thee, except a man be born of water, and of the Spirit, he cannot enter into the kingdom of God. That which is born of the flesh is flesh; and that which is born of the Spirit is spirit. Marvel not that I said unto thee, Ye must be born again." This passage is admitted on all hands (except the Disciples) to be a very difficult one; they are very clear about it. They say that the being born of water here referred to means baptism; therefore, say they, unless a man is baptized he cannot be saved, for he cannot enter the kingdom of God, and there is no salvation out of it. They see right through the thing; like the owls, they seem to see best in the dark. Let us look at this passage: "Except a man be born of water and of the Spirit he cannot enter the kingdom of God." There are several interpretations given by commentators; I will give you some of them. Some say that the passage should be rendered, "Except a man be born of water, *even the Spirit*, he cannot, &c." The word in the Greek (*kai*) which is here used is often translated in that way. They say that water is here employed as a symbol of the Spirit, and therefore the symbol and the thing symbolized are both put together, the one exegetical of the other.

Others again say that the being born of water refers to baptism, but that it is here put for what baptism represents, the burial and resurrection of the believer with Christ, a union which is the real source of their new life. We often find in the Word of God cases in which something is said of the type that is not true of it, but of the antitype; and something said of the symbol which is true only of the thing symbolized. David says: "They pierced my hand and my feet," and again, "they gave me vinegar to drink." Here David affirms things of himself which were only applicable to his great antitype.

The Scriptures frequently view the type and the antitype as one. Again our Lord says of the bread in the supper. "This is My body." He affirms something of the symbol which is true only of the thing symbolized.

I shall only mention one other interpretation of the passage. It is that being "born of water" means Christian baptism; and that our Lord in addressing this Jewish ruler informs him that there were two things necessary in order to an entrance into that kingdom which He had come to set up in visible form upon the earth; a new birth by the operation of the Spirit of God, as well as an initiatory ordinance, which represented the way in which this new life is obtained; namely, by a union with Christ, in His death, burial, and resurrection. In other words that they only have entered Christ's Kingdom, as it is fully and visibly set up by Him upon earth, who have been the subjects of regeneration and baptism. As none could enter the Kingdom of Israel but by circumcision, so none can enter the Kingdom of Christ as it is visibly set up by Christ, unless born both of "water and of the Spirit." But this does not by any means imply that none but those who have entered the visible kingdom in the prescribed manner can be saved. There were many in Old Testament times, who never entered the Kingdom of Israel by circumcision, who were nevertheless the worshippers of Jehovah, proselytes of the gate, so there are multitudes of true worshippers now, who, like the dying thief, never enter Christ's visible kingdom of baptism.

REPLY.

Friday, Sept. 11*th,* 3.30 *p.m.*

(MR. SWEENEY'S NINTH REPLY.)

I shall endeavour to review my opponent's speech in the order in which it was delivered, as nearly as I can. He still insists that I am bound to take up every passage he has brought forward bearing upon the doctrine of the "divine decrees," and show that it does not prove what he claims it does, or I am defeated. Why! I am not bound to discuss the *doctrine* of the "divine decrees" at all, much less to notice every passage that he may think bears upon the subject! What did we come here to discuss? Has he forgotten? Did he not come here and set out to show us, first, what "Campbellism" is, and then to show that it is unsound and false? And he attacked what he calls Campbellism as to its teaching upon the question of Spiritual influence in conversion, and was driven back step by step till he landed upon his own doctrine of decrees, or unconditional election: and now he tells you that if I do not notice every passage he may quote as bearing upon that doctrine I am defeated! The man is bewildered! I am defeated! I say the Holy Spirit, in the conversion of a sinner, operates through the truth, and he has *admitted it*, repeatedly. That's the only point in issue, so far in our discussion, to which I sustain an affirmative relation. He affirms that the Holy Spirit also operates *immediately* in the work of conversion. This I have denied. This is the only issue yet made out. He has been fighting and retreating all the while. The doctrine of divine decrees is just about the "last ditch;" and whether to follow him into that is a question I am at perfect liberty to decide for myself, and can do so either one way or the other with perfect safety to my own position. But, by the bye, I believe I have examined about all the passages he has adduced even bearing upon election, and shown that his construction of them is not only not necessary, but not even the most natural one. I may have omitted a few,—one occurs to me just now. Acts xiii. 48. "As many as were ordained to eternal life believed." This passage he quotes, coming down with tremendous emphasis upon the word "ordained," as if it were here taught beyond all question, that no one can possibly believe who was not chosen from all eternity and unconditionally ordained to eternal life. But no such thing is here taught. The Greek word *Lasso*, translated in the common version of the Scriptures "ordained" may just as well be translated "disposed," or "determined," or even "inclined:" so that the passage only teaches that such Gentiles as "were determined upon eternal life, believed." This same word is translated in the New Testament both by "determined" and "addicted," as the gentleman well knows—as, for instance, (1 Cor. xvi. 15) where it is said of certain persons, "they have *addicted* themselves to the ministry." I believe myself that one must be disposed to, or determined upon eternal life, before he will believe in Jesus Christ.

When the gentleman says that the doctrine of Divine decrees has necessarily an important bearing upon the question of Spiritual influence in conversion, he is manifestly in error. The doctrine of Divine decrees, as he holds it, might be true, and yet his affirmation, that the Spirit operates immediately in conversion, be false. Could not God *decree* the salvation of certain men without such an operation of the Spirit as the gentleman contends for ? It seems to me that he could, and could save them without the Holy Spirit altogether, if He chose to do so. So that if the gentleman had proved his doctrine of decrees, he would yet have to prove his doctrine of spiritual influence in conversion all the same. His theory of conversion involves the doctrine of unconditional election, I grant; but the thing doesn't work the other way. The doctrine of unconditional election, if true, would not involve the truth of his theory of spiritual influence in conversion; I have run him into unconditional election and am satisfied, without spending much time on that old error. Who believes that old doctrine now? And if it be true—that is, his doctrine of the divine decrees—why need he try to convince anybody, or fear the effect of anything I can say ?

The Professor comes back to John i., 12. He admits that the passage teaches only that believers have the *privilege of becoming* sons of God. But he says he quoted the passage to show that believers .become the children of God without baptism. But, I submit, that the passage says nothing about *how* believers become children of God. *It* only says that all who believed received the power, or privilege, *to* become the Sons of God. The language of Paul (Gal. iii., 26, 27) might throw a little light upon the question as to *how* believers become children of God : " For ye are all the children of God by faith in Christ Jesus; for as many of you as have been *baptized into Christ have put on Christ*." How are these persons said to have put on Christ ? How did they put on the new man ? How did they *become* children of God in Christ Jesus ? By being "baptized into Christ." Faith is often spoken of in the New Testament as the *principle* upon which persons are justified and accepted as opposed to "blood," or "works of law," that is, perfect obedience; but it is never opposed to repentance, or confession, or baptism, or any *acts of faith*. On the other hand it includes all these. Faith is not unfrequently put for the whole Gospel system, as opposed to the law. We are justified upon the *principle* of faith, as opposed to the principle of works. We are justified by faith, rather than law. We are the children of God by faith, rather than by flesh or blood. But faith is never opposed to the appointed acts and expressions of faith. On the other hand, when it is said that any one is justified by faith, faith always implies, or includes, such acts as are necessary to its *actual*, real existence. Faith that is not *actual* is no faith at all. It's dead. Faith unexpressed is as a thing unborn. And this brings me to two passages of Scripture to which I am specially solicitous of his attention : James ii, 20, "But will thou know, O vain man, that faith without works is dead?"

1. Now, James is not speaking here of "works of law," to which Paul opposes faith ; but of works *of faith*. He is speaking of such acts as are necessary to its real, *actual*, and objective existence ; as are, in fact, part of itself.

2. He speaks of faith *generally*. He does not say a *Christian's* faith, a church member's faith, or anybody else's faith in particular; but *faith*— faith wherever and whosoever it may be—faith anywhere and everywhere—*without works is dead. Whose* faith ? *Faith. What* faith ? FAITH, all faith, without works is dead. That's it.

Now, the second passage is John xii, 42: "Nevertheless, among the chief rulers also many believed on Him; but because of the Pharisees they did not confess him, lest they should be put out of the Synagogue; for they loved the praise of men more than the praise of God." Now will Professor Crawford say that these persons, who were afraid of the Pharisees, afraid of being put out of the Synagogue, and who loved the praise of men more than that of God, were justified and saved? I hardly think he will. But they "*believed* on him"—that is, on Jesus. One of two things is true, then. Either, first, more than simply believing on Jesus is necessary to justification; or, secondly, these persons were justified in their miserable, craven, cowardice. What shall we say? It will not do to say that the persons here named didn't believe; for that would be a square contradiction of the inspired writer, and I will not look for that from a Professor of Biblical Interpretation in Woodstock University. Now, one of these passages lays down a rule, namely, that "*faith without works is dead;*" and the other furnishes a plain case under the rule—in which persons believed, but would *do* nothing, and hence were not justified. The gentleman must give attention to these passages, as I hold that they do, beyond question, preclude the possibility of his proving that persons are justified by faith, without any *expression* of it, or profession of it—by faith, without any action of faith; and hence by faith that is not *actual* faith at all. These passages certainly do lie in the way of any such a doctrine. I submit the following passages now for my learned friend's consideration, as opposed to his doctrine of justification without baptism. John, iii., 5: "Except a man be born of water and the Spirit he cannot enter into the Kingdom of God." That "born of water" here means baptism needs not to be argued. It never was questioned for hundreds of years after the Saviour uttered the language. It is not questioned now by the best critics, and most candid scholars. It is only questioned by men in controversy, when it gets in their way. There is no other fair and honest interpretation of the passage, than that which makes "born of water" mean baptism. The passage looks to the future, when the Kingdom should be established, and the Gospel preached to Jews and Gentiles. "The Kingdom of God" is a state of justification, or salvation from sin; and hence the passage teaches baptism in order to justification or salvation. Mark xvi., 16: "Go ye into all the world, and preach the Gospel to every creature; he that believeth and is baptized shall be saved." Here is the same doctrine without a figure. He who believes and is baptized is born of water and of the Spirit. And here salvation is promised to the person who believes and is baptized. Comment couldn't make it plainer.

Acts ii., 37, 38. "Now when they heard this they were pricked in their heart, and said unto Peter and the rest of the Apostles, men and brethren, what shall we do.? Then Peter said unto them, 'Repent and be baptized every one of you in the name of Jesus Christ for the remission of sins, and ye shall receive the gift of the Holy Ghost.'" Here, persons who have been taught, and who believe, and ask for their duty, are told to repent and be baptized in the name of Jesus Christ for the remission of sins. I have now only a word or two upon this passage. It teaches beyond all question baptism *for the remission of sins in some sense*. This, it were folly to deny. Can it be determined by the passage itself in what sense it makes baptism *for* remission? I think it can. You will observe that there are two imperatives in the passage—two things the Apostle commanded the people to do —to "*repent* and be *baptized.*" These two things were to be done "*for* remission." "For," then, expresses not only the relation of baptism to remission, but that of repentance also. Now as to the relation of repentance to remission of sins we have no controversy. It goes before remission always. Its relation to remission is that of an antecedent. And so must be that of baptism, for it is expressed by the same word, in the same place, and at the same time. "For" stands here between the two imperatives, repentance and baptism, telling their relation to remission of sins: Can it at once mean *in order to* as respects repentance and something wholly different as respects baptism? Impossible! The gentleman will not say it can. Then the fact that repentance is in this passage coupled with baptism, determines the relation of the latter to remission to be that of an antecedent. And that's exactly what my brethren teach.

Titus iii., 5, " Not by works of righteousness which we have done, but according to his mercy he saved us, by the washing of regeneration and the renewing of the Holy Ghost."

All critics are agreed that by "the washing of regeneration" here the Apostle means Baptism. This passage settles two things, then: 1. That baptism is not to be classed with what Paul called "works of righteousness;" for here he clearly sets them over against each other: Not by works of righteousness, but by (the washing of regeneration)—baptism. This is the language of contradistinction. Very well, then: When the

Apostle expressly excludes "works of righteousness," "works of law," "works" from justification, he does not mean thereby to exclude baptism. This passage settles that question. 2. It also says "He (God) *saved* us by the washing of regeneration and the renewing of the Holy Ghost." This connects baptism with salvation, as a means. And if we would know *how* this is so, we have only to look back at the passages I have already cited : " Except a man be born of *water* and of the Spirit, he cannot enter into the kingdom of God ;" "He that believeth and is baptized *shall be saved;*" "Repent and be baptized every one of you in the name of Jesus Christ, *for the remission of sins ;*" " For as many of you as have been *baptized into Christ* have put on Christ," these passages, I say, show clearly enough, it seems to me, how " He saved us by baptism." Now, that, by "the washing of regeneration," the Apostle meant baptism, there is, I think, but one voice among all the first-class critics—such as Bloomfield, Dean Alford, Macknight, and on down to Wesley.

The Professor persists in an effort to make the impression that Mr. Campbell taught that "baptism *is* regeneration," in the present current sense of the word regeneration. This, I think, is at the expense of his own reputation for fairness. Did I not read you from Mr. Campbell that when he uses baptism for regeneration, or conversion, it is upon the well recognized principle of rhetoric, that the *last act* of a process may be put for the *whole* process ? I have to say, and I wish to say it very emphatically too, and once for all time in this discussion, that Mr. Campbell never taught that regeneration, in so far as it is an *internal*, or *moral* change, is effected by baptism. He did'nt believe it. He taught quite distinctly otherwise. And so do my brethren generally.

Why does the Professor persist in quoting such Scriptures as predicate justification or salvation of faith, without naming any other cause or instrumentality? Does he not know that if such passages exclude baptism because they do not name it, that they exclude everything *else* that they do not name also? But he tells us that repentance, love, prayer, and everything of which salvation is predicated, excepting *only* baptism, is essentially connected with faith, and therefore understood or implied in such passages! Indeed! Who said so? Why, *he* did! That's all the authority we have for so arbitrary a statement. I freely admit that where justification or salvation is predicated of faith without naming repentance, that repentance is implied—implied because elsewhere in Scripture it is made a condition of salvation. And just so of everything else, not excepting baptism. If there is but one passage that teaches that a given thing is a condition of pardon in the Gospel plan, that given thing is implied in every case of pardon, according to the Gospel plan, whether named or not. If this is not true the Bible can be ruined in an hour in the estimation of intelligent people. Of course, Paul told the jailer at Philippi to "*believe* on the Lord Jesus Christ, and he should be saved." But did he tell him to believe and *stop there* and he should be saved? To believe was the first step in the process, and the step without which he could take no other, and without which it would be useless for him to be told any other. But when Paul had spoken to him the Word of the Lord, the means of faith, then did he not at once take other steps, even "the same hour of the night?' Why then should this case be cited to prove salvation by faith, as a mere conviction, without anything else? If the jailer had believed and done nothing else his case would have been like that of those gentlemen referred to in John xii. 42., and as little would he have attained to the salvation he sought. I can't get my opponent to see this. I would like it even if I could get him to see it "in the dark;" for I hold that it is better even to "see like an owl" than not to see at all.

Now, it is known to every thoughtful scripture-reader that justification or salvation is by the divine writers and speakers, predicated some times of one and some times of another of the causes or instruments of salvation, just as the one or another of these causes or instruments may be under consideration at the time of writing or speaking. If, for instance, Grace is the matter under consideration, it is said, "For by Grace are ye saved"—if Faith, it is said, "Being justified by faith;" if Hope, it is said, "We are saved by hope;" if Repentence, then it is said, "Except ye repent ye shall perish," implying that we are saved by repentance. And if baptism comes prominently forward, the inspired writer says, "Even baptism doth also now save us." Now, if a farmer were at one time to say, a certain *field* had yielded him so much corn; at another time so much *seed corn* had done it; at another, two *horses* had done it; at another, two *boys* had done it; at another, two *plows* had done it; just as he chanced to be speaking of the one or another of the causes at the time, would we have any difficulty in interpreting him? When he predicated the whole result of the field without then naming any other cause, would we argue that he meant to exclude other causes because he did not name them at that time, though he had named them at other times? Surely not. If he were to say that one bushel of seed corn had brought him so much crop, would we understand him that the seed corn alone had yielded the crop? without any land, or plows, or work of man, or beast? Oh, no! We should none of us have any difficulty with a matter of the kind, take it out of theology and into farming. When salvation is predicated of Grace, nothing is excluded that is not *expressly* excluded, or that is not necessarily *opposed* to Grace. So, when it is predicated of the blood of Christ, or of Faith, or of Obedience, or of anything else. It seems to me that an owl ought to see this, even in daylight!

What wonderfully mysterious language that in John iii., 5, has got to be! And there are so many plausible interpretations of it! And the Professor don't know which is most plausible! How long has this passage been so profoundly mysterious? How long have these various interpretations been in existence? Not very long. Ages and ages rolled away into the past, before this passage had but one interpretation. The "water" part of the passage meant baptism without a question, for centuries upon centuries. The Baptists never had any trouble with it till they got heterodox upon the subject of Baptism —till they entered into a tacit agreement with Protestant pedo-Baptists to call Baptism a "nonessential," for the sake of making a show of unity upon the essentials in Christianity. Dr. Gale and Baptists of his day had no trouble with the passage. The troubles of Baptists began after they departed from the Truth. I have no trouble with it. It is in perfect harmony with all the unfigurative teaching of Scripture as to the design of baptism. Is it not in harmony with the commission, "He that believeth and is baptized shall be saved?" Is it not in harmony with Peter's first discourse under this commission, wherein he told believers who desired to know what to do, to "Repent and be baptized in the name of Jesus Christ for the remission of sins?" Indeed it is in the most perfect harmony with the whole New Testament teaching upon the subject. What necessity, then, is there for all the different interpretations to which the Professor treated us? Could not any passage in the Bible be treated in the same way?

The gentleman severed the kingdom of God in twain, and made two births of one to break up the force of this passage! What authority is there for saying there are two kingdoms, the visible and the invisible, and two births, one "of the Spirit" into the invisible kingdom, and another " of water," into the visible kingdom? Where is there anything in Scripture about all this? Nowhere! Nor is there one word of truth in it. Has God ever revealed anything about the "invisible kingdom" the Professor talks about? Has he ever *seen* this *invisible* kingdom? Certainly not. Then, if such sheer, bold assumption is received by any one for argument, that's a case I can't reach. I give it up. Such a case is beyond any treatment I know.

ADDRESS.

(PROF. CRAWFORD'S TENTH ADDRESS.)

Friday, 11th Sept., 4 o'clock, P.M.

Prof. Crawford.—My opponent again refers at the beginning of his speech to the Divine Decrees. He says it is unnecessary for him to discuss that point, or to disprove the doctrine of election; because that in introducing this topic I have got off the true question at issue, the doctrine of the Spirit. Why, then, did he drag me into the question at all? Why? Just because he thought justly that if my doctrine be true on that point it is true also on the other—the doctrine of the Spirit's influence. If I prove the one I necessarily prove the other; if the one be admitted, so must the other. I say, then, if he intends to disprove my views as to the influence of the Spirit, it will be necessary for him to go through all the passages I have brought forward in support of the doctrine of the Divine Decrees. He has also spoken of faith; I maintain there is a wide distinction between a dead and a living faith, between a mere historical belief in the facts of Christianity and that belief which implies Divine light, and which brings eternal life. Many in the world believe in the former sense, but yet have no saving knowledge of the Truth; have not that Truth which brings salvation. So that we are agreed on this that faith implies everything that is necessary to salvation. This is implied in the very idea of faith.

He dwelt for a long time on the many virtues that are essentially connected with faith, and I admit them all. His illustration about the farmer who raised so much corn I will also admit so far as it justly applies, but it is scarcely appropriate to this matter, inasmuch as baptism is *not* one of those virtues inseparably connected with faith. I admit that all the graces upon which my opponent has been spreading himself to such an extent are essentially connected with and implied in faith; but there is just this screw loose: he will have to show that baptism is one of these implied graces, for that is just what I deny. To take this for granted is to beg the whole question. What is the real object of this faith, the real ground of the sinner's justification? It is the righteousness of Christ Jesus. The sinner needs this righteousness to make him just, to enable him to stand justified before the Throne of God. And what is the great instrument which God has appointed to enable the sinner to connect himself with that righteousness? What is *essentially* necessary to connect him with that righteousness? We say it is faith.

My oppenent has failed entirely in proving that I was wrong in any one of the interpretations I gave of that passage in John. I take the interpretation that makes it refer to water baptism. He says that all the passages refer to baptism. I say they do not. But if in this case it refers to water baptism when it says, "Except a man be born of water and the Spirit he cannot enter the kingdom of God." What is meant by the kingdom of God? I say that it cannot refer to the inward and invisible kingdom of God, because there are many passages in the Scripture where admittance to this kingdom is promised without water baptism—in fact, where the meaning is plainly and undoubtedly the inward kingdom, baptism is not mentioned as indispensable. It is "Believe on the Lord Jesus Christ and thou shalt be saved." The simple act of faith is necessary and sufficient to secure eternal life, and to make us true subjects of Christ's spiritual and everlasting kingdom; but, as we understand it, baptism is an ordinance, a figure of the believer's union with the Saviour in his burial and resurrection, and is used in connection with the kingdom of God in this world as the initiatory ordinance of the Christian Church. Most Christian denominations so regard it, and will not, therefore, admit to the privileges of church membership such as have not been in their esteem baptised.

I will now refer to some of the passages of Scripture which have been quoted against me: Titus 3, 5: "Not by works of righteousness which we have done, but according to His mercy He saved us, by the washing of regeneration and renewing of the Holy Ghost." I admit that in this passage the commentators generally are against me, but that does not make their interpretations true. I might show many views and interpretations held for ages, which are now generally admitted to be wrong. The fact that commentators hold certain views on certain passages does not prove these views to be correct, and I am not bound to accept their views. I say that it is more natural to suppose, taking the other passages bearing on the subject into consideration, that the washing of regeneration here refers to the cleansing of the soul, by the application of God's word and spirit, in the fountain opened in the House of David for sin and uncleanness, than that it means water baptism. This washing in the blood of the Saviour is inseparably connected with regeneration; the other, I have shown from many passages, is not. As this is one of my opponent's proof-texts, I have gained my point if I submit an interpretation as natural and as likely to be correct as his. As he is affirmative in regard to this question, the burden of proof lies on him to demonstrate that his interpretation is necessarily the correct one. But suppose we admit, for argument's sake, that baptism is here meant. Let us read the passage again, "According to His mercy He saved us by the washing of regeneration and the renewing of the Holy Ghost." The question then comes up, is the washing of regeneration used in a literal or in a figurative sense. If we take it in its literal sense then we may just as well take in its literal sense the passage where Christ says "This is my body." But we never think of saying that Christ literally means His body when He uttered these words; I say I don't believe there is any baptism referred to in this passage; but, if so, it is merely that figuratively baptism washes. Does baptism save effectually or merely in a figure? Moreover, granting that baptism is necessary, something else is necessary, namely, the renewing of the Holy Ghost. But according to the view of the Disciples, considered in the early part of this debate, there is no renewing of the Holy Ghost in the question. There is no Divine influence according to their doctrines. So that even on his own interpretation my opponent gets himself either on one horn of the dilemma or the other. The next passage quoted by my opponent is the commission given to the apostles: Matt. 28, 19, "Go ye, therefore, and teach all nations, baptizing them in the name of the Father, and of the Son, and of the Holy Ghost." Mr. Campbell, in explaining this passage, (and my opponent agrees with him) says the commission for converting the world teaches that immersion is indispensable to salvation. He says we have an imperative mood : "Go ye, therefore, and teach all nations," followed by an active participle, "baptizing them, &c." He claims that in all cases in which the imperative is followed by the active participle, the latter shows the manner in which the command is to be carried out. He says he knows no exceptions to this rule. He gives as examples, "Cleanse the house sweeping it," and "clean the garment washing it." These he gives in support and illustration of his view. Suppose, on the same principle, we say, "Cleanse the house batting it," would he argue from this that the manner of cleaning the house is by batting it? Yet we have here the active participle following the imperative mood. Let us take the other case. Suppose we say, "Cleanse the garment, putting a frill upon it," does the active participle in that case indicate the manner in which the command is to be carried out? You thus see that Mr. Campbell's rule, involves a false principle of interpretation, and would lead to very ridiculous mistakes. I say that there is no such meaning in the passage as that drawn from it by Mr. Campbell. Jesus says, "Go ye, therefore, and teach (or make disciples of) all nations, baptizing them." Does that mean that the apostles were to baptize *all nations*? Certainly not. Any man with even a smattering of Greek will not give the passage that interpretation, for the word "nations" is in the neuter gender, while the pronoun is masculine. "Go and make disciples, *baptizing them*," that is the disciples, not in order to make them disciples, for they were so by supposition already. They are made disciples by the influence of the Holy Spirit, through the preaching of the Gospel, before baptism and not by being baptized. Then Acts 2, 38., " Then Peter said unto them, Repent and be baptized every one of you in the name of Jesus Christ for the remission of sins, and ye shall receive the gift of the Holy Ghost." The argument of the disciples is that the baptism brings about the remission of sins. The question is this, When we are baptized, does the baptism procure for us the remission of our sins, or is the remission of sins only signified figuratively in baptism ? We say that baptism in a figure places us in the position of being one with Christ, " buried with him by baptism, and so justified and pardoned in him." It is just the same as when we eat the Lord's flesh and drink his blood in a figure ; though He says, " This is my body." We do not believe that is literally the body of the Saviour that we eat at the Lord's Supper. I hold that the Roman Catholics are far more consistent in this matter than are the Disciples. They take the literal meaning of both passages, while the Disciples accept the figurative meaning in one case and reject it in the other. The word rendered for in this passage is the preposition, the primary meaning of which is *into* or *unto*. The believer, therefore, according to this passage, is represented in his baptism, as being placed in a state of union with his once crucified but now risen Lord ; and by virtue of that union, as obtaining remission of sins. We have a parallel passage in the Gospel of Matthew; one which will assist us in the interpretation of the one under consideration. Mat. iii., 8 to 11," " Bring forth, therefore, fruits meet for repentance : And think not to say within yourselves, We have Abraham to our father ; for I say unto you, that God is able of these stones to raise up children unto Abraham. And now also the ax is laid unto the root of the trees: therefore every tree which bringeth forth not good fruit is hewn down, and cast into the fire. I indeed baptize you with water unto repentance: but he that cometh after me is mightier than I, whose shoes I am not worthy to bear: he shall baptize you with the Holy Ghost, and with fire." In the words "*unto* repentance," the very same proposition is used as in the other passages quoted. Where it is rendered "*for*," John baptized them *into* repentance, just as in the other passages they were baptized *into* remission of sins. But observe that these whom John baptized into repentance, were required by him, to be true penitents before he would baptize them. "Bring forth," said he "fruits meet for repentance." His baptizing them unto repentance, therefore, did dot make them penitents, but only in a figure, represented them as already brought into the state of penitents. He says "bring forth fruits meet for repentance, for I cannot baptize you till you show the fruits of sincere penitence for sin." Just as I or any other minister would not think of receiving into church membership, or of baptizing any one without his bringing forth fruits meet for repentance. I say to every applicant manifest by your works, or give full and satisfactory evidence that you are truly penitent, and then I will represent you as washed from your sins, by the figure or symbol of baptism. Now just as John's baptism to repentance did not make the subjects of it penitents; but only in a figure represented them to be such, so to baptize a believer for (or unto) the remission of sins does not give him pardon, but only represents what, in reality, he had received when first he believed the Gospel. Baptism represents him as one unto Christ in His death, burial, and resurrection; and by this union he obtains both pardon and justification. But when did this union really take place? Was it not when he *believed?* It is faith not baptism which unites us with Christ; by whom we obtain both pardon and justification, and eternal life. "He that believeth on the Son hath eternal life." John iii., 36. Paul was a converted man before he received the command, "Arise and be baptized and wash away thy sins." He was converted on the way to Damascus when the Lord appeared unto him in the way, and changed his hostile and persecuting heart. So that when Ananias came to him he addressed him as a brother. Surely it does not mean that his sins were not pardoned, or that his sins were literally to be washed away by water baptism. Nothing but the blood of Christ can wash away sins, and it is all sufficient for that purpose. The command given to Paul was as much as to say "Thy sins have been forgiven thee through thy faith, but now thou must obey God's command, and profess that Faith by submission to his ordinance of baptism, by which is figured the cleansing of thy soul from sin through the Saviour's blood. It is my opponent's place to show that baptism is not a figure or symbol. Until he has done this he has failed to prove his doctrine from these texts.

REPLY.

(MR. SWEENEY'S TENTH REPLY.)

Friday, Sept. 11*th*, 4.30 *p.m.*

Mr. Sweeney.—One thing, I think, is becoming quite clear as our discussion progresses, and that is, that my opponent is satisfied he is not going to sustain his cause without "works." I think he is pretty thoroughly aroused on that point. Well, I like to see a man in earnest when defending his faith. I like to debate with a man, when I do debate, that rubs me closely.

Now that he is on baptism he would like to get me to remain on election, it would seem. Well, I am not going to do it; I am going to be *with* him along the whole line of his attack upon my works. He has now attacked what he calls "Campbellism" on the doctrine of "baptism for remission of sins," and there I am ready to meet him, and mean to meet him. I am perfectly satisfied with what has been said on the question of "Spiritual influence in conversion." The gentleman has about convinced me that he is not a safe reasoner. He says that if the doctrine of "divine decrees," as he holds it, be true, then his doctrine of immediate Spiritual influence in conversion follows. But this is a blunder. Could God have decreed the conversion of certain persons from all eternity *only by an immediate operation of the Holy Spirit?* Could he not have decreed that sinners should be converted by *means of the Truth?* The Professor is confused. He did not expect to get into the doctrine of "election" when he began the discussion of Spiritual influence; he told us so. Indeed, in his last speech, he says I "dragged" him into the "divine decrees." And now he wants me to "drag" him *out*; I can't do it. The fact is, he found himself forced back into the doctrine of "decrees" in his effort to defend his own position on Spiritual influence; and now he thinks the doctrine of decrees ought to force him back again, to the point from which he started! He thinks, I suppose, that it is a "poor rule that will not work both ways." Well, that's just the kind of rule he is working by. It only works one way, and that's directly into fatalism; and then it will not work back.

But the gentleman seems to assume that he made an argument for the doctrine of election, or Divine decrees, as he holds it, that I have not replied to. But I deny that this is so; I claim to have defeated him even on that remote question, in a very few words.

The Professor says I must show that baptism is "essentially connected" with salvation.

Professor Crawford—(correcting)—I say, and have proven, that repentance and other virtues are essentially connected with salvation; and it is your duty, in order to maintain your views, that you should show that baptism is essentially connected with faith.

Mr. S.—I don't know that I understand the gentleman. He claims anyhow, that I must show that baptism "is essentially connected with faith." Will he deny that it is? Is there any such thing as Christian baptism without faith? It is not always and everywhere essentially connected with faith, I grant. Neither is repentance. One can believe without repenting. But in the plan of salvation about which we are contending they are all connected together, and all connected with salvation; and they are so connected by the word of God. And "what God hath joined together let no man put asunder." I have not said that baptism is "*essentially* connected" with salvation. Nor has he shown that faith is. And when he does show it he will then and thereby show that all infants, according to his view of their natural condition, are damned. Will he not?

By the way, the gentleman has repeatedly spoken of the *virtues* of repentance, faith and so-forth, and I refer to this little matter only to say that I do not approve of the language. In a very limited sense the language may be admissible, but I prefer not to use it.

The Professor tells us that the question is, "Can a man be saved without baptism?" I ask his pardon! I am discussing no such question. I suppose God could save one without faith, repentance, or baptism, or any other condition upon the part of the creature. I would discuss no such question. But I suppose that in the Gospel God has submitted a plan upon which he proposes to save men; and I deny that men are at liberty to depart from that plan. In that plan I contend that baptism, with other things, is by the divine authority connected with the remission of sins. That's the question. The gentleman admits that some things are in the Gospel connected with salvation; but denies that baptism is. Now, I put this to him: Let him show where anything—I will not except the blood of Christ—is connected with remission of sins in language stronger than that by which baptism is so connected. Here is work for him. Let him go at it. When we talk about what God *can* do, or cannot, or what is, and what is not, *essentially* connected with salvation, we are simply wasting time and breath. What has God *said*, as to the matter in hand. That's the question.

The gentleman tells us there is a vast difference between mere "historic faith" and "saving faith." Of course, he sees a clear distinction here. He can tell just where "historic faith" leaves off and "saving faith" sets in. I wish, now, I could get him to see the Scripture distinction between living faith and dead faith. He can see a clear distinction where the Bible makes none, but where the Bible makes a clear distinction he sees none! Isn't that just a trifle queer?

He says faith is *essentially* connected with our justification, because we are justified by the righteousness of Christ, and that faith is the instrument of our connection with Christ. Well, I grant that faith is the instrument of our connection with Christ, but *dead* faith is not. Will faith, without repentance, connect us with Christ? I think not. And I am slow to believe that since Jesus said, "He that believes and is baptized shall be saved," any one can believe and stop there, refusing to be baptized, and by such faith be connected with Christ. Baptism is faith acting and connecting the penitent alien with Jesus Christ. Many people have been taught to look upon the doctrine of baptism for the remission of sins as opposed to justification by faith; whereas the fact is that baptism for remission of sins *is* justification by faith. What is baptism disassociated from faith? It is nothing. What is Scriptural baptism but faith in Christ acting, reaching out and taking hold of Christ? When you see a person Scripturally baptized you *see* faith in Christ.

The Professor tells us that persons are "saved by baptism *in a figure.*" What does he mean by that? Does he mean to *figure away* this Divine ordinance? I Hope not. Who said that the relation of baptism to remission is a figurative one? Have we any sufficient authority for such a statement? Suppose I were to say that we are saved by the blood of Christ "in a figure;" and then suppose my opponent were to ask me to prove it; and suppose I were to say the proof of it is in the same chapter and in the verse following the one that says, "we are saved by baptism in a *figure*." Then what do you suppose he would say next? In this manner, my friends, every doctrine, every fact, if not every person of the Bible might be *figured away!* The Universalists figure away the Divinity of Christ, figure away the devil, and figure away hell and heaven, before getting more than fairly started to figuring away! Men begin this figuring business generally who get into close places trying to defend their errors. Was Peter talking *figuratively* to those people at Jerusalem who wanted to know what to do to be saved, when he said, " Repent and be baptized every one of you in the name of Jesus Christ for the remission of sins?" That looks very little like figurative speech to me. Nor was it a suitable occasion for figurative speech. The apostle had before him thousands of men who were in their sins, and whom he had convinced of the fact, and who had just asked him and the rest of the apostles what they must do, desiring to be saved; and he told them *literally*. It might be said with as much reason, and quite as much truth, too, that the relation of repentance to remission here is only a figurative one.

" Born of water," in John iii. 5, he tells us may mean baptism; but in that case it is only the visible, outward kingdom that is entered thereby. But I suppose that if it could be determined that "born of water" means something else in the passage, then the kingdom of God heed not be split—then it might mean the whole kingdom ! Truly, the conception of the "visible" and the "invisible" kingdoms is a convenient one, when one gets into a close place.

The Professor admits that most of the commentators and critics are against him on Titus iii, 5, when he denies that the "washing of regeneration" means baptism. And so they are. Reason and common sense are against him too. And what is still worse for his cause, the general teaching of the New Testament upon the subject is against him, with tremendous force. And it is just because of the general teaching of Scripture upon the subject, and because all writers of the early centuries interpreted the phrase "washing of regeneration," or "*laver* of regeneration," of baptism, that all respectable critics and commentators do so interpret it now. And is it not in perfect harmony with all the other passages I have cited? Is it not in harmony with John iii., 5, "born of water and of the Spirit;" with the commission, "He that believes and is baptized shall be saved;" with Acts ii., 38: "Repent and be baptized every one of you in the name of Jesus Christ for the remission of sins;" with Acts xxii., 16, "Be baptized and wash away thy sins, calling on the name of the Lord." It certainly is. But then the gentleman says, that if he can name another interpretation that seems to him natural, I am bound to give up mine—the one universally received in all ages—because I am in the affirmative as to the passage! That's a singular rule, indeed. And if, after all, the phrase in question does mean baptism, then the salvation in connection with it is only "figurative." But supposing the phrase "washing of regeneration" to refer to the washing of the soul in the fountain opened in the house of David for sin and uncleanness, as he thinks it does, *then* what about the salvation in connection with it? Then I suppose, it is literal! Now, isn't the "figurative" method of interpretation of great service to my opponent? When baptism is found in connection with salvation in a passage he "figures" out the baptism always first, if he can; but if he fails in that, then he "figures" the salvation! He interprets a good deal as the hunter shot, when somewhat in doubt as to whether his game was a deer or a calf, and he aimed so as to hit if it was a deer, and miss if it was a calf. When salvation is connected with baptism, he allows the salvation to be literal if he can figure away the baptism, but if he can't do that, then the salvation is a figurative one, even though it be connected with repentance, or the renewing of the Holy Spirit, in the very same passage. So, I suppose, he teaches "Biblical Interpretation" in Woodstock University.

The gentleman took up Matthew's record of the commission, and dwelt upon it at length as one of my proof-texts, when I had not referred to it at all. I read only Mark's record of it. He told you what Mr. Campbell had said upon the passage—misrepresenting him, as usual—and then proceeded to reply to him. He says Mr. Campbell holds that in the phrase, "Teach all nations, baptizing them," and in all such constructions, the participle explains the manner of performing the thing indicated by the verb. I think that Mr. C. did not say that such is *always* the case. However, that's immaterial. Mr. C. gave illustrations, as, for instance, "cleanse the house, sweeping it"—that is, *by* sweeping it.. But how does the Professor upset the rule? Why, by applying it to a phrase that *has no sense in it!* That's

decidedly rich! Such phrases as he named are
not to be interpreted by any rule. However good
a rule may be for interpreting language, it must
not be expected to bring sense out of nothing!

But my opponent thinks a fair interpretation
of the Commission by Matt. would give us about
this: "Make disciples of all nations, baptizing
them;" that is baptizing the *disciples.* Well, I
am inclined to think he is not far wrong in this
interpretation. I think persons are first to be
taught, instructed, made believers, and then to
be baptized. I deny, however, that the word we
here render *disciples,* or *make disciples,* necessarily involves pardon, or salvation. Indeed, we
know it does not; for Mark, in his record of the
Commission, while he, like Matt., has teaching
or instruction before baptism, puts salvation *after*
baptism. " Preach the Gospel to every creature;
he that believes and is baptized *shall be saved.*"
What the Professor said about the gender of
" nations" (*ethnas*), and " them" (*autous*), is correct. " Them" cannot refer to " *nations,*" as
its antecedents, because *autous* (them), is masculine, and *ethna* (nations), is neuter. But all that
doesn't affect the question between him and myself, as to the design of baptism.

I have already given you my criticism of Acts
ii. 38, " Repent and be baptized in the name of
Jesus Christ *for the remission of sins.*" I want,
now to show you that I am sustained in this position by the very best critics of Europe and America. I will read first Dr. Hackett; first because he is a scholar, and secondly because he is
a Baptist. In his commenting on the Acts, of
the Greek phrase rendered in our version "for
the remission of sins," he says, giving the Greek
phrase: "*aphesin hamartioon, in order to the forgiveness of sins* (Matt. xxvi. 28; Luke iii. 3.)

We connect, naturally, with both the preceding verbs. This clause states the motive or object which should induce them to repent and be baptized. It enforces the entire exhortation, not one part of it to the exclusion of the other." I might read to the same purport Dr. Barnes, Olshawsen, Lange, and others, but I will not consume time to do so unless my statement that they agree with Dr. Hackett, substantially, shall be questioned. Why does the gentleman tell you that I only *assume* that baptism is one of the things connected with remission of sins? Is it so, that I only assume this? There is not the "screw loose" about my argument that he seems to think there is. But he gets on, and at once *slides* away from this passage to another one, and these are very smoky as to the meaning even of the other passage! But did I not show that the two imperative verbs, "repent" and be "baptized" are in this passage *connected together*, and then the relation of both to remission expressed by the same preposition? Why does he not notice this fact? I tell him again, that whatever the relation of repentance to remission is, in this passage, *that must be* the relation of baptism. Does "for" here mean one thing for repentance and another for baptism? It cannot be so?

I invite my friend's attention now to Acts xxii. 16. "And now why tarriest thou; arise and be baptized and wash away thy sins, calling on the name of the Lord. This is the language of Ananias to Saul. You are all doubtless familiar with all that had gone before this in Saul's conversion. A few days before he had left Jerusalem for Damascus a virulent and furious foe of Christ and his disciples. On the way, Jesus himself appeared to him, and in such a manner as to convince him that he was alive, and was the Christ indeed and in truth. Saul fell upon his face before the glorious and divine presence ; and, like the brave and true man that he always was, cried out, " Lord, what wilt thou have me to do ?" The Lord told him to arise and go into Damascus, and there it should be told him what he " *must do*." Saul arose and went. Then the Lord appeared to Ananias and directed him to go to Saul, " For," said he, " behold he prayeth." Now, Saul was three days in Damascus waiting to be told what he " must do ;" and when Ananias came, he told him, as we have read, " Arise and be baptized, and wash away thy sins, calling on the name of the Lord." But, was not Saul a believer before this ? Was he not a *penitent* believer before this ? Did he not *pray* before this ? Did not the Lord *hear* his prayer before this ? " Behold he *prayeth*," said the Lord to Ananias, when he sent him to Saul. Then, what have we in this case ? We have a believer, a penitent believer, a praying, penitent believer, a praying, penitent believer, whose prayer the Lord had heard ; such an one told to " arise and be baptized, and *wash away thy sins*, calling on the name of the Lord." Professor Crawford believes, and preaches, that if a penitent believer prays, the Lord will hear him and pardon him, without his being baptized ; and he wants me to believe and preach so, too ! He will have to get this case of Saul's out of the book before ever I can do it, however. Why did not the Lord pardon Saul when first he believed ? Was not Saul a believer when, upon his face, he cried, " Lord, what wilt Thou have me to do ?" Yes. Was he not penitent ? Yes. Did he not pray ? Yes. Did not the Lord hear this prayer ? Yes. Then, why did he not pardon him then? Why must Saul wait to see a preacher, and be baptized? Why, he might have died within that three days? Well, we may ask as many questions as we please, my friends, and still here are the facts—the stubborn facts—of this case. The man was not pardoned till he was baptized, though he had believed, and was penitent, and had prayed for three days before. And, by the way, the Baptist brethren want me to believe that this same Saul afterward in his letter to the Romans, and in other letters, taught justification by Faith *only* ; taught that persons might believe and be pardoned without being baptized! Surely there is some mistake about that! The Apostle could have never so taught without forgetting, or palpably contradicting, his own personal experience. Did he ever so entirely forget that *three days* of prayer and waiting for Ananias, as to teach other sinners only to believe, and thus would be pardoned without baptism? It cannot be so. And I would advise Professor Crawford, and these other preaching brethren who agree with him, hereafter to interpret Paul's doctrine upon this point, in his epistles, in the light of his *experience*. They believe in " experiences ;" so they must not object to my pressing upon them Saul's experience, as calculated to throw much light upon his teaching on those very matters involved in his experience.

I can think of but one reply to the argument from Saul's case, and that is the " figurative one." That would come in here most handsomely.

Now, I feel that the passages I have cited clearly teach that for which my brethren have been judged heterodox, that is, baptism for remission of sins. Yet the Professor tells you I have not shown, and cannot show, that baptism is connected with salvation in any sense. Let us try a simple illustration. Suppose that a man of this community, of great wealth and strictest integrity, were to issue a proclamation that whoever believes in him and is baptized shall have ten thousand dollars; do you think anyone would deny that baptism is in any way connected with, or necessary to, the enjoyment of the ten thousand dollars? I think not. Just put ten thousand dollars in place of salvation, or remission of sins, in the passages I have quoted, and all my opponent's difficulties will disappear as the frosts before the rising sun. "He that believes and is baptized shall have ten thousand dollars;" "Repent and be baptized every one of you in the name of Jesus Christ for ten thousand dollars." Now, if the passages read so, would any of us have any difficulty about how to get the money. Would we listen to Professor Crawford, or to anyone else, who would endeavour to dissuade us from being baptized? Would the Professor endeavour to do so? I think he would conclude that the language does, some how, establish some sort of connection between baptism and the money. I don't think he would even trouble us even with the "figurative" method of interpretation. He would conclude that the conditions upon which so much *money* is to be enjoyed, would barely be put in figurative language.

ADDRESS.

Friday, Sept. 11th, 5 p.m.

(PROF. CRAWFORD'S ELEVENTH ADDRESS.)

Prof. Crawford:—My opponent has never touched upon the argument I brought forward that the promises of salvation are made only to Faith and to virtues that are *necessary* to, and *essentially* connected with Faith. For instance, salvation is promised to repentance, but repentance is essentially and necessarily connected with Faith,—in fact there could not be Faith without it—and it is by Faith we are justified. And, therefore, we might say that we are saved, when we are truly penitent, because we cannot have true repentance without at the same time having that faith that produces repentance, and by which we are justified. Faith in the Saviour is the very foundation of our salvation. We have no righteousness of our own; we have salvation only through the righteousness of Christ. But how is the sinner's soul to reach and get hold of the Saviour's righteousness? How is he to connect himself with that righteousness? By Faith. Just as the Israelites who were bitten by the fiery serpents were saved by even a single look on the brazen serpent, so the sinner is saved by looking to Christ in Faith. Therefore, we are justified by Faith—a living Faith. Not the mere historical Faith which Simon Magus had, but the Faith that James speaks of as a Faith that " wrought with works, and by works was made perfect." We freely admit, therefore, that salvation is promised to everything that is *essentially* connected with Faith. Now, if my opponent wishes to show that baptism is necessary to secure eternal life, he will have, in the first place, to prove that baptism is *essentially* connected with or inseparable from Faith. I will show you instances where Faith is not connected with baptism, and yet Faith, as we have seen, secures eternal life. Acts 10. 43, 48, " To Him give all the prophets witness, that through His name *whosoever believeth on Him* shall receive remission of sins. While Peter yet spake these words, the Holy Ghost fell on all them which heard the Word. And they of the circumcision which believed were astonished, as many as came with Peter, because that on the gentiles also was poured out the gift of the Holy Ghost. For they heard them speak with tongues and magnify God. Then answered Peter, Can any man forbid water, that these should not be baptized, which have received the Holy Ghost as well as we ? And he commanded them to be baptized in the name of the Lord." Here you perceive that these gentiles had the Word preached to them ; they had received the Holy Ghost, they spake with tongues and magnified God, while yet unbaptized. Does the Almighty give the Holy Ghost and the gift of tongue, and give Grace to enable man to magnify Him, and yet the recipients of these blessings are unsaved men ? Their sins *must* have been remitted, for " whosoever believeth on his name *shall receive* remission of sins ;" they believed, for the Holy Ghost fell upon them, and they magnified God. Yet it was after and apart from this that Peter says, " Can any man forbid water ?" Does not this show plainly that baptism was not a virtue *essentially* connected with Faith, but an ordinance that was administered after they had believed, and received the remission of sins. Will any one say that if these men had died after they had received the Holy Ghost, spoken with tongues and magnified God, *before* they were baptized, that they would have been lost. That's the point we are contending for. If baptism is essential to salvation, they certainly would have been lost, although true believers, and although they had received both the gift and Grace of the Holy Ghost. And in the case of the thief on the cross; was there not here also saving faith unconnected with baptism? Yet the Saviour's own promise was, " To-day shalt thou be with me in Paradise." But if baptism is essentially necessary to salvation, eternal life would have been impossible. My opponent has never even made an attempt to meet this case. I say it is as clear as any demonstration in Euclid, both from the case of Cornelius and that of the dying thief, that eternal life may be obtained without baptism. Both men had every qualification which God has declared essentially necessary to eternal life, the one before and the other without baptism.

Let us take another case, for I want my opponent to face this point squarely, instead of beating around it, and leaving it untouched as he has been doing so far. Take the case of Philip and the Eunuch, Acts 8. 27, 39. In the 35th verse it is stated, " Then Philip opened his mouth and began at the same Scripture, and preached unto him Jesus. And as they went on their way, they came unto a certain water; and the Eunuch said, See, here is water; what doth hinder me to be baptized? And Philip said, If thou believest with all thy heart thou mayest. And he answered and said, I believe that Jesus Christ is the Son of God." You see that Philip would not baptize him without faith, but he had believed before he was baptized, and God's Word declares that whosoever believes shall be saved. Faith and baptism are here plainly shown to be two things which may exist separately. The latter is not essentially connected with the former. Here is the point that has been evaded all along, though a great deal of time has been spent talking about it. This is my argument, that the promise of eternal life is made to many virtues that are necessarily and essentially connected with saving Faith. I have proved, on the other hand, from several passages, that baptism is *not* essentially connected with saving Faith. All that fine illustration about the farmer's plow, &c., amounts to nothing. It is quite inaplicable and a waste of time. There is just one link lacking in my opponent's argument ; he has not shown that baptism is essentially connected with saving Faith. Whenever the sinner's mind is drawn away from the great Truth, that Faith, in the blood and righteousness of Christ, is the ground of his justification, and the importance of baptism is unduly magnified, his soul's safety is endangered. I teach baptism, I urge baptism to those who believe, and whose sins are already remitted, but if a sinner becomes anxious about salvation, is troubled about his sins, wants to know what he is to do to obtain eternal life, I say, " Believe on the Lord Jesus Christ and thou shalt be saved." Christ must be held up to him as his only hope ; ordinances are of no avail. It is in this that I find such fault with the doctrines taught by the Disciples, that they have a tendency to draw away the sinner's attention from his only hope of acceptance with God, Faith in the crucified and risen Saviour.

He has called on me to prove my views from

writers and commentators. Now, I have just to say that I bind my Faith to no man's creed. Let God be true and every man a liar. Yet I will engage to bring forward quotations from many commentators and eminent scholars and critics who regard baptism as a figure, or symbol. But I never expected to have such a preposterous demand made by my opponent; or I would have come furnished with the proof. Instead of my views being a novelty, it would be difficult to find any respectable Protestant author or commentator who does not treat baptism as a figure, or symbol. The only author at present within my reach is Dr. Adam Clarke, who, in commenting on Tit. 3. 5, says, "Baptism is only a *sign*, and, therefore, should never be separated from the thing signified." Here, you see, that Dr. Clarke makes baptism only a sign or symbol. He differs from us, indeed about what the sign or symbol signifies; but, nevertheless, he makes it a symbol. He takes it to symbolize the operation of the Spirit; we, the union of the believer with Christ in his death, burial and resurrection. The candidate is put under the water, which figuratively sets forth our death and burial with Christ; we have him in a figure, not literally, buried with Christ. And when he is raised out of the water it signifies, figuratively, his being raised with Christ. My opponent may deride the idea of a figure or symbol if he chooses; it is just the same plan as the Papists adopt. When we say that Christ's words, " This is my body," is to be taken in a figurative sense, they sneer at us. The mind which cannot see that it is a figure is very obtuse indeed. I will engage to get plenty of our best writers who treat baptism as a figure, but I will now give you a better authority than any of them. 1 Peter 3. 20, 21,

" Which sometime were disobedient, when once the longsuffering of God waited in the days of Noah, while the ark was preparing, wherein few, that is, eight souls were saved by water. *The like figure*, whereunto even baptism doth also now save us (not the putting away the filth of the flesh, but the answer of a good conscience towards God) by the resurrection of Jesus Christ." I think that is authority which my opponent will scarcely dispute. After speaking of the eight souls that were saved in the ark, he goes on, " the like figure whereunto even baptism doth also now save us." " The like figure" —no language could be plainer. What was the figure in the case of the ark ? A judgment for sin had fallen upon the world. Those that entered the ark were lifted out of the water, in which the rest of the world were destroyed. Of what is this a figure ? The flood—a type of the final judgment—and their deliverance from the flood was a type of our deliverance from the consequences of sin, through union with the Saviour. We are saved by virtue of our union with the risen Christ, just as they were saved in the ark as it rose out of the waters of the flood. But, says my opponent, " baptism doth also now save us." Yes, of course, *by a like figure* we are not efficiently saved by this ordinance, only in a figure. He says, " Oh, you say it's a figure." Of course I do, for the text says so. Just a like figure ! Here we have him forced to admit it, for the Holy Spirit, speaking by Peter, says, It is a figure ; the temporal deliverance was a figure of the eternal, and this is a like one. There are only two figurative or symbolical ordinances in the Christian Church, baptism and the Lord's Supper. Baptism sets forth how we obtain life ; we obtain it by virtue of our union with Christ in his death, burial, and resurrection. The other ordinance shows how this life is to be sustained, and they are both figures or symbols. As the elements of bread and wine do not in themselves, but in a figure, sustain our spiritual life ; so baptism does not, in itself, secure to us that life, but in a figure. Then, with regard to the passage in Titus, where it speaks of the " washing of regeneration;" it yet remains for my opponent to prove that baptism is meant here. I say it means the regeneration, not by water, but by the word and spirit of God, applying the blood of Christ—their being made the sons of God, and it would be a misnomer to call it baptism. It means the change that is effected by the Holy Spirit, acting upon the soul through the instrumentality of the Truth. I do not care a straw for the opinion of commentators, when they outrage common sense and the Word of God ; they are but men, and we are to call no man our father. I claim that this interpretation which I have given of the passage is the most natural and most in accordance with the teachings of God's Word on this subject in other passages. And as this is one of his own proof texts, it is only necessary for me to show that his rendering of it is not sufficient to carry the point he is trying to prove. If I show that it possibly means a washing in the blood of Christ by the instrumentality of his word and spirit, instead of water baptism, he has failed in his argument.

Then, with regard to the commission given to the apostles, " Go and make disciples, baptizing them," I showed that by the Greek, the word them could not refer to nations, one word being in the masculine, the other in the neuter ; but that the meaning of the passage was that baptism was to be administered *after* they were made disciples and, of course, saved. I do not wish to overlook any passages he may cite in support of his views. I want to face them all.

He alludes to the passage where Peter says: "Repent and be baptized every one of you for the remission of sins." The primary meaning of the Greek word here rendered "for," is "into," so that the passage properly reads, "Repent and be baptized every one of you *into*, or unto, the remission of sins." The question is, is this "baptizing them into the remission of sins" a figure, or is it to be taken in a literal sense. It must be understood either one way or the other, and there is a vast difference in the meaning. I hold that the baptism into the remission of sins is a figure; the text I cited from Peter, "the like figure whereunto even baptism doth also now save us," I think plainly proves this. And the very same preposition (eis) is used in the original where John the Baptist says, "I indeed baptize you with water unto repentance." The passage from Peter, if nothing more was given, shows that in this as in the other case the baptism was merely a figure. The evident signification is, that as a person in baptism is plunged into or buried in the water, so the believer is in reality by his faith made one with him who was crucified and buried, but who on the third day arose triumphant. I take the Greek preposition in its all but universal meaning, as any Greek scholar knows, and I give the passage a perfectly natural interpretation. The baptism of John "unto repentance" was unquestionably only figurative, as we have seen that genuine repentance was required of them by John before he would baptize them. So I maintain that Christ requires no less than John. He requires in every candidate for his baptism saving faith and genuine repentance. Now when these believers are baptized they are not literally but figuratively placed in the position of pardoned and justified, for these they have already by faith to which the Holy Scriptures invariably ascribe eternal life.

REPLY.

(MR. SWEENEY'S ELEVENTH REPLY.)

Friday. Sept. 11th, 5.30 p.m.

Mr. Sweeney—I am not certain that I understand just what my opponent means by what he calls virtues that are "necessary to" and "essentially connected with faith." He says "salvation is promised to faith," and therefore only such things as are essentially connected with it are necessary to salvation; but baptism is not essentially connected with faith; therefore, baptism is not necessary to salvation. That's about what he calls his argument, as I understand it. Now, it is true that salvation is promised to faith, but never to faith *only*. Salvation is promised to obedience, is it not? It is promised to baptism in the very same language, in the very same verse, in which it is promised to faith. "He that *believes and is baptized* shall be saved." There it is. Now, why should my opponent say that it is promised to faith any more than it is to baptism? Then again, on the day of Pentecost, Peter told *believers* to "repent and be baptized in the name of Jesus Christ for the remission of sins," which shows that although one believes, in so far as faith is a mere psychological condition, he must yet repent and be baptized for remission. What, therefore, the gentleman calls his argument here turns out to be nothing but an assumption. He assumes that faith secures salvation; that salvation is promised to faith for its *own sake*, and that anything else can be necessary to salvation only as it may be related, and necessary, to faith. This is not only an assumption, but it is directly in the teeth of adverse facts, as I think I have quite sufficiently shown. He tells us the faith he is talking about is not mere historic faith; not such faith as Simon Magus had. How did he find out what kind of faith Simon Magus had, I should like to know? The Holy Spirit says he "believed," and the Holy Spirit used the same word it uniformly used to express "believed." Now Professor Crawford assumes that he had a different kind of faith from the other people who believed the preaching of Philip at Samaria. It would perhaps be well for him to tell us all about what the Holy Spirit omitted to mention as to Simon's faith. The Professor says the faith to which salvation is promised is that faith James speaks of, that is "*made perfect by works.*" That sounds pretty well. Now, would he be willing for it to *begin* to work, and hence begin to be made perfect, *in baptism.* That's the first act assigned to it in the Great Commission. If faith is to be made perfect by works, as James and Professor Crawford both say, and if it is to begin where the Lord assigns it its first act, that will bring baptism in before salvation in spite of everything!

Then the gentleman goes to Acts x. 43, to show that salvation, or remission of sins, was secured by faith without baptism. But the passage teaches nothing of the kind. He read, "To him give all the prophets witness, that through his name whosoever believeth in him shall receive remission of sins." Now, does this passage teach that whoever believes in Jesus Christ, shall, without repentance, without any public profession of faith, without prayer, without anything but bare belief, receive remission of sins? No; the gentleman himself does not believe it. Then why quote it? Simply, I suppose, because remission of sins is mentioned in connection with faith, and baptism is not named in the same verse! The language only teaches that whoever believes in Jesus Christ shall receive remission of sins *"through his name,"* without specifying everything that is to be done. Did not the Apostle immediately after command the persons to be baptized *in the name of Jesus Christ?* By the way, I suppose the gentleman knows that there is pretty good proof that this forty-eighth verse of the chapter, in the oldest manuscripts, reads thus: "And he commanded them to be baptized in the name of the Lord *for the remission of sins.*" Irenæus so understood and so wrote it, and he must have read from manuscripts one hundred and fifty years older than any we now have.

But the gentleman dwells with emphasis upon the circumstance that the Holy Spirit fell on Cornelius and others, who with him heard the word, before they were baptized. Does that prove that they were pardoned before they were baptized? I think not. The gentleman assumes that it does, but it is only assumption. I suppose that this miraculous outpouring of the Holy Spirit was meant to signify to Peter and the Jewish Christians who were with him, that the Gentiles upon whom God now sent the Spirit, were to be baptized and received into the Kingdom of Christ, and made partakers of the blessings thereof, one of the first of which was remission of sins. They were *baptized into Christ* after this miraculous testimony of the Spirit, and you know it is "*in* him we have redemption through his blood, even the forgiveness of sins."

The gentleman says "the point he is contending for" is that if these persons at the house of

Cornelius had died before they could have been baptized they would not have been lost. Well, that's not the point I am contending about. The point is this: Did they come to the *promise* of salvation, or remission, before they were baptized? That's it. Peter was preaching on this occasion under a commission whose express terms are, "he that believeth and is baptized shall be saved;" and under this commission he said to the people in his first discourse, who wanted to know what to do, "Repent and be baptized every one of you in the name of Jesus Christ for the remission of sins." Now, did he promise these persons at the house of Cornelius remission upon their faith *without baptism?* I can't believe it. The fact is he had no right to do so. Here, we have the commission under which Peter preached to both Jews and Gentiles; let the gentleman show that it authorized Peter to preach as he supposes he did. He cannot do it.

The Professor gets back to the thief on the cross. Here he thinks he has a case of pardon without baptism. He thinks also that I have not attempted to reply to his argument derived from this case. I think differently. *Is this a case under the Gospel rule?* Had Christ given the commission that sent his Apostles with the terms of salvation to all nations, when the thief died? No! Then why go to this case to learn the plan of salvation? And, as I think I have already said, even if the thief had lived and died in the Christian dispensation, becoming a believer as he did when it was impossible for him to be baptized, his case would hardly fall under the rule; but would be considered one falling within the divine equity rather than the law.

Next the gentleman calls our attention to the case of the Ethiopian eunuch, converted on the way from Jerusalem to Gaza. But what he sees in that case bearing upon his cause is more than I can see. Of course the Ethiopian believed, in so far as faith is a conviction of the mind and heart, before he was baptized. But was he pardoned before he was baptized? Did the gentleman show that? No. Why then did he bring up this case? Does he think my brethren do not require sinners to believe with all the heart before admitting them to baptism? If so, he is wrong. We require them to believe with all the heart before baptizing them, and before promising them pardon we require them to believe with all the heart *and body too.* There is no evidence that the eunuch was pardoned before his baptism. The presumption is against it, in fact. The fact that he desired to be baptized so soon after hearing the word, and the fact that he "went on his way *rejoicing*" *after* his baptism, are both proofs that Philip preached in accordance with the commission that says, "He that *believeth and is baptized* shall be saved."

The gentleman thinks our teaching has a tendency to draw the mind and heart of the sinner away from Christ to the ordinances. Does he understand us to teach that a sinner should be baptized for the remission of sins *without reference to Christ?* Surely not. The ordinances of the Gospel, properly observed, direct the mind and heart *to Christ.* Indeed this is their chief design. Baptism is for remission only as it is "*in the name* of Jesus Christ," and "*into* the name of the Father, and of the Son, and of the Holy Spirit," only as it proclaims the penitent believer's faith in the burial and resurrection of Jesus Christ. Does the Professor think that we hold baptism for the remission of sins *dissociated* from Christ? I suppose not.

He tells you that he believes in baptism himself! Indeed! I suppose he felt that it was *necessary* for him to tell you so. He "urges baptism upon those whose sins are already remitted." But who authorized him to do so? Where is his commission for baptizing such as are *already saved?* I want it. I demand the document. Who authorized him to baptize pardoned persons? Where is his example in the New Testament? Where is an example there for commanding persons who are saved to "repent and be baptized in the name of Jesus Christ *for the remission of sins.*" And where is there an example for commanding a pardoned believer to "arise and be baptized and *wash away thy sins,* calling on the name of the Lord." And there is a precedent there for teaching that "baptism doth also now *save* us." But where is the authority for baptizing a person *already saved?* That's what I want.

There is this thing that seems strangely inconsistent in my friend's theology. He will have it that persons are pardoned before baptism, not merely in exceptional cases, but as a rule; that persons are saved and fit for Heaven without baptism; and yet he will not receive them into the Baptist Church without it. There is just that one good and holy place that no one can enter without baptism. It is true, in a most literal sense, that "except a man be born of *water* and of the Spirit he cannot enter into the"— *Baptist Church!*

The Professor is in trouble with his "figurative" method of interpretatiion. The Saviour said of the loaf, "this is my body," and Protestants generally deny that he meant to be understood in a strictly literal sense; therefore we are at liberty, the Professor seems to think, whenever a passage does not suit our theory, just to say it is figurative! And that disposes of the troublesome passage effectually! What a fine thing it is for schismatics and errorists among Protestants, that the Saviour said of the loaf, "this *is* my body," and of the cup, "this is my blood." The circumstance bridges all the rivers of their difficulties!

The gentleman produces one commentary (that of Dr. Adam Clarke, by which *almost* any doctrine can be proved) that calls baptism a "sign," or symbol," and although he does not agree with his witness as to what baptism is a "symbol" of, he claims that he has proved that the *relation of baptism to remission of sins* is only a figurative one! Does his witness say that? The question is not as to whether baptism itself is a sign, or symbol, of something; but whether all those *passages* that connect it with salvation or remission are only figurative. For instance, "Repent and be baptized in the name of Jesus Christ for the remission of sins;" is that figurative language? Does "for remission" here admit of the "figurative" interpretation? If so, then repentance is for remission only figuratively; and are we ready for that conclusion? "For" can't be interpreted here as expressing a figurative relation to remission as to baptism, and a literal one as to repentance. That would be worse than nonsense. As to the passage in 1 Peter iii. 21, "The like figure whereunto baptism now saves us;" it certainly does not say that the relation of baptism to salvation is only figurative. Indeed, it does not call baptism a "figure." The Greek word from which the word "figure" in the common version comes, as I suppose the Professor knows very well, is *antitupon*, and might better be translated anti-type than figure.

What I object to is not his saying that baptism has a symbolic character, or that it is a sign; but I do object to his making all the language which connects it with remission or salvation figurative language; as if every promise connected with it can be enjoyed as well without it, it being designed merely to signify the fact that such promises, or blessings, are already possessed and enjoyed. And this he seems inclined to do, and to do, as it seems to me, arbitrarily— that is, simply because his theory makes it necessary. I am certain that baptism was not so looked upon primitively. It was put in connection with Faith in the commission by our Lord, and both it and Faith were, as antecedents, connected with salvation. It was accordingly, by the Apostles, required of all penitent believers, and connected with remission, or salvation, by the same words that Faith and repentance were, as I think I have shown. Then, where the Apostles preached the Gospel and persons believed, we find that they were baptized straightway—on the highway, or the same hour of the night. In Scripture style, " *When they believed* they were baptized, both men and women." And, furthermore, when any joy, or rejoicing, are mentioned it comes in invariably after baptism. It was after the Samaritans were baptized that there "was great joy in that city." It was after the Ethiopian nobleman was baptized that he " went on his way rejoicing." It was after the Philipian jailor was baptized—having been baptized " the same hour of the night" in which he believed—that he set meat before Paul and Silas, and "rejoiced, believing in God with all his house." All this and more that might be noticed is entirely inconsistent with my opponent's notion of the ordinance, while it is entirely consistent with mine. And in this connection I wish to say that my friend's view is comparatively a new one. I know it is now the view of most of the large bodies of Protestants, but none of them have long entertained it. My learned opponent will not deny that all the Apostolic fathers, and all the church fathers, for centuries after, taught baptism for remission of sins. Nor will he deny, I presume to say, that the doctrine is in the literature, and even the creeds of the churches of to-day. Luther and Calvin both taught it, and so did both Wall and Gale. True, Luther taught the doctrine of justification by faith only, but he did not mean by "only" to exclude *baptism* from faith. Let us hear the great Reformer on this point:—" Paul saith, 'All ye that are baptised have put on Christ.' Also, 'According to his mercy he saved by the washing of regeneration and renewing of the Holy Ghost"—Titus iii, 5. For besides that they who are baptized are regenerate and renewed by the Holy Ghost to a heavenly righteousness and to eternal life, there riseth in them also a new light and new flame; there riseth in them new and holy affections, as the fear of God, true faith, and assured hopes. . . . Therefore, the righteous of the law, or of our own works, is not given unto us in baptism, but Christ himself is our garment. . . . Wherefore, to be appareled with Christ according to the Gospel is not to be appareled with the law or with works, but with an incomparable gift; that is, with remission of sins, righteousness, peace, consolation, joy of spirit, salvation, life, and Christ himself." Luther on Galations : Phila., 1801, 8vo., p. 302.

Calvin taught baptism for remission in language very much stronger than that of Luther, as I presume my opponent very well knows and will not deny. And we have already seen that Dr. John Gale, the great English Baptist, taught the same thing, and is hence so unacceptable to the Professor. Besides, why is it that the Baptists generally to this day refuse to commune with *persons* who have not been immersed? Is there any reason in it, if, as Professor Crawford contends, baptism is in no essential sense connected with the Kingdom of God, with remission of sins, or even with faith itself? Certainly not. But, my friend, this custom of the Baptists comes down to us from a time when they looked upon this ordinance as of some real, unfigurative, and essential importance; as connected with the Kingdom of God; as, indeed, the initiatory rite of the Kingdom, and hence necessary to the remission of sins and Christian fellowship and communion. Baptist doctrine, upon this point, has undergone a change. That's the trouble.

I don't know that I am prepared here and now fully to prove it, but I will, nevertheless give my opinion as to the reason of this change. It was gradually made. It was made in a spirit of what is called *charity*. It was made in order to a show of Christian unity; that it might be said Baptists and Pedobaptists are one in all *essentials*, differing only as to non-essentials. Romanists, you know, have all along paraded their unity—a sort of slavish unity, a sort of unity such as we may find in grave-yards, it is—as an evidence that they constitute the true Church of God. They could tell Protestants, you are divided—divided about the very initiatory rite into the Church—and hence you are wrong; are not the Church of God. To meet this, Protestants have come to claim a unity in all essentials of the Church of God, and to make this claim good it must, of course, be agreed that baptism is a non-essential. So they have a sort of show of unity—better than that of Romanism, I grant—but it has been reached at the expense of about all that is real and significant in the divine ordinance of baptism. Yes! Baptism with them is now but an empty shell—and the Pedobaptists have given up nearly all the shell itself! Well, I love union ; but I am not willing to have it in that way. The Word of God, in every jot and tittle, must be maintained *first*. Then union upon that is desirable. If the ordinance of baptism, as connected with remission of sins, or salvation—as the initiatory rite of the Church—may be "figured" out of the New Testament, then anything and everything else it teaches may be figured out by the same method. And then what would unity be worth ?

ADDRESS.

(PROF. CRAWFORD'S TWELFTH ADDRESS.)

Saturday, 12th Sept., 10 o'clock, a.m.

Prof. Crawford.—The topic of this debate as it now stands is : Whether we can be saved without baptism, Whether the omission of that ordinance is damnation to the soul ; that is the point to be decided. I affirm that while God expects his people to obey every command which he has laid down, and that baptism is one of his requirements, yet if through ignorance his people omit that ordinance, just as they may not from a similar cause obey other commands which he has given, they are not, on that account, condemned to all eternity. We say that faith in Jesus Christ as the Son of God, and in his offices as the Saviour of men, is the only essential requirement for the sinner's acceptance with God. This is a reasonable doctrine. The sinner is lost and ruined for want of righteousness ; he has none of his own. Christ died on the cross as the substitute for the sinner ; " by his stripes we are healed." It is only by having imputed to him the righteousness of the Lord Jesus Christ, that the sinner can find acceptance at the throne of God ; and faith is the only means by which the sinner reaches and appropriates the righteousness of the Saviour. My opponent has tried to show that this is not sufficient to save the soul, and because certain virtues, as love, charity, patience, &c., are essentially connected with faith, and consequently have the promise of life attached, he claims that baptism, too, is included in saving faith. I have shown that this ordinance is not essentially connected with faith, that there can be faith without baptism, while the other virtues cannot exist without faith. I have demanded of him some proof, something more than the mere assertion that baptism is essentially included in faith. He has failed to produce any proof of this, and I say that as his whole argument is based on this assertion, if it is not established his entire fabric falls to the ground. He has indeed brought forward some passages of Scripture, but not one of them proves or hints that a man is damned if not baptized.

He says that I affirm that repentance is essential to faith: and if there be eternal life promised to faith, and repentance is included, he says without repentance we are lost. Most certainly, but not without baptism. It is true, he asserts, that we are saved through faith; but what, he asks, becomes of infants? I hold that this is merely shuffling the question before us; we are speaking of those to whom the Gospel comes. I might ask him, if we are saved through the preaching of the word and baptism, how is the salvation of infants accomplished? If there be any difficulty it bears equally upon his views. We believe that they are saved through the influence of the Holy Spirit without means, applying the merits of Christ. We believe that faith is necessary in the case of those to whom the Gospel is sent.

He says are there not some persons who are said to have faith without having repentance? And here he quotes John viii. 31, where those Jews whom our Lord addressed are said to have believed, and yet he tells them in verse 44: "Ye are of your father the devil." It is said that many believed and yet went away, for they were not true penitents. When I was on that point I said that genuine saving faith is implied when life eternal is promised; it must be more than mere historical faith, the faith of a Simon Magus. We are not talking of that kind of faith; we all know that that dead faith will save no man. It is "Believe on the Lord Jesus Christ and thou shalt have eternal life," and this must be more than a mere historical belief. Spiritual knowledge of Christ, the object of faith, is here implied. Such a misinterpretation of my evident meaning as my opponent has taken up is merely for the sake of making capital: it is scarcely fair. Then he says you cannot prove that Cornelius was saved before he was baptized. He says this because the Bible does not assert in so many words that Cornelius was saved. Yet he had that faith to which the Bible time and again promises eternal life; the Holy Spirit had fallen upon him; he "had spoken with tongues," and magnified God. Besides, it was said of the Roman centurion, before his baptism, that his "prayers and his almsdeeds had come up for a memorial before God;" but "without faith it is impossible to please God." If this be not genuine saving faith having eternal life attached, I would like to know who has got saving faith? I ask any unprejudiced man if this is not plain—so plain that we can scarcely call it an inference—that Cornelius was a saved man. I say that most undoubtedly he was in the condition of saving grace, and that this is a plain case of a man receiving eternal life before baptism. I believe, on the authority of Holy Scripture, that he would have gone to heaven just as surely as the dying thief did, and we have the Saviour's own words for that: "To-day shalt thou be with me in Paradise." The case of Philip and the eunuch is another proof of the same fact, that men can be saved without baptism. He believed in Jesus Christ, the Son of God, and had received eternal life before he went into the water. My opponent says that I cannot give proof that the dying thief had saving faith. I reply that Christ himself recognized faith expressed in the rebuke which the thief gave the other malefactor, and in his prayer, "Lord, remember me when thou comest unto thy kingdom." He acknowledges his belief in the Saviour's power to save him when he uses these words. He believed in him; he had that faith that brings eternal life, and the Saviour, recognizing this, says, "To-day shalt thou be with me in Paradise." My opponent says again, How do we know he was saved? Can he want any stronger proof of that than the promise of Christ himself? "To-day shalt thou be with me in Paradise." He certainly could not get to Paradise if he was not a saved man. He asks again, "How do you know he was not baptized? One thing is certain, he was a malefactor, living in a state of open rebellion against God and His baptism, if he had ever been baptized while living in that state would be but a mockery of God's ordinance and not Christian baptism. What good would such a baptism be? This style of quibbling is unworthy of an honest disputant, and surely the side which my opponent is here to defend must be a very weak one, when it obliges him to resort to such shuffling.

He takes another little fling at close " communion." The evident object of this is to get a little sympathy from our Pedobaptist friends. Because he, as a Campbellite, would allow them to sit with him at the Lord's Supper, although I must confess that I did not know before this that the Disciples were open communionists, I confess that I have my doubts about this ; and if my doubts are well founded my opponent is dishonest in wishing to leave this impression on the mind of the audience ; but if he would receive them to the Supper then I say the more shame to him if they are, according to his doctrines, damned individuals. How could he allow them to the Communion with him if he believes them unpardoned, unsaved ? The reason we don't allow Pedobaptists to sit down at Communion with us is simply because we have no authority in God's Word for so doing. According to his own doctrine if men are not baptized they are not saved, they are not justfied or sanctified, they have no access to the blood of Christ, yet he would allow them to the Table of the Lord— unsaved men at the Lord's Table. But he says, I must show that the term regeneration is aplied to the inward change. Suppose we take just this passage : 1 John 4. 7, " Beloved, let us love one another ; for love is of God ; and every one that loveth is born of God, and knoweth God."

Mr. Sweeney.—The word "regenerate" is not in the passage at all.

Prof. Crawford.—You say always "give me Bible words." I say that when a man is *born again* he is regenerate ; the word means exactly the same thing, and what else can it mean ? It refers to the new birth ; that is, regeneration. Besides in the original the word is the same. I could ask him of a great many things which he believes but for which he could not give me the exact Bible words. The Sadducees said to Christ, you cannot show us that the resurrection of the dead is taught in the Scriptures. But though the exact words were not there they were held accountable for their unbelief, because God had said, "I am the God of Abraham and of Isaac and of Jacob, and he is not the God of the dead but of the living." They would say as my opponent says, that's an inference and we will have nothing to do with inferences. Yet they were held responsible for their unbelief and "not knowing the Scriptures." Here is another passage, John v, 18: "We know that whosoever is born of God sinneth not; but he that is begotten of God keepeth himself, and the wicked one toucheth him not." I contend that regeneration means the second birth, the being "born of God." And then he said that no respectable authorities could be produced who regarded baptism as a figure. He made quite a swagger over it. I could produce a hundred authorities who so regard it, and can give him a dozen of them to-day. He knew very well that I had not the books by me at the time, as I never dreamed that he would question this, hence his swagger. I could puzzle him very easily in the same way. Suppose I assert here to-day that Napoleon was never banished to the Island of Elba. He believes he was, but can he produce the proofs? This just shows his plan of argument, when he knows I had not the books at my hand. It does not look like a man contending for the truth, but as if his only object was to get his antagonist in a close place, a thing very easily done if one does not happen to have at hand every authority that may possibly be required, but which no one would expect to be needed. I will first quote from the works of John Bunyan: "Reason of my practice and worship." Question—"But why then were they baptized?" Answer—"That their own faith by that *figure* may be strengthened in the death and resurrection of Christ."

Here it is, you see, in the very words. John Milton held the same view, as the following quotations from his works will show:—"Hence appears that baptism was intended to represent *figuratively* the painful life of Christ, his death and burial, in which he was immersed."

I will next quote from the "Baptist Quarterly:"—"When John the Baptist is said historically to have baptized his converts in the Jordan, literally dipped them into Jordan, we have the bare and literal fact. When he is said to baptize into repentance we have a *tropical* use of the very same language." I would here observe that I have made this quotation from an article in the "Baptist Quarterly," in which some pages are occupied in proving the absurdity of Dr. Hackett's translation of the preposition *eis*, in Acts 2, 38. He translates the passage, as Mr. Sweeney has told you, "Repent and be baptized every one of you, *in order to* the remission of sins." This translation the article in the Quarterly most justly condemns, and shows that if the preposition were translated so in every place in the New Testament where it is construed with the word *baptizo* it would make perfect nonsense. Were Dr. Hackett here I would rebuke him for this translation, and I would demand of him a single example in the Greek tongue where the preposition *eis* must necessarily have this meaning; I give it here its common and appropriate meaning, and I don't believe it has any such meaning as that assigned to it in this passage by Dr. Hackett. But, even if we must accept of this rendering, "Repent and be baptized in order to the remission of sins," I would still ask Is it the repentance or the baptism by which this repentance is expressed in a symbol, that would secure the remission of sins? Most unquestionably it is the repentance and **not the baptism.**

I will quote next from " Whedon's Commentary " : " ' Wash away thy sins.' By the external symbol just as the Holy Spirit has already done the work in the eternal reality."

Then in the "Madison Lectures": lecture IV. by Dr. Boardman, "Baptism is a symbol, not a power ; a shadow, not the substance." I might give hundreds of the same kind, but I have not the works here. Instead of finding any difficulty in finding an author who treats baptism as a figure or symbol, I have scarcely found a sensible Protestant author who regards it otherwise; the Disciples stand almost alone here. He says the Wesleyan body do not teach that it is a figure. Let us see what the great founder of Methodism, Wesley himself, says on the subject : " Father Wesley," if he desires him to be called by that name, though my opponent is only using it to get a little sympathy ; for, according to his own views, Wesley was a lost man ; he was unbaptized, therefore unsaved! " Wesley's Works," vol. 6, p. 16 : " This clearly represented the cleansing from sin which is *figured* in baptism."

Another from Wesley :—Vol. 6. p. 14 :

" Even to give them a clean heart and a new spirit, to sprinkle clean water upon them (of which the baptism is only a figure)." So you see Father Wesley does not teach as my opponent does on this matter. And in the Wesleyan Discipline, 17th Article, page 7 :—"Baptism is not only a sign of profession and mark of difference whereby christians are distinguished from others that are not baptized, but it is also a sign of regeneration or the new birth. Hence it appears that baptism was intended to represent *figuratively* the painful life of Christ, his burial, in which he was immersed as it were for a season." It is called here a sign : just what we are contending for. But suppose these authorities had been against me; that is of little consequence. We must go to the Bible for the best proof. My opponent contends that the washing of regeneration, spoken of in Titus iii, 5, is baptism. I say that baptism is never spoken of in the Bible as regeneration, and have shown furthermore, that there are no other washings spoken of in the Bible besides baptism. But this is one of my opponent's proof texts: it is his place as he affirms to prove it. I have given an interpretation natural, and more in accordance with the teachings of God's word elsewhere. It is his duty to disprove my interpretation. Then Mr. Campbell's argument regarding the Divine commission, which my opponent accepts, viz. that the active principle after the imperative denotes the manner of carrying out the command goes for nothing. They were made disciples first, and being disciples they were afterwards baptized. This my opponent has at last been forced to admit, but says that although they are disciples before baptism; and are baptized *as disciples,* they are not regenerate disciples until baptized. Well, suppose we grant this for arguments sake, can we not see that he has by this admission given up the argument about the active participle following the imperative. All the time taken up therefore in defending Campbell on this point has been wasted; for he now abandons the whole thing. They were not made disciples he now admits by baptism, but they were first made disciples; and then, as such, were baptized. But he still maintains that they were not regenerate disciples before baptism. This is just what he has to prove, and to assert it without proof is just simply to beg the entire question.

Then Mark xvi, 15, 16, and He said unto them "Go ye into all the world, and preach the Gospel to every creature. He that believeth and is baptized shall be saved; but he that believeth not shall be damned." It does not say that he that is not baptized shall be damned, but it is he that believeth not. God expects us to obey Him by observing His ordinance of baptism, but He does not say that all who neglect to do so from inadvertence or ignorance shall be damned. I do not quote this as a proof text in support of my doctrine ; it is one of his, and it is therefore his duty to show wherein it proves his doctrine. Suppose I am called to the bedside of a dying sinner, an unconverted man. I would like to unfold the truths of the Gospel to him, to point him to the Cross of Christ, and tell him the blood of the Saviour cleanses the soul from all sin. But there is no means of baptizing the man—it is impracticable,—and what is the use of tantalizing him by directing him to the Cross of Christ, if he cannot be saved without baptism. This may be Campbellism, but it's another Gospel ; It's certainly not God's Word. You remember the Israelites tried to make an idol out of the brazen serpent and it was taken away from them, but this is making an idol of baptism. I do not undervalue baptism, but it will never save the soul, and I wish to assign to it its proper place. Then with regard to that passage, Acts ii., 38, "Then Peter said unto them, "Repent and be baptized every one of you in the name of Jesus Christ for the remission of sins, and ye shall receive the gift of the Holy Ghost." The Greek preposition *eis* occurs in the original, and I defy my opponent to show that there is any such meaning as "in order to" given to that word in the whole Greek language. The writer in the *Quarterly* as we have seen, rebukes Hackett for ever giving it such a translation. The great question is this: Does baptism really wash away sin or only in a figure. The general opinion of the Christian Church is that it is only in a figure, and that nothing but the blood of Christ applied by the Word and Spirit, can cleanse the soul from sin. The Jews have just as valid right to contend that the blood of bulls and goats really washed away the sins of the people because they are frequently said to make an atonement, but we know that these were only types of the great sacrifice on the Cross. "The blood of bulls and of goats cannot take away sins." So with baptism; it is a figure of the believers burial with Christ, and afterwards rising with Him; but no more than the Jewish sacrifices can it take away sin.

REPLY.

(MR. SWEENEY'S TWELFTH REPLY.)

Saturday, Sept. 12*th*, 10.30 *a.m.*

Without any preliminaries I shall address myself to the speech of my opponent, to which you have just listened to so patiently. And, first, I may be allowed a remark or two as to its spirit, which, I am sorry to say, was not the very best. My friend is evidently not in a good humour this morning. If he had made use of those hard words yesterday in the heat of the day and in the heat of discussion, I could have made greater allowance for them. But they come in his speech this morning, after a night's rest and sleep, and after a pleasant ride in the cool morning air; and hence seem studied. I fear he has been out of temper all night. I have no doubt he is worried, and I am heartily sorry for him; but I can't help him out of his trouble. He is contending against the Truth, and that will give any man trouble. He is off after the "herring" he told us about, having fallen back into the "foolishness" of his boyish days, and followed the "*pups*" off!

He says the "topic" of this discussion is, "*Can* any one be saved without baptism?" What a mistake! Did I not correct him yesterday as to this matter? He thinks that, while God expects of us obedience to all his commandments, yet if on account of honest ignorance or other cause over which he has no control, one fails to be baptized he may yet possibly be saved; and he would have you believe I am here to deny that. No indeed. The debate is about, or should be about, the *place* of baptism in the Gospel plan of salvation. I affirm, as my brethren do generally in preaching upon the subject, that it is connected with salvation or remission of sins as an antecedent, just as faith and repentance are; while Professor Crawford holds that it is—well, the fact is, I should not like to have to tell just what he does hold, further than that most passages of Scripture in which it occurs are *figurative*. He holds that faith, and only faith, is "essentially connected with salvation"; and he thinks this quite reasonable, while it would be shockingly unreasonable to have baptism so connected. *Why unreasonable* that baptism should be for remission? Oh, he thinks some honest soul "might through ignorance omit the ordinance," and then, of course, he must be lost eternally! Well, I wonder if no honest soul in this world will ever through ignorance fail to *believe?* But he informs me that he is not talking about infants and heathens that *can* not believe; but about persons who *can* believe—faith is essential to *their* salvation. Very well: I accept that qualification of his doctrine. Now, will he allow me to tell him again, that when I say baptism is for the remission of sins, I mean to such as *can* be baptized; and my affirmative goes no further than this. What did I read Hall, Gale and others for, in my first speech on this question, but to show that extraordinary cases do not make void a standing rule.

He thinks—why I do not know—that to maintain my position, I must show that "baptism is essentially connected with faith." Has he shown that nothing is necessary to salvation that is not necessarily and essentially connected with faith? *He has not.* He never will. But he says he has shown that there can be faith without baptism. Who ever questioned it? Of course, there can be faith without baptism. And what's death to his cause is, there can be faith *without salvation.* Have I not shown it? But he tells us that in such cases the faith is not genuine saving faith; but is "dead, Simon Magus" faith. Very well; what kind of faith is "genuine faith?" We have agreed already, I think, that it is faith *made perfect by works.* But faith cannot work without doing something. Abel's faith was made perfect at the altar, when he offered more excellent sacrifice than Cain; because he did what God required of him. Abraham's faith was made perfect when he offered up his son upon the altar, " and the Scripture was fulfilled which saith, Abraham believed God and it was counted to him for righteousness ;" and his faith was thus made perfect because he did what God required of him. Now, where shall a sinner's faith be made perfect? Jesus said, " Go ye into all the world and preach the Gospel to every creature ; he that believeth *and is baptized* shall be saved." Now, we are agreed that the sinner's faith must *work* before he will be justified. I say that to be baptized is the first act of Faith that is required of him. Will Professor Crawford tell us what work is required of Faith before baptism? If he knows he ought by all means to tell, else the people will begin to suspect that he is defeated. For he is compelled to say that Faith that does not work is dead ; that Faith is made perfect by works ; now he must show us in what Faith works before baptism, under the Gospel. There is no use for him to talk about mere historic Faith, and genuine saving Faith, as it is unscriptural language, and as we are agreed on what is Scriptural—" Faith made *perfect* by works," and "Faith without works is *dead*, being alone." This all can understand, and then as it is confessedly and expressly Scriptural, it is sure not to mislead anyone. But the gentleman amused me when contending that it was unreasonable that baptism should be for remission, because that some one might through ignorance omit that ordinance, and so be lost eternally. I wonder if he had forgotten his doctrine of "divine decrees"—of "unconditional election and reprobation?" Of course, that's altogether reasonable! But, is it not amusing that the Professor should think it quite unreasonable that the scheme of salvation should be such as that one might possibly be lost on account of an unintentional omission; that is, might be lost for not doing what, under the circumstances, was impossible; when at the same time he believes that every man's fate was decreed from all eternity, "without any foresight of Faith or good works," or anything else in the creature? I suppose that, to him, looks altogether reasonable; though I say to you that to my eyes reason turns pale in its presence.

He says that not one of the passages I have quoted to prove baptism for remission says or hints that a man will be *damned* if he is not baptized. But, I beg him to bear in mind that I am not trying to tell anybody how to be damned. To refuse to be baptized is not the only way to be damned. The passages I have referred to speak of the connection of baptism with *salvation or remission of sins*. If the Professor wants to get into a discussion as to what is and what is not a condition of *damnation*, he can for the present, have it all his own way.

I showed that according to my opponent's doctrine as to infants, and that which he advocates as to faith—that it is *necessarily* and *essentially* connected with salvation—they will all be lost. And he says that I am in the same difficulty, Well, if I am I am unconscious of it. I have not said that infants are sinners, or that they are lost; neither have I said that faith is necessarily and essentially connected with salvation. His assertion, therefore, that I am in the same difficulty that these two doctrines involve him in, needs to be labored a little, to make it plain.

The Professor comes back to the case of Cornelius the centurion, to tinker up his argument thence derived. What I said before I repeat substantially. The gentleman argued that Cornelius and those with him were saved before their baptism from the fact that the Holy Spirit came upon them in miraculous power before. Now, the *miraculous* gift of the Holy Spirit, was confined to primitive times, and had no *particular place*, in reference to the remission of sins, or to baptism, in the scheme of salvation. At Jerusalem the first disciples received this gift after they had been baptized and were saved persons. But at the house of Cornelius the case was different. The persons there receiving it, being Gentiles, Peter would evidently have hesitated to baptize and receive them into the church, and the disciples generally, being all Jews up to this time, would not have approved it, had not they received this testimony from God, before they were baptized. Peter so interpreted the matter in his defence of his conduct, made afterward.

But in his last speech my friend argues that Cornelius was saved before he sent for Peter, from the fact that in the former part of the chapter it is said of him that his prayers and alms had gone up before God for a memorial. He thinks that if that does not imply that he had saving faith it would be very difficult to know who has got it. Now, it is true, as he says, that the angel that appeared did tell him that his prayers and alms had gone up for a memorial before God; but he did not tell him that this was evidence that he was already a saved man. On the contrary, he told him to "Send men to Joppa, and call for Simon, whose surname is Peter, who shall tell thee *words* whereby thou and all thy house *shall be* saved."— Acts xi, 13-14. Does not this imply that he was not yet saved? And yet, in the very teeth of this language, the worthy gentleman infers that he was a saved man already, because of what was said of his prayers and alms! And what is seriously damaging to his whole position upon this question is, that he says if Cornelius did not have saving faith before he sent for Peter that it would be difficult to know who has got saving faith. Well, we have seen that he *was not* saved at that time, but had yet to send for Peter and hear words whereby he might be saved; and hence we see that with the Professor's view of the matter one cannot "know who has saving faith." And this is because he is in error, and error always brings confusion.

A word or two about "regeneration." I may have said in the early part of this discussion that the word regeneration is not used to indicate that inward moral change that is now almost universally called regeneration. Anyhow, I think it is a fact, whether I said it or not. Mr. Campbell said something of the kind, too, I think, and you know my distinguished opponent is debating about as much with Mr. Campbell as with me. I repeat that it is true, that the word regeneration does not in the New Testament indicate in a single instance what regeneration popularly means now. Now, do not understand, please, that I do not believe in what is now called regeneration, for I certainly do, and so do my brethren, and so did Mr. Campbell. Mr. Campbell never questioned the *fact* of the moral change now called regeneration, but chose to designate it in other words, using the word regeneration in what he believed to be its Scriptural sense. The gentleman was simply mistaken as to the word regeneration being in the passage he read from John. Regeneration is not in the English of it, nor is the Greek New Testament word for it in the original. The Greek word translated "regeneration" occurs but twice in the New Testament, is in both instances translated regeneration, and in neither means a personal moral change, such as is now called regeneration. But this is a matter about which I feel little concern, further than that you should know that when Mr. Campbell used the word baptize to indicate regeneration, he did not mean to indicate regeneration in its present current sense. It is but just to him that this should be said.

The gentleman comes in with several quotations from men somewhat distinguished in the world of letters—none of them specially so, however, for criticism, that I have ever heard of—to prove that baptism has a figurative or symbolic import. But that's not the figurative question between the Professor and myself. I do not deny that it has both a symbolical and a commemorative character. What I deny is, that it has only a figurative or symbolic connection with remission of sins. I deny that such passages as clearly connect it with remission of sins or salvation are all to be interpreted as figurative passages. Baptism may be a sign or symbol of something, and yet be *really* connected with remission.

He tells us how some Baptist *Quarterly* has shown the absurdity of Dr. Hackett's translation and criticism of Acts ii., 38, and how that if he had the Doctor here he would certainly rebuke him. Well, fortunately for the Doctor, he is not here. But did the Professor *show* us the absurdity of Hackett's rendering and criticism ? Did he even read it from the Baptist *Quarterly* ? No. He only *said* the *Quarterly* had shown it, and that if Hackett were here he would rebuke him. The Doctor's book is here containing the translation and criticism. Let the Professor take hold of the matter and show that the Doctor blundered if he can. It amounts to nothing to say that there are places in the New Testament where *eis* is construed with *baptizo*, where it would do not to translate it *in order to*. No doubt the *Quarterly* did this. So the Professor can do. But this is not meeting the question. The question is, how must *eis* be translated in *this passage !* It is not claimed that it should be so translated in *every* passage. But in *this* passage *eis* means "*in order to*," and must be so interpreted, on account of its connection here with repentance.

But the Professor says that even if the phrase in Acts ii. 38. must be translated as Hackett has translated it, then he would ask whether it is the repentance or the baptism that is in order to remission ? Well, I tell him *both*. That's just the *point* of the criticism. Repentance and baptism are connected together in the passage, and then the *one* preposition expresses the relation between *both* of them and remission of sins. And, as it cannot be denied that repentance is *always* in order to remission, it follows that *in this passage* the preposition *eis* must have that meaning ; and that makes baptism in order to remission. Dr. Hackett *saw* this point ; some people do not. Hence some people, and some *Quarterlies* even, nibble round the edges of the question merely.

Next, the gentleman is found quoting from Wesley to show that remission of sins is figured in baptism. This he quotes, of course, on account of the word figure. But did even Mr. Wesley mean, when he said baptism was figurative of remission, that it has no necessary or real connection with it ? Certainly not. His quotation from Wesley, then, may keep company with another from the same author : "Baptism, administered to real penitents, is both a *means* and *seal* of pardon. Nor did God ordinarily, in the primitive church, bestow this on any, unless through this means."—*Wesley's Notes*, on Acts xxii, 16.

I did admit that a fair interpretation of Matt. xxviii, 19, yields the conclusion that the apostles were to "make disciples of all nations, baptizing *them ;*" that is, baptizing the *disciples*. This has been my view of the passage for years. But does it follow that when persons are taught so far as that they may be called disciples that they are therefore saved, or pardoned? I think not. One may be a disciple in the sense of the commission, and yet not be saved. Mark's record of this commission throws sufficient light upon the point of difference between us : instead of "make disciples of all nations," as in Matt., Mark says, "Preach the Gospel to every creature." These phrases must be equivalents to harmonize the two records. What Matthew means by "make disciples of all nations" Mark expresses by the phrase "preach the Gospel to every creature." But one may be *taught*, as according to Matthew, or preached to as according to Mark, and not yet be saved. This is made clear by Mark, for he adds (having said preach the Gospel to every creature) "he that believes and is baptized shall be saved." So we see that the baptism comes in after the teaching, and "saved" still after the baptism.

I hope the gentleman will give attention to my arguments and criticisms, rather than spend so much of his time replying to Mr. Campbell. Or, if he prefers to reply to Mr. Campbell, then I hope he will allow me to make use of my own arguments rather than Mr. Campbell's; I understand them better, and can handle them with greater safety.

Professor Crawford thinks Saul was pardoned before he was baptized, because when Ananias went to him he called him "Bro. Saul" before baptizing him. Well! that surprises me just a little. Now, Professor, if you will turn and read in the third chapter of Acts the account of Peter's second sermon, you will find that he addressed his hearers as "*brethren*," and then afterward said: "Repent ye, therefore, and be converted, that your sins may be blotted out."

ADDRESS.

Saturday, Sept. 12th, 11 a.m.

(PROF. CRAWFORD'S THIRTEENTH ADDRESS.)

Professor Crawford. My opponent says that the three thousand on the day of Pentecost believed before they had repented; and that, therefore, Peter urged them to repent and be baptized, *after* they had expressed their faith. But where does the passage inform us that they had believed before the apostle had urged them to repent? It says, indeed, that "they were pricked in their heart:" they were deeply convicted of their sin, in crucifying the Messiah; but conviction is not saving faith. It was not when they had believed; but when, in their distress of mind, they cried out, "men and brethren what shall we do" that Peter said, "Repent and be baptized." They were first to repent, which implies faith; and then to profess that faith, and repentance, in the ordinance of baptism. This is the scripture order, as well as the common sense order. I emphatically deny, therefore, that this passage, any more than the one which my opponent advanced from John's Gospel, or any other passage in the word of God, proves that there may be saving faith without repentance. There may be a dead faith without repentance: and there may be, and often is, baptism without either.

Mr. Sweeney says that I omitted to come back to the passage in Peter, where baptism is called a "like figure." He need not be the least afraid that I am going to let his remarks on this passage pass unrefuted. I was just coming to this topic, when my address closed; but I shall examine his arguments presently.

My opponent charges me with making baptism a non-essential. I do not undervalue this ordinance of our blessed Lord. It is very true that I affirm that baptism is not essential to salvation; although I believe, and teach, that the observance of this ordinance is essential to good obedience. I say, moreover, that the man who neglects, or refuses to obey, this divine command, imperils his soul's salvation. All sin, whether of omission or commission, is perilous. But I do not teach the unscriptural doctrine, that the omission of baptism, from whatever cause, necessitates a man's eternal damnation.

Mr. Sweeney perseveres in affirming that I cannot produce commentators who regard baptism as a figure or symbol. I have read several quotations to this effect this morning, and I have quite a number of others here which I could read, if it did not consume too much of my time. But, as I have said, the assertion of my opponent is preposterous in the extreme, as any man, even moderately acquainted with theological literature, knows. Why, there is scarcely a respectable Protestant commentator who does not treat baptism as a symbol. I might ask my opponent if he could produce any respectable Protestant author who denies that baptism is a figure or symbol? I still maintain, therefore, that when it is said, in Acts ii, 38, "Repent, and be baptised unto (*eis*) the remission of sins," the meaning is, that baptism only *symbollically* places the believer in the condition of one whose sins are remitted, by virtue of his union with Christ in his death, burial and resurrection. I have shown that John's baptism unto (*eis*) repentance, placed those who submitted to it in the position of penitents only in a symbol. It did not really make them penitents; and, for the very obvious reason, that they were penitents before their baptism; for John would not receive them to this ordinance until they had first brought forth fruit meet for repentance; and, if John's baptism was only a symbol, what reason have we to regard Christ's baptism in any other light?

Let us now turn to Eph. v, 25-27 :—" Husbands love your wives, even as Christ also loved the Church, and gave himself for it: that he might sanctify and cleanse it, with the washing of water, by the word, that he might present it to himself a glorious Church, not having spot or wrinkle or any such thing: but that it should be holy and without blemish." The Disciples make the "washing of water" baptism. Well, let us, for the sake of argument, suppose that it is baptism. I still ask, does baptism *really* wash away sin, or only smybollically? I hold that sins are only washed away through baptism in symbol; and before my opponent can build an argument on this passage and it's parallels, he must show that baptism is not a symbol; and I am far mistaken if he does not find, notwithstanding all his reckless assertions, that nearly all Protestant theologians are against him.

I contend, however, that baptism is not the thing signified in the passage before us. The Apostle is here employing a beautiful, but, in Scripture, a common figure, in which he compares the Church to a bride, prepared for her husband. She is to be purified and presented to Christ, without spot or wrinkle. It is not her pardon, nor her justification, but her sanctification, therefore, to which the Apostle refers. This is evident, not only from the nature of the figure employed, but it is equally obvious from the word by which it is expressed. The word *hagiozeio* to sanctify, and the word *hagios*, holy, are invariably employed in Scripture to signify sanctification, and not justification, or pardon. What, then, is the figurative bath, or washing, by which the Church, as the bride of Christ, is sanctified? Why the Apostle himself explains the figure. He says that is "*by the word*," ver. 26. And this interpretation is also confirmed by the words of our Lord himself, when he says, "Sanctify them through thy truth; thy *word is truth*," John xvii. 17.

Let us now look once more at 1 Peter iii. 21: "The like figure whereunto even baptism doth also now save us." Mr. Sweeney quotes with approbation, from Parkhurst, I believe, to show that the word *antitupon* rendered in the text, "a like figure," should be translated *antitype*. To this I would reply that we cannot, at all times, follow the derivation of a word, as words very frequently depart, in meaning, from their derivations. Take our word candlestick as a familiar example. At first it signified a *stick* to hold a candle; but, in process of time, the word was applied to any candle-holder, whether of brass, or silver, or glass, or earthenware. Now the word antitype, although derived from *anti* and *tupon* has not the meaning of the Greek word *antitupon*. And, I ask, is it not absurd to call baptism the antitype of the salvation from the flood? The salvation in the ark of Noah was no type of baptism. It was a type of our deliverance from the final judgment, through our union with the risen Saviour; and baptism, as the Apostle affirms, is a like figure, symbolizing the same deliverance by our union with Christ, in his death, burial and resurrection.

I defy my opponent to produce a simple example, either in the Greek classics, or in the New Testament, where the word *antitupon* has the meaning of antitype. There is but one other passage in the New Testament, where the word is found. Let us see what it's meaning is in this passage, Hebrew ix., 24, "For Christ is not entered into the Holy places made with hands, which are the figures, *antitupa*, of the true ; but into Heaven itself, now to appear in the presence of God for us." Here the meaning is evident. The Holy places made with hands are the *antitupa*, or, figures of the true, or "Heaven itself." My opponent will hardly venture to argue that the Holy places made with hands is the antitype of Heaven ! This passage, then, settles the meaning of the word. It means, a type, symbol, or figure, *answering* to the reality or thing figured. This is the true force of the preposition *anti* in composition. Is it not as clear, therefore, as the light of Heaven, that baptism is a figure, or symbol ? The ingenuity of Satan could not set aside the meaning of the word *antitupon* in this passage ; and there is absolutely no example in the Greek tongue, where it signifies antitype, the meaning for which Mr. Sweeney contends. Baptism, then, only saves in a figure, and should never be observed by any man, who has not previously undergone that saving change, of which it is the symbol ; otherwise it would be but an empty form, without the power. It is union with Christ by Faith, through the operation of the Holy Ghost, revealing that Saviour to the soul, that really saves ; and, without this, all the waters in the Atlantic can never wash away sin. While we believe, and teach, that baptism should always accompany Faith ; or, in other words, all who believe should profess that Faith in the ordinance of Christian baptism; yet we believe there are, and have been, through false teaching on this subject, thousands of excellent Christians, such as Luther, Whitfield, Wesley, and Chalmers, who were never baptized; yet of whose salvation I have no doubt. To deny salvation to these devoted servants of Christ, because they were in error about the nature, and obligation of Christian baptism, is not only an unscriptural, but, in my opinion, an *abominable* doctrine. However important the ordinance may be, this is to make an idol of it; and the tendency of this doctrine is, to put baptism in the place of that of which it is but the symbol.

There will not be time for me to follow up this topic any farther, as I am anxious, before this debate closes, to draw attention to another important error, held, and taught, by Campbell and his followers. I refer to his views on saving Faith.

Mr. Campbell teaches that all that is essential to saving Faith is belief in the bare fact "that Jesus, the Nazarene is the Messiah." Had he taught that the belief in the *Truth*, contained or implied, in this statement, was saving Faith, I would not have so much fault to find; for then it would be implied that the man understands who Jesus the Nazarene is; and what is the nature of his office, as the Messiah, the prophet, priest and king of his Church. In other words, this would imply that the man's mind has been enlightened by God's Word and Spirit. But Mr. Campbell has, when treating on this subject, distinguished between the *Truth* and the *fact*, and it is belief in the *fact*, according to his doctrine, which constitutes all that is *essential* to saving Faith. Now, this I regard as another Gospel. But let us hear Mr. Campbell himself,

"Christianity Restored," p. 118, 119: "The grandeur, sublimity, and beauty of the foundation of hope, and of ecclesiastical and social union, established by the author and founder of Christianity, consisted in this, that the *belief of one fact*, and that upon the best evidence in the world, *is all that is requisite, as far as faith goes to salvation.* The belief in this *one fact*, and submission to *one institution*, expressive of it, is all that is required of heaven to admission into the church. A Christian, as defined, not by Dr. Johnson, or any creed maker, but by one taught from heaven, is one that believes this *one fact*, and has submitted to *one institution;* and whose deportment accords with the morality and virtue of the great prophet. The one fact is expressed in a single proposition, *that Jesus, the Nazarene, is the Messiah.* The evidence upon which it is to be believed is the testimony of twelve men, confirmed by prophecy and miracles, and spiritual gifts. The *one institution is baptism* into the name of the Father and of the Son, and of the Holy Spirit." Here you see that all that is requisite, "as far as faith goes to salvation," is belief in the bare fact "*that Jesus, the Nazarene, is the Messiah,*" and submission to *one institution*, baptism.

Now, I maintain that, if this be sound doctrine, we are bound to receive Arians, Socinians, Mormons, Christadelphians, and a host of other heretics; for these all admit the one fact that Jesus the Nazarene is the Messiah; and most of them are quite willing to submit to the one institution, baptism. Indeed, Mr. Campbell appears willing to accept of this inference from his teaching. Let us read again from "Christianity Restored," p. 123: "What is a Unitarian? One who contends that Jesus Christ is not the Son of

God. Such a one has denied the faith, and therefore we reject him. But, says a Trinitarian, many Unitarians acknowledge that Jesus Christ is the Son of God in a sense of their own. Admit it. Then, I ask, How do you know they have a sense of their own ? Intuitively, or in words ? Not intuitively, but by their words. And what are these words ? Are they *Bible Words ? If they are, we cannot object to them ;* if they are not, we will not hear them ; or, what is the same thing, *we will not discuss them at all.* If he will ascribe to Jesus all Bible attributes, names, works and worship, we will not fight with him about scholastic words ; but if he will not ascribe to Him everything that the first Christians ascribed, and worship and adore Him as the first Christians did, we will reject him ; *not because of his private opinions,* but because he refuses to honour Jesus as the first converts did." There is not time to read the whole passage ; but it goes on to deal in the same manner with the Universalists. He is willing to receive, both to baptism, and to the Church, Arians, Universalists, provided they only dissemble, or hold these soul-destroying heresies as *private opinions.*

Then a large party of Unitarians, with their leader and preacher, the Rev. Mr. Stone, who had openly and in print, as I am prepared to show, denied the proper Deity of Christ and the doctrine of the atonement, were received ; and Stone worked with Campbell, as a recognized leader, in the Bethany Reformation.

Indeed, these views were practically carried out by Mr. Campbell. In the year 1828 a Universalist preacher, the Rev. Mr. Raines, was received and baptized for the remission of sins, and this with the full approbation of Mr. Campbell ; and at whose suggestion it was resolved,

"That, if these peculiar opinions were held as *private* opinions, and not taught by his brother, he might be, and constitutionally ought to be, retained."

Again, Dr. Thomas, the founder of that miserable sect of heretics, the Christadelphians; who, with other damnable heresies, deny the proper deity of Christ, was a fellow labourer with Campbell. Campbell called upon the Church of Dr. Thomas to exclude him, not for his doctrines, if he was only willing to hold them as *private opinions*; but Thomas would teach them; and his Church would stick to him; and, after Campbell had debated with him for three days, he agreed to a compromise, while each held to his own opinions.

Indeed Campbell was less offended with the heretical doctrines of Dr. Thomas than with his insisting on re-baptism, in the case of those who had not been baptized in order to the remission of sins; or, in other words, according to the ancient Gospel restored by the reformers. Now, while I entirely dissent from the views of both Campbell and Thomas, I must say, that Dr. Thomas was the more consistent. According to Mr. Campbell's own teaching, Dr. Thomas was right in insisting on re-baptism.

Let us hear Mr. Campbell. Debate with Rice, p. 439. "Now if baptism is for any other end or purpose than was that to which Paul submitted, it is another baptism, as much as bathing for health is different from a Jewish ablution for legal uncleanness, or impurity. The action has a meaning and a design; and it must be received in that meaning, and for that design, else it is another baptism." Now does it not follow from this, that all those, who have not adopted the peculiar views of the Bethany Reformation, have received a baptism, which, in the esteem of Mr. Campbell, is of no more avail than a bathing for health: but, according to his doctrine, baptism is necessary to salvation. Therefore if they were to partake of salvation they ought to be re-baptized as their first was invalid.

Here I would observe that, if his doctrine be correct, Mr. Campbell ought to be re-baptized, as he was baptized before he discovered the ancient Gospel, before he could have been baptized with the right object; and consequently, it was of no more avail than bathing for health! It would appear, according to his own teaching that he is lost, for he was never baptized in order to the remission of sins!

As the debate is drawing to a close, and my time is nearly up, I feel that I cannot do justice to this topic which I have thus introduced at the close of the discussion, because I was unwilling to omit it. It would in fact require a whole day, fully to discuss this question of saving faith. Besides, I find that the quotations, which I would like to read, have got mixed up with others, which there is not time to read during the few minutes which remain.

I intended also to prove the inconsistency of Mr. Campbell and his followers; but I can do no more than hint at a few things, which I could prove by abundant documentary evidence, had I time. I would briefly state, then, that when Mr. Campbell first commenced his crusade against the sects, he, in the most bitter manner, condemned nearly all the evangelical institutions of the day; but, when he found himself at the head of a new sect, he adopted many of the very things which he had before opposed.

Sabbath Schools and Bible Societies were denounced by him and the reformers. "I have for a long time," says he in the *Christian Baptist*, p. 80, "viewed both Bible Societies and Sunday Schools as a sort of recruiting establishments, to fill up the ranks of those sects which take the lead in them."

If time permitted I could read several passages to show that he also denounced Missionary Societies; and his denunciations were not without effect. A Kentucky correspondent in the *Christian Baptist*, p. 144, writes, "Your paper has well-nigh stopped Missionary operations in this State."

Again, Mr. Campbell denounced colleges for the education of young men for the Gospel Ministry. Let us read one or two quotations: "Baptists, too, have got their schools, and their colleges, and their Gamaliels, too—and by the magic of these *marks of the beast*, they claim homage and respect; and dispute the high places with those very Rabbis whose fathers were wont to grin at their fathers." Again, "The sermon is intended to proclaim that it is the duty of the Church to prepare in her bosom pious youth for the Gospel Ministry. Now, this is really a new message from the skies; for there is not one word, from Genesis to John, which says that it is the duty of the Church to prepare pious youth for the Gospel Ministry."—*Christian Baptist* for 1826, p. 221.

Although both common sense and the Bible teach that ministers of the Gospel should be supported by the churches; that "they who preach the Gospel should live by the Gospel;" and "we are not to muzzle the mouth of the ox that treadeth out the corn;" yet Mr. Campbell and his followers denounced, as hirelings, all who received any remuneration for their evangelical labours. "Every man," says Mr. Campbell, "who receives money for preaching the Gospel, or for sermons, by the day, month, or year, is a hireling in the language of truth and soberness." And, even in the present day, we hear the Disciples sometimes denounce, as hirelings, those who receive support for preaching. And yet I think it is pretty well known that they sometimes yield to common sense and Scripture and support their preachers. I cannot say what my opponent's private circumstances are, whether he has, or has not, property of his own, to enable him to labor without support from the churches; but I would ask him whether he can say, that he receives nothing for his services from his church in Chicago? No, he cannot. Why, then, do the Disciples denounce other donominations for supporting their ministers, according to the Word of God?

REPLY.

(MR. SWEENEY'S THIRTEENTH REPLY.)

Saturday. Sept. 12th, 11.30 a.m.

Mr. Sweeney.—The fact that the three thousand on the day of Pentecost already believed when Peter told them to repent and be baptized in the name of Jesus Christ for the remission of sins, is in Professor Crawford's way, as I expected it would be when I called attention to it. He denies that it is a fact, as I thought it quite probable he would, and asks me where in the record it is said that they believed when they asked what to do. Well, it is not said at all. But is that sufficient proof that they did not? If so, then it would be difficult to prove that they believed at all before their baptism. Is the proof ready for that? "Where does the passage say they believed" before they were baptized? It doesn't say it at all. We have to infer that they did. And I offer two facts from which I think we may very safely make the inference that they believed before Peter told them to repent and be baptized. First, the fact that they asked Peter and the rest of the Apostles, "What must we do!" Would they have done this had they not believed that Jesus whom they had crucified was the Christ? Did they ever consult these friends and Apostles of Jesus before, as to their duty. No! they had crucified the Master and stopped the mouths of his Disciples; and had they not been convinced—had they not *believed* —that Jesus was risen, and made Lord and Christ in Heaven they would never have "said unto Peter and the rest of the Apostles, Men and brethren, what shall we do?" Secondly, we may fairly infer that they believed from the fact that Peter told them to "repent and be baptized in the name of Jesus Christ." Would he have so instructed *un*believers? Will Professor Crawford say he would? It is certain that these persons, when they asked what they must do, either believed, or they did not. If they did not, as the Professor contends, then Peter told unbelievers to "repent and be baptized in the name of Jesus Christ for the remission of sins," promising them thereupon "the gift of the Holy Spirit!!" But if they did believe, then Peter told *believers* to "repent and be baptized in the name of Jesus Christ for the remission of sins," which is the fact in the case. And from this fact two others follow. First, that repentance comes after faith; and, second, that both repentance and baptism come before remission of sins. But the Professor says that they did not believe, when they "heard" and "were pricked in their heart;" that they were only " convicted of their sin, in crucifying the Messiah." But I submit that this could not have been had they not *believed* that he whom they had crucified *was* the Messiah. Truly, this passage is a hard one for my opponent!

The gentleman denies that he makes "baptism a non-essential;" but in the same breath almost he says, "it is not esential to salvation!" He only makes it "essential to good obedience." Then, I suppose "good obedience" is not essential to salvation. That's it; is it?

Have I said that the "omission of baptism, *from whatever cause*," necessitates one's eternal condemnation? Have I not particularly and repeatedly denied that my brethren do so teach, or that they ever did. I believe my opponent is sincere, but he does *most strangely* misunderstand me and my brethren.

The gentleman ventures to translate *eis*, in Acts ii. 38, by the English preposition "unto." This translation, with me, is not seriously objectionable. But I shall hold him to the fact that baptism is *unto* remission of sins in the same sense that repentance is. If *eis* is to be translated "unto" in the passage, then it will read, "Repent and be baptized in the name of Jesus Christ unto remission of sins." Now, in what sense must a sinner *repent* unto remission of sins? Must he not repent to *bring* him unto remission? Certainly. Then, so he must be baptized unto remission. Does unto have two different meanings in the one occurrence? It cannot. So the gentleman only shifts the difficulty, without getting rid of it. He might just as well take Dr. Hackett's rendering after all; for it is more elegant than his own, while it affords him no less aid in his extremity. It matters very little how we interpret *eis* in the passage where it is said John baptized (*eis*) unto repentance, so far as it respects our controversy concerning its meaning in Acts ii. 38. I am not bound to show that it means precisely the same in both passages. I believe, however, that John baptized the people *into repentance;* repentance in that case meaning a *state* of reformation, or preparation, to receive the Christ when he should come.

As to baptism merely "symbolizing" what was possessed and enjoyed before and without it, the learned gentleman has as yet proceeded no farther than *bare assertion*. He has found one passage of Scripture that he thinks calls baptism a "figure"—"the like figure whereunto baptism doth also now save us." Now, granting that "figure" is a correct rendering of the Greek word *antitupon*, (though I do not believe that it is) it does not get rid of the fact that baptism now *saves* us." A thing may itself be a figure, or a symbol, of something else, and yet be really connected with salvation as a condition. The passage does not say, nor can it be be made to say by any possible translation, that baptism is a figure, or symbol, of *salvation already possessed*. Then, how does all he had to say about *antitupon*, even if correct, afford him any aid in his effort to get rid of the connection between baptism and remission of sins? Can any one tell?

But I say that the Greek word *antitupon* does literally mean *antitype*. It means antitype in the passage in question, and it means the same in the passage in Hebrews, to which he referred with such emphasis. Let us see if it does not have this meaning in Heb. ix, 24. I admit that the gentleman is correct in saying that the Apostle there calls "the Holy places made with hands the *antitupa* of Heaven itself." But I do not agree with him that it would be absurd to render *antitupa*, in this place, *antitypes*. What is there so absurd about it? What *is* an antitype? It is something which is formed according to a model or pattern, and bearing strong features of resemblance to it. The model, or pattern, or type, must always exist *before* there can be an antitype. Well, did not Heaven itself exist *before* the Holy places made with hands? And is it absurd to say that the Holy place was modeled, or patterned, in some sense, after Heaven itself? I cannot see the absurdity. Indeed the Apostle says as much in the verse next preceding this, in which he calls the Holy places "*antitupa* of Heaven." Let us read: "It was therefore necessary that the *patterns of things in the heavens* should be purified with these, [that is, with the blood of animals] but the heavenly things themselves with better sacrifices." So we are bound to understand the word *antitupa* in this passage in the sense of antitype. The Holy places made with hands were *antitypes* of things in the heavens. And this is precisely the sense of the word in 1 Peter iii, 21 : "Eight souls were saved by water; the antitype to which, baptism, doth also now save us." The eight souls were saved by water *before* any one was ever saved by baptism. The salvation by baptism need not answer to the salvation of eight souls by water *in every particular*, any more than the Holy places made with hands needed to answer to things in the heavens in every particular.

Eph. v, 26: "Husbands love your wives as also Christ loved the Church and gave himself for her, that he might sanctify her, *having purified* her by the laver of the water in the word." I have read Dean Alford's translation in his critical New Testament; and with it agree substantially all the critics. Christ proposes to sanctify (*hagiasee*) the Church for the marriage of the Lamb, *having* purified (*katharisas*) her by the laver of water (*baptism*) in the Gospel. This makes the purification from sin perfect, and the sanctification present and future. All critics known to me make the *laver of water* here mean baptism. Among scholars there is just simply no doubt about it. But the gentleman says "baptism does not literally wash away sins." Well, does the blood of Jesus literally wash away sins? Blood literally washes nothing. But shall we, therefore contend that the blood of Jesus is not really connected with remission ? Surely not. The same may be said of baptism.

It matters not that the doctrine of baptism for remission of sins is, in the gentleman's judgment, "an abominable doctrine." That's a matter of *education*. There have always been those in the world who have looked upon remission of sins *by the cross of Christ* as an unreasonable and an abominable doctrine. But my opponent and I suppose their education is wrong. But why my opponent should be horrified at baptism for remission, with his "abominable" view of election and reprobation is, to me, a little mysterious.

Next the Professor takes up what he calls Mr. Campbell's "view of saving *Faith*." I regret that we have so short a time left in which to examine this question.

I shall not review the passages he read from Mr. Campbell on this point. Suffice it to say, that we require persons to "believe that Jesus is the Christ, the Son of God," in order to baptism, and reception into the Church. This is a divine proposition. This is the creed of the Church. When Peter said to Jesus, " Thou are the Christ, the Son of the living God," Jesus answered and said unto him, "Blessed art thou Simon, son of Jona; for flesh and blood hath not revealed it unto thee, but my Father who is in heaven. And I say also unto thee, that thou art Peter, and upon this rock I will build my church, and the gates of hell shall not prevail against it." (Matt. xvi. 16-18.) This teaches that the divine creed upon which the church is founded is the divine proposition, "*That Jesus is the Christ, the Son of the living God.*" We do not say this " *bare* " proposition ; but *this proposition* in all its length and breadth, heighth and depth ;

in all its comprehensiveness and divine fulness, is all that is necessary, as to faith, in order to baptism, and admission into the church.

When John had written his story of Jesus he said, "Many other signs truly did Jesus in the presence of his disciples, which are not written in this book; but these are written that ye might believe *That Jesus is the Christ, the Son of the living God*; and that believing ye might have life through his name." (John xx. 30-31.) This divine proposition contains all necessary truth. It has life and death in it. It has Jesus in it, as Prophet, Priest, and King. It involves the truth of all he ever said. It involves the truth of all his inspired Apostles said. It involves the truth of the Old Testament and the New. It is the only divine confession of faith. It is the creed given by God himself to men. It includes what He holds to be essential as to faith, and excludes what is really not essential. Men have all adown the ages been disposed to make more essentials than God has made, as to faith. This has been the prime cause of most of the schisms in the church, as well as of the mighty flow of innocent blood. I am not only willing to defend the position of my brethren upon this point, but I am proud of it. I will baptize any one who believes with all his heart that Jesus is the Christ, the Son of the living God. I am not so afraid of receiving "heretics" as my worthy opponent seems to be. There has been too much time worse than lost in legislating against heretics. If a man believes in Jesus with all his heart, it is his right to be baptized, and so received into the church. No man has the right to hinder him one moment. When the Ethiopian nobleman said to Philip, "See water; what hinders me to be baptized?" the inspired preacher said, "If thou believest with all thine heart thou mayest." And when the nobleman said, "I believe that Jesus Christ is the Son of God," the inspired preacher baptized him. So all preachers should do now. We have no divine authority for requiring more. When a man requires more as to faith. he presumes to intermeddle with what is strictly a divine prerogative.

If Professor Crawford feels authorized, as I doubt not he does, to require more of the sinner than to believe with all his heart in Jesus, as the Christ, the Son of the living God, I hope he will find time yet to give us the passage in the word of God upon which this feeling is grounded. I want it. His brethren would, no doubt, like to see it. His practice requires that he should produce it.

He thinks we are bound to receive Unitarians, Universalists, Christadelphians, and other heretics, unless we require more than the simple faith of the Gospel, as already noticed. Well, now, I put the whole matter to Professor Crawford in this way: 1. Is there any Divine authority for requiring more of aliens, as to faith, than we require; that is, to believe with all the heart that Jesus is the Christ, the son of the living God? 2. Can a man believe in Jesus thus with all his heart, and not be a *Christian* at heart? 3. If one is dishonest, is really not a believer in the Christ, but desirous of getting into the Church, at least apparently, can it be hindered by requiring more of him than the simple faith of the Gospel? If one will say he believes with all his heart in Jesus as the Christ, the Son of the living God, when he does not, then will he not tell as many lies as you may require, if his object really be to get into the Church for some unworthy purpose?

As to the reception of Aylett Raines, who had been a Universalist, upon the profession of faith in Jesus and a promise to hold his Universalism as merely private opinion, I think that the church in Paris, Ky., did exactly right.

As to the case of Dr. Thomas, I can not see how our brethren could have gotten along with him better or gotten rid of him easier, if they had been governed by the best human creed and Discipline in the world. Does the gentleman mean to say that in respect to such matters, the Baptists never have any trouble? Do the parties who have, wisely as he supposes, adopted human creeds to prevent heretics getting in among them, and preventing difficulties with troublesome men—never have any such troubles as we had with Dr. Thomas, and have had with a few others? Ah! it's an easy matter to point at *other's* troubles, and if only this could prove that we ourselves have none it would rid the world of a world of trouble.

From the case of Dr. Thomas, Professor Crawford switched off the track and got on baptism again. He thinks Dr. Thomas was more consistent than Mr. Campbell. Mr. Campbell, he thinks, to have been consistent, "should have been re-baptized." But Mr. Campbell was not re-baptized; and I suppose, therefore, that he did not see that his duty or his consistency required it of him. I suppose that Mr. Campbell understood himself quite as well as the Professor understands him. I suppose Mr. Crawford does not *perfectly* understand Mr. Campbell's views as to faith or baptism. I have learned already, and I am not near as old a man as Professor Crawford, that it is a very easy matter to sit in judgment on men, even great men, that are dead, and to tell wherein they were and wherein they were not consistent. And it is sometimes the case that the less one knows of such great dead men the easier it is to pass judgment.

We are not bound to receive Unitarians, Mormons, Christadelphians, or Trinitarians, *as such*, but all men *as believers in Jesus;* and as believers in Jesus we are bound to walk together without judging each other's doubtful private opinions. If one believes with all his heart that Jesus is the Christ the Son of God, and makes this confession with his mouth, I will receive him to baptism and to fellowship, without requiring him to tell just *how* Jesus is the Son of God. I don't believe Arius or Alexander either one knew just how Jesus is God's Son. I don't believe that either Unitarians or Trinitarians can explain this matter with infallible certitude. Indeed, I doubt gravely about even Professsor Crawford being able to analyze the God-head, and tell us just *how* this thing and that thing are thus and so. We are authorized to require persons coming to baptism to believe that Jesus is the Christ, the Son of the living God, but we are not authorized to make them explain how it is so, or endorse any of our theories as to the how of the matter. Here is where the "non-essentials" come in. Untaught questions as to the *how* of the Truths and Facts of revelation are nonessentials.

The Bible says God appeared to Moses in a burning *bush*. I believe there was a bush there. I am bound to believe that, for it is expressly said that there was; but I am not bound to accept any man's theory as to what kind of a bush it was. One man may very honestly think it was a cedar bush; another, with equal honesty, may hold that it was an oak; and my opponent might possibly, without jeoparding his orthodoxy, hold *tamarach*. It is essential that we should believe it was a bush, for the Bible says so ; but, as the Bible does not say what kind it was, I suppose we are all at liberty on that point. God requires us to believe that " Jesus is the Christ, the son of the living God," for he has revealed that, and demonstrated it; but as he has not told us just *how* Jesus is His son, I suppose it is not essential that we should know.

But now a few words as to the " inconsistency of Mr. Campbell and his followers." The gentleman tells us that when Mr. Campbell started out in his " crusade upon the sects," he, with great bitterness, denounced Sabbath schools, theological colleges, missionary societies, and the salaried clergy ; but that we have turned about, and now favour all these things ; that is, we are doing among ourselves what Mr. Campbell denounced " the sects " for doing. Well, I submit now, that after all, there are two or three ways for accounting for all the facts there are in the case without making us out any worse than a *growing* people, at the very worst.

1. Possibly Mr. Campbell went to an extreme in his opposition to those things, and afterward modified his views of them. That, if true, wouldn't make a very bad case of it.

2. Possibly Mr. Campbell aimed what he said against such things, *as they existed and were used at the time of his opposition*, and not as they were favoured afterward by himself and his brethren. That might be the case.

3. Even if our present position in relation to matters named were wholly different from, and entirely inconsistent with, the early views of Mr.

Campbell and his co-adjutors, that would only prove that we have changed a little in reference to some matters of expediency. And even that would not make out a very ugly case.

And now, will the gentleman deny that Baptist views, in reference to the very same matters, have undergone a change? I think not. Have not all Protestant parties developed the same or similar phases in their history? Then why does he throw this thing in the face of my brethren particularly. Are there not Baptists now who "denounce as hirelings all who receive anything for preaching the Gospel?" Certainly there are. And when my opponent was on the "divine decrees" yesterday, I thought his "breath smelt" very much like he belonged to that branch of his "Father's children." If his doctrine of election and reprobation be true, what need have we for "Sabbath Schools," "Missionary Societies," "Theological Schools," or a paid ministry.

But if I have brethren who refuse to support the ministry, they are of all people most inconsistent and wrong, and I shall certainly not undertake to defend them against any reasonable attack the Professor may choose to make upon them in that respect. I will remind him, however, that he is the wrong man to lecture my brethren or any other people for being anti-missionary; and that, even if he were the right man, he can find plenty of that kind of work nearer home—even among his Baptist brethren.

And has it come to this, that the Professor can say nothing worse of what he calls "Campbellism" than that Mr. Campbell and those he choses to call his "followers" have, in their history, developed some inconsistencies in reference to Sunday schools, theological schools, missionary societies, and a paid ministry? It would seem so!

ADDRESS.

(PROF. CRAWFORD'S FOURTEENTH ADDRESS.)

Prof. Crawford.—According to arrangements I am entitled still to ten minutes before the debate is brought to a close. I regret that we have not a longer time, especially that we might more fully discuss the last topic introduced. I refer to the nature of saving faith. This is a question of vital importance; and I have had barely time to hint at some of the errors involved in the doctrine upon this subject, as held by Mr. Campbell and his followers. I have furnished myself with abundance of materials to establish all that I have asserted upon this topic, but time prevents me from exposing the erroneous views of the sect upon the subject of saving faith.

I felt the difficulty of dealing with the materials which I had prepared, especially in so short a time as remained, and had to hurry in order to bring forward as much as possible before closing. There are many things in my opponent's last address which I should like to deal with, but this is impossible.

He is very unwilling to give up I Peter iii. 21, where baptism is called a "like figure." But I ask has he to make my arguments? As I have said; he cannot produce a single example, either in the Greek classics or in the New Testament, where the word *antitupon* has the meaning of our English word antitype. I have shown also that the only other place where the word occurs in the New Testament it means type or figure, and is so translated. How could it be translated in any other way? Let us read the passage again. "For Christ is not entered into the holy places, made with hands, which are the figures (*antitupa*) of the true; but into heaven itself now to appear in the presence of God for us."—Heb. ix, 24. Now, I ask, is it not as clear as day, that the tabernacle, or holy places made with hands, is the figure or type, and "heaven itself" the anti-type? But my opponent's interpretation would reverse this order. According to the meaning which he would force upon the word in question, heaven would be the figure or type, and the tabernacle, or holy places, made with hands, would be the antitype! This is certainly a new order of interpreting types and figures! It is simply preposterous to attempt thus to force a meaning upon a word which it has not got in the language, and which would make nonsense if so translated, in the only other passage where it occurs. No amount of ingenuity, therefore, can silence the clear testimony of the passage under consideration. Baptism, then, is a "like *figure*" to the typical salvation in Noah's ark. That temporal salvation typified the still more important salvation by Christ, and baptism also sets forth this salvation in a "like figure." Baptism saves, but only in a figure. The real salvation is through our union with Christ, in his death, burial, and resurrection; of which baptism is the figure.

It is a faith, not a dead faith, but faith wrought by the Spirit of God, and through the instrumentality of Divine truth, which unites us to Christ; and this faith we profess in our baptism. Hence, eternal life is inseparable from saving faith; and is, consequently, promised to faith, and also to repentance, as well as to every grace or virtue, that is essential to, and inseparable from, saving faith. There can be no eternal life without faith, nor without repentance, which is ever conjoined to faith; because there can be no union with Christ, the only source of life, without these. But baptism and eternal life are not inseparable; nor are baptism and saving faith inseparable. All believers, that is, all who truly possess saving faith, ought, indeed, to profess that faith in the ordinance of Christian baptism, because Christ has appointed it; and he says, "If ye love me keep my commandments;" but many excellent Christian people, owing to the confusion and darkness which have gathered around this doctrine, through the unfaithfulness of the Church, have, unfortunately, misunderstood the design and wish of God on this point; yet, being, by Divine grace, changed in heart and life, through the belief of the truth, and by the operation of God's Spirit, they are saved through the blood and righteousness of the Saviour.

I have shown you that Mr. Campbell, when he first commenced his reformation, attacked nearly every evangelical movement: and, among others, colleges for the education of pious young men for the ministry, and which he denounced as one of the "marks of the beast." But, let us hear how inconsistently with this he writes, when he felt the need of such institutions for his own sect.

In the "Millenial Harbinger" for 1854, he thus writes, in a letter addressed to his wife, p. 40:—"Since I last wrote to you I have been almost constantly on the wing, pleading the cause of man's redemption in the department of an educated ministry. That this is one of the Lord's ordinances cannot rationally be doubted by any student of nature and the Bible. . .

We want not higher authority to teach or to constrain us to raise up—to educate and train men in human and Christain science, that they may be able to teach others also. . . . . We are pleased to see that every form of Protestantism, Quakerism alone excepted, is intent on the proper education of its itinerent ministry."

But, Mr. Chairman, my time has expired. I have only to remark that the Disciples cannot say that they have not been well represented in Mr. Sweeney. They could not have procured the services of an abler advocate of their views.

I have, before sitting down, also to thank the audience for their patient and orderly attention to both speakers throughout this lengthened debate.

REPLY.

(MR. SWEENEY'S FOURTEENTH REPLY.)

Mr. Sweeney.—The gentleman does not regret more than I that we have so short a time for the discussion of the question as to *the Faith*. But he has had that matter all his own way. I have not said anything as to how much time we should devote to the whole discussion, or how much to any particular topic. Even yet he can decide the question as to time, and I shall try to remain till he is perfectly satisfied.

Still he hangs on *antitupon,* denying that it ever anywhere means antitype. Well, I say it does always and everywhere mean antitype. It occurs but twice in the New Testament; once besides in the passage in controversy, and I think I showed in my last speech that it there most unquestionably means antitype. Any proper authority upon such a question will tell us that the type must always exist *before* there can be an *answer* to it, or an antitype. And was not heaven before the holy place made with hands? Was not the holy place made with hands *patterned* after things in the heavens? Paul says so. My learned opponent tells us, however, that the holy place made with hands was the type, and heaven itself the antitype. Then, I suppose the holy place made with hands was *before* heaven itself, and heaven was modeled after it!! That's decidedly new. The gentleman calls on me to show where in classic Greek literature the word *antitupon* means antitype. I have neither the time nor the Greek literature now at my disposal. This I will say, however; that *all* the Greek lexicons give it that meaning, substantially, as any of you can see by examining them.

The gentleman says that "Baptism saves, but it saves only in a figure." Well, he only *says* that. It is not in the Bible. I suppose he feels at liberty so to interpolate God's Word. I do not.

He repeats again that it is Faith that unites us to Christ—not dead Faith, but living Faith;" that " repentance is essentially connected with Faith," and, therefore, necessary to unite us to Christ; but that baptism is essentially connected neither with Faith nor salvation." I suppose that looks very much to him like sound teaching. But I pronounced it, as an argument, untrue, and extemporized. I ask again if Faith is *necessarily* connected with salvation, what will he do with infants, idiots, and all honest and sincere persons who have died without Faith? They will all be lost! According to his view, not an infant or an idiot will ever be saved. That's a heresy equal to that of the "Christadelphians," at which he is so horrified. Faith is necessary to salvation, because God requires it in His Word, and not because God cannot *save* without it. The same is true of repentance, confession and baptism.

The gentleman tells us again that Mr. Campbell in the beginning of his reformation "denounced almost every evangelical movement;" among other things, "colleges for the education of pious young men for the ministry;" and yet, afterwards, feeling the need of such things, he became an advocate of them. Now, as respects this matter, one of two things must be true, if Mr. Campbell is fairly represented. Either, first: Mr. Campbell's mind underwent a change upon the subject, in the interim; or, secondly: the colleges he advocated for the education of young men for the ministry were *not the kind of institutions* he had previously denounced. And I suppose the latter is the fact in the case. I have never read all Mr. Campbell's works, but I will venture to say that I cannot be shown that he ever opposed the education of pious young men to preach the Gospel. He may have criticized the popular method of educating preachers. He may have denounced the divinity schools, as conducted at that time, and he may never have become an advocate of *such* divinity schools in all his life. But I do not believe it can be shown that he was ever opposed to the proper education of young men for the ministry. If it can, however, I shall not hesitate to say that I think he was *wrong* that time.

In conclusion, my friends, you have heard what my learned opponent could say against what he calls "Campbellism." You have heard what he could say against the teaching of my brethren, as to "spiritual influence" in conversion; as to the *design* of the ordinance of baptism; as to "saving faith": and you have heard what he could say about our "inconsistency." Imperfect as have been the replies to his studied addresses, I am not sorry that you have heard the discussion. Take what you have heard home with you. Ponder it well, and compare it with what you read in the Bible, and I shall have no fears as to the result of our discussion.

I thank you, one and all, for the good order you have observed during our debate, and for the marked attention you have given to all we have had to say. And should we meet on earth no more—which is highly probable—may we all meet in heaven to part no more, is my sincere prayer in the name of the Lord.

www.ingramcontent.com/pod-product-compliance
Lightning Source LLC
Chambersburg PA
CBHW032052220426
43664CB00008B/974